CW00969264

WHAT MADE THE SOUTH DIFFERENT?

What Made the South Different?

Essays and comments by
SHEARER DAVIS BOWMAN
ELIZABETH FOX-GENOVESE
GEORGE M. FREDRICKSON
EUGENE D. GENOVESE
RICHARD GRAHAM
STEVEN HAHN
EDWARD L. AYERS
MICHAEL CRATON
BARBARA JEANNE FIELDS
RICHARD H. KING
PETER KOLCHIN

Edited by
KEES GISPEN

UNIVERSITY PRESS OF MISSISSIPPI
Jackson and London

The paper in this book meets the guidelines for permanence
and durability of the Committee on Production Guidelines for Book
Longevity of the Council on Library Resources.

Library of Congress Cataloging-in-Publication Data

What made the South different? : essays and comments / by Shearer
    Davis Bowman . . . [et al.] ; edited by Kees Gispen.
        p.   cm. — (Chancellor's symposium series ; 1989)
        "The 1989 proceedings of the Porter L. Fortune Chancellor's
    Symposium on Southern History at the University of Mississippi"—P.
    Includes index.
        ISBN 0-87805-454-5 (alk. paper). — ISBN 0-87805-455-3 (pbk. :
    alk. paper)
        1. Southern States—Civilization—Congresses.   I. Bowman, Shearer
    Davis.   II. Gispen, Kees, 1943-   .   III. Porter L. Fortune
    Chancellor's Symposium on Southern History (1989 : University of
    Mississippi)   IV. Series.
    F209.5. W47   1990
    975—dc20   90-12611
                                                                CIP

British Library Cataloguing-in-Publication data available

Contents

Acknowledgments

This volume contains the 1989 proceedings of the Porter L. Fortune Chancellor's Symposium in Southern History at the University of Mississippi. These annual conferences, originally known simply as Chancellor's Symposium in Southern History, were renamed in 1984 in honor of Chancellor Emeritus Porter L. Fortune, who had championed them since their inception in 1975. Porter Fortune's death shortly before the 1989 meeting saddened the university community and conference organizers, but in keeping with his commitment to higher education the conference took place as planned, and will continue as a yearly memorial to his vision and pursuit of excellence.

In organizing the symposium I received help and support from many people. Foremost among them is Cora Norman, executive director of the Mississippi Humanities Council, an agency whose financial assistance made the symposium possible. I would like to thank Chancellor Gerald Turner for his support and interest in the symposium. I am indebted to Dale Abadie, dean of the College of Liberal Arts, and Ann Abadie, associate director of the Center for the Study of Southern Culture, for their hospitality to the symposium participants. Barbara Fields and Robert Haws, chairman of the history department, provided valuable advice, as did my colleagues Charles Eagles, Winthrop Jordan, Ted Ownby, and Charles Wilson. The conference also owed much to the contributions and the professionalism of the panel moderators, Professors James C. Cobb, Kenneth Goings, Johnpeter H. Grill, Richard H. King, and Robert J. Norrell. Arthur Kinnard of Mississippi Valley State University gave valuable support.

I received important clerical help from Virginia Williams and Janet Smith in the History Department office, as well as logistical assistance from Krista Agnew, Robert Ginn, Greg Hospodor, Bruce MacTavish, Matt Pearcy, Wiley Prewitt, Deanna Rummage, and especially Lisa Speer, graduate students in history, whose voluntary efforts on behalf of the meeting constituted an initiation into the history profession, which depends so heavily on the uncompensated labor of its junior members. Finally, I owe gratitude to Seetha Srinivasan, editor-in-chief of the University Press of Mississippi, who has done so much to make this volume possible. Thank you all.

Introduction

The theme of these essays is the American South in comparative perspective. This choice of topic resulted from certain peculiar circumstances. The volume's editor, who teaches at a university and in a department that lavish attention on southern history and southern culture, is not himself a student of the South. On the contrary, as a European historian in an environment pervaded by the primacy and uniqueness of all things southern, I have had frequent occasion to advocate a less inward-looking, more comparative and cosmopolitan approach. Such challenges eventually resulted in my mission as a complete outsider to organize the annual symposium in southern history.

This situation, coupled with my scholarly interest in comparative history and my personal experience of the region's peculiarity, made the comparative theme an obvious organizing principle for the conference. Perhaps a comparative symposium would help redress the problem I had identified and also answer some of the large, speculative questions that had surfaced over the years in casual discussions with friends and in moments of private reflection. For example, in light of Max Weber's *The Protestant Ethic and the Spirit of Capitalism* I have often wondered why the culture of this overwhelmingly protestant region resembles so little the European or Yankee capitalism with which I am familiar. Or does it? On other occasions I have asked myself—with some exaggeration but typically after reading newspaper accounts of bizarre acquittals or failures to prosecute—why does this seem to be a region of men (and women) rather than of laws? Why, reflecting on Ferdinand Toennies's famous dichotomy, does it occur to me that the South is more about *Gemeinschaft* ("community") than *Gesellschaft* ("society")? Why, when I hear colleagues talk of the industrialization of the South, do I catch myself thinking that my dominant impressions of the region are about as far removed from the ideal type of industrial society as can be imagined by someone not acquainted with the so-called Third World? To be sure, I live in Oxford, Mississippi, not in Atlanta or in Nashville, and even here things are much affected by the presence of a university and Japanese cars. Still, my guess is—and it would be intriguing if such things could really be measured—that the socioeconomic distances between small-town Mississippi or Alabama and the metropolises of the New South are larger than those between, say, rural Burgundy or Bavaria and the large urban-industrial centers of France and Germany.

Or, to take a question inspired by the literature in my own area, why is the class-based interpretation of southern slavery so authoritative when it is generally acknowledged in German history that Marxist historiography is probably at its weakest in addressing the problem of Nazi racism and genocide in the Third Reich? And why should slavery and capitalism be considered mutually exclusive in southern history when few if any historians in my field dispute the reality of their combination in the case of, say, I.G. Farben at Auschwitz or, to take something less extreme, the modern serfdom created by the authoritarian and paternalistic social-welfare measures of nineteenth-century German big businessmen in the industrial development of rural Westphalia? What exactly do we mean by the word capitalism, and why?

Posing those questions, some of which are addressed directly in the chapters that follow, is not to suggest that the uninformed outsider should set the agenda for southern history. Nor is it true that an outsider is inherently better situated to ask meaningful questions than the insider, although Alexis de Tocqueville certainly demonstrated that it can be done. It is rather to draw attention to the fact that familiarity with one subject matter, applied, however crudely, to another one, inevitably yields fresh perspective. Questions—and answers—more or less force themselves upon the mind. If this is true for an amateur, it can be imagined how much more valuable the comparative method should be when practiced systematically, informed by expert knowledge and careful scholarship. The essays collected here are a case in point.

Eugene Genovese establishes one component of the region's distinctiveness in the unique, comparative interpretation of world history advanced by southern conservative intellectuals from the first half of the nineteenth century to the present. As Genovese points out, by anchoring the South within the larger development of western civilization, southern conservatives could trumpet the moral benificence not just of slavery but also of the provincial and communal Christian social order that the free-labor system of industrial capitalism and godless liberalism were devouring in the North and in Europe. Like their counterparts and exemplars in Europe, southern conservatives eagerly espoused the themes of patriarchalism, social harmony and the organic community that had allegedly governed medieval and ancient society.

Proclaiming themselves the "only true Europeans left," southern conservative intellectuals differed, however, from the real thing when it came to slavery. This, it seems to me, raises the problem of their ingenuousness, as well as the paradox that the conscious propagation of traditionalist ideology is itself an integral part of modern society. Even so, their hatred of bourgeois liberalism was undoubtedly sincere—as sincere as that of the Marxists, whose critique of capitalism they largely shared. Surely it is this affinity that explains why Marxist scholars such as Genovese were attracted to southern conservatives in the first place. Ironically, the attraction may have acquired added meaning from recent global developments. The southern conservatives' awareness of being on the losing side and their lament about a vanishing world would appear to parallel closely the historical predicament of many a Marxist today in the midst of capitalism triumphant.

Where Genovese assesses the role of pens in shaping southern culture, Shearer Davis Bowman concentrates on the impact of swords. Specifically, Bowman seeks to determine the cultural significance of dueling in the nineteenth-century South by comparing it with the same practice in contemporary Prussia, a state

xii   Introduction

whose reputation has long been synonymous with saber-rattling
militarism and with a peculiar symbiosis of tradition and modernity often deemed significant for understanding the South. Of
course, Bowman does not analyze dueling for its own sake, but as
an index of a specific concept of premodern honor and a propensity
to physical violence, which in his view are crucial components of
southern distinctiveness. Bowman addresses the question of how
such "Prussian" values could have evolved in the South, in many
ways the antithesis of that European state. He draws attention to
their similarity as colonial frontier lands, settled by men who saw
no contradiction between serfdom and slavery on the one hand
and their role as entrepreneurs on the other. Returning to the
social role of the dueling-type of honor, Bowman concludes his
essay with an intriguing hypothesis about their different paths and
functions in Prussia and the South.

Although it would be tempting to engage here in a dialogue with
Bowman—and with the volume's other authors—that pleasure has
been reserved for their commentators, whose remarks immediately follow each essay.[1] In the case of Bowman's paper, Edward
Ayers raises several penetrating questions. Referring to recent
German historiography, Ayers calls into question the value of
comparisons and parallels between allegedly outdated, inaccurate
interpretations of nineteenth-century Germany and the American
South. He reviews the social roles and histories of their respective
martialisms, thereby casting doubt not only on the alleged tradi-
tionality and importance of the dueling-type honor but on the
usefulness of the so-called Prussian Road argument in general.

If Ayers's comments make the South resemble other parts of the
nation more rather than less, Elizabeth Fox-Genovese returns to
the theme of southern uniqueness. Her analysis of conservative
women intellectuals against a background of European and northern conservatism demonstrates that the values of these women
writers of the Old South dovetailed closely with the ideology of the
male authors studied by Eugene Genovese. The women, too, built
their intellectual constructs on a foundation of modern tradi-

tionalism, the female version of which tended to emphasize the virtues of biblical Christianity, inwardness, and domesticity. More importantly, it also included an ardent defense of slavery as well as explicit arguments for woman's subordination to man.

With the exception of proslavery arguments, Fox-Genovese points out, much of this resembled the conservative view of and by women that prevailed in other parts of the transatlantic world. However, according to Fox-Genovese—and Barbara Fields in her comments in no way disagrees—there were certain subtle differences, notably in constructing the logic of paternalism. Whereas northern or European conservatism increasingly relied for this on biology, domesticity and the need to preserve a shrinking sphere of community, the southern version rooted primarily in the women's determination to uphold slavery and therewith civilized society. That sounds plausible enough, although it remains an open question whether, as Barbara Fields suggests, southern conservatives were closer to the truth than it is now fashionable to admit when they claimed to be upholding civilized society.

The next two essays, by Steven Hahn and Richard Graham, focus on the political economy of the South in comparative perspective. Hahn concentrates on the effects of emancipation on the South's agricultural economy, forcefully arguing that the discontinuity in labor relations in the South was much greater than elsewhere and resulted in a radical and speedy transition to capitalist agriculture. Whereas a Brazil, a Germany, or a Cuba made this conversion "unevenly" and in such a way that noncapitalist social relations continued to exercise a powerful influence on the economy long after emancipation, Hahn's planter South underwent a radical transformation from pure slave economy to pure capitalism. The reasons for these different paths, according to Hahn, include the success of landed elites elsewhere—as opposed to the failure of southern planters—to maintain economic and political power at the national level, as well as greater use of migrant farm workers and the existence of more entrenched peasantries in those other societies. In short, the brutality and thoroughness of "deregulation" in the South created a vacuum filled immediately by uncontrolled market forces in labor relations. This in turn affected the economic and political history of the entire nation.

Peter Kolchin accepts Hahn's thesis of radical discontinuity but does not agree with his tendency to reduce it to a question of labor relations. To give the "case for emancipation as a bourgeois revolution" a broader foundation, Kolchin probes what he views as inconsistencies and problems in the details of Hahn's argument. Analyzing Hahn's use of the term capitalism, he draws attention to the differences between historians who define capitalism strictly in terms of labor relations and those who stress profit maximization. Kolchin believes that Hahn, an exponent of the labor-relations definition, comes close to tautology when stating that the abolition of slavery gave rise to capitalism. To avoid that truism, claims Kolchin, Hahn is forced into several problematic positions, which he could have avoided by adopting a broader organizing principle, such as general societal dislocation in the wake of emancipation. The upheavals of Populism, for example, should be explained not as the consequence of an unregulated market in labor relations but rather as a more general, political phenomenon. Discontent and unrest sprang from countless broken promises and shattered hopes—hopes first raised by the prospects of radical Reconstruction—in a development that Kolchin likens to the dynamics of nineteenth-century Russia's "great reforms" and the Societ Union's current "perestroika."

Where Hahn detects massive discontinuity, Richard Graham appears to find almost the opposite. That at any rate is the obvious implication of this economic historian's intriguing comparison of the South and Brazil in the days of slavery. The Brazilian perspective transforms the pre-civil war South from a quasifeudal system in Hahn's interpretation into a paragon of bourgeois enlightenment and economic development in Graham's. And slavery, the crux in the one interpretation, is reduced to the role of minor player in the other. Could this be true, or is it merely an optical illusion? As someone who is unfamiliar with the history of the South as well as Brazil, I am not prepared to answer that question, though it seems to me that regardless there is great heuristic value in Graham's essay.

It demonstrates that everything is relative, and that one's choice of referents relates directly to what one will find and what one seeks to explain. If it is Brazil's economic backwardness, comparison with the U.S. South would indeed suggest that slavery is not the most important cause, because the South—with double the number of slaves—was so far and indisputably ahead of Brazil. But the same comparison does not prove that relative to the North or the developed parts of Europe the South was progressive. On the contrary, its relative backwardness in this regard has not been explained at all by the Brazilian comparison and may therefore well have been due to slavery. Even so, comparing the South and Brazil serves an important purpose. It is a powerful reminder of the danger of emphasizing the differences between North and South so much that they appear as mutually exclusive, totally alien economies and forms of society. From the Brazilian perspective, and probably others as well, it is obvious that what separated North and South must be balanced against what they had in common: a cultural heritage of capitalism, individualism, and Puritanism, and, for the white population, a social structure more like that of north-western Europe than Spain or Portugal.

As an intellectual historian Richard King applauds Graham's weighting of cultural factors but regrets his failure to explore them in greater depth. Three aspects of the cultural differences between Brazil and the South in particular might have received greater attention: racial composition and ideology, religion, and political culture. King's points are well taken, especially so considering that Graham himself is the one who ventures into the territory of other specializations. Still, no one can be an expert in everything, and making broad connections is more important than filling in the gaps, which is precisely why the dialogue and the cross-fertilization attempted in this collection are so important.

The volume's final essay is a contribution by George Fredrick-

son, who surveys the trajectories of black-white relations in South
Africa, Brazil and the United States since emancipation. The main
purpose of that exercise is to show that in those three countries
"politics and power are crucial to understanding evolving patterns
of race relations," a position that in turn provides the basis for their
comparability. That is to say, Fredrickson seeks to demonstrate in
the first instance that political action and race are historical forces
that operate as independent variables rather than as functions of
class (though he by no means denies the impact of economic
conditions on race relations). More importantly, Fredrickson argues that an autonomous cultural racism is not static or immutable,
but changes its meaning, shape and intensity depending on the
political situation. American and South African politics in turn are
typically framed in terms of race, thereby perpetuating the latter's
evolving historical role.

All this is argued on the basis of a "thumbnail sketch," which in
Michael Craton's view remains a bit too much on the surface. A
believer in microhistory, Craton qualifies Fredrickson's sweeping
conclusions with observations inspired by his own intimate knowledge of the British West Indies. He draws attention to anomalies
and complications such as the great differences among the United
States, Brazil, South Africa, and the Caribbean in the ratios of
blacks and whites, the internal stratification of the subordinate
ethnic groups, the presence of non-African ethnic minorities per-
forming indentured labor, and variations in the legal status of
indigenous and settler peoples. These and other factors in Craton's
comments add up to a very different vision of race relations—one
in which Fredrickson's massive agency of political history and
political events is much reduced. In the end, what remains is the
old alternative of race or class, the latter of which Craton—not
necessarily for scholarly reasons—much prefers.

To return, finally, to the volume's original theme, what made the
American South different? It seems to me that despite their different questions, interpretations and answers, the contributors
collectively bring into sharp focus the contours of Southern pecu-

liarity. What emerges time and again from their analyses is the overwhelming importance of incongruity. The contradictions of unfree labor relations and cash nexus, of rational means-ends calculation and quasifeudal attitudes, of white supremacy and democratic values, produced an historical situation that is impossible to capture accurately with neat, mutually exclusive ideal types. The South was not a case of capitalism *or* slave system, tradition *or* modernity, bourgeois liberalism *or* patriarchal conservatism, but rather their simultaneity, confrontation and amalgamation: capitalism *and* slavery, tradition *and* modernity, liberalism *and* conservatism, shading into one another as though aligned in a continuous spectrum and combining in the unexpected ways of a hybrid. Reconciling those incongruities became a formative experience for the South, which ended up preserving them in a culture distinguished by extraordinarily high levels of value conflict and tension between the multiple levels of reality.

K.G.

WHAT MADE THE SOUTH DIFFERENT?

The South in the History of the Transatlantic World

EUGENE D. GENOVESE

The comparative method in southern history is of recent origin, but only for the historical profession. In contrast, the southerners we historians write about—those without Ph.D.s—have been interpreting their history comparatively and in world perspective for centuries. As for professional historians, who, as is well known, are slow learners, we must make an honorable exception for Carter Woodson and the black historians associated with him. Early in the century they waged a lonely battle for comparative history, but not until the 1960s did the historical professions deign to notice their work. The profession, it seems, was, as always, in hot pursuit of academic excellence and had no time for no-'counts.

The comparative method, while now reputable, remains on the defensive and has not yet passed much beyond comparison of the Old South with other slave societies. There has still been little effort to study the South in world-historical context, notwithstanding the general recognition that slavery, throughout the New World, arose and fell as an integral part of world capitalist development. Yet, it ought to be clear that an understanding of slavery, to say nothing of Reconstruction, requires close attention to the international context of industrialization, nationalism, imperialism, state centralization, and the demise of the great European landed classes.

In speaking of comparative history, we often confuse two separate matters—confuse the international context of the southern experience with the comparative method of analysis. The context requires the method, but not vice versa. In consequence, even much comparative analysis proceeds narrowly and obscures the larger context.

First, the context: The history of modern slavery constituted a chapter in the history of capitalism—of the rise, expansion, and world conquest of a new social system based upon the freedom of labor and capital in a competitive world market, and, paradoxically, the tightening or reintroduction of slavery and servitude in the colonies and even in Eastern Europe. That is, notwithstanding some important qualifications for Russia and elsewhere, modern servile labor systems arose as tributaries to the burgeoning world market and the rising demand for foodstuffs, raw materials, and markets that marked a new and self-revolutionizing social system in Western Europe and North America. Thus, not only do we confront an increasingly integrated world economic history, but a political and intellectual history as well. For if the metropolitan countries fastened slavery and serfdom on every part of the world—or alternatively, subordinated existing systems to the domination of Euro-American capital—they also created a world marketplace of ideas and ideologies. Western ideas of individual freedom and the ideology of individualism are commonly associated with the Renaissance and the Enlightenment, but they were already rooted in the Christian concepts of a personal God and His direct, personal relation to each individual. And they could not be kept at home. They quickly penetrated the colonial ruling classes, however much those ruling classes tried to deny the benefits to the lower classes, to the colored races, and to women.

In time, those ideas fired the imagination of the slaves, who, for the first time in world history, rebelled not merely to liberate themselves but to destroy slavery as a social system. The rise of abolitionism, in its black and white aspects, thereby represented a revolutionary movement in what was emerging as a worldwide civil war.

As Robert Paquette has especially well shown in his masterly book, *Sugar Is Made with Blood*, even the apparently local politics of a small country like Cuba inescapably became intertwined with European and American politics, including southern politics, in an intensifying struggle for world power. And here, Paquette's use of the comparative method—significantly, he is also a historian of the South—draws our attention to the extent to which comparative history, like southern history and American history in general, is being steadily reduced to a narrow, ideologically sanctioned social history that features increasingly antiquarian studies of the lower classes and oppressed races, as if they themselves could be understood in isolation from the classes that dominated them and that stood astride society as a whole. Paquette's book does illuminate the social history of the Cuban slave regime, does illuminate the lives of slaveholders and slaves, and of the intermediate classes. But it does so in a manner that demonstrates the importance of transatlantic intellectual life, much as the work of Michael O'Brien has been doing for the intellectual life of the Old South. It does, that is, what social history was supposed to do in the first place—not substitute a new and ideologically loaded antiquarianism for the politics that alone justifies the study of history, but, rather, it demonstrates that the essential political history can only be understood in relation to the daily life and thought of society and its constituent parts. For, as Eric Hobsbawm has insisted, our object should be not social, or economic, or intellectual, or political history, but an integrated history of society.

Now, there is a marvelous irony in the continued resistance to a world-historical perspective and the comparative method, and especially to the lingering fear that they invite a loss of "feel" for the South itself. For educated southerners have always understood themselves as participants in a transatlantic culture as well as a transatlantic economy. Here, as a necessary shorthand, I shall single out two principal subjects to illustrate the point: first, the emergence of a unique proslavery world view that had no analogue in Brazil, Spanish America, or the Caribbean, but that nonetheless matured in the context of the proslavery theorists' study of world history and of the social systems of Eastern as well as Western Europe and of Asia, Africa, and Latin America; and second, the emergence in the twentieth century of a southern traditionalist or communitarian conservatism, self-consciously linked to Europe and concerned to relate traditional southern values to the struggle for a new social order appropriate to the modern world as a whole.

Notwithstanding the received New England stupidity, according to which southerners have had no mind, only a temperament, the Old South had a vigorous intellectual life. As a symptom, it had proportionately more young men in college than the North, and by the 1840s was even making long strides in the education of women. More to the point, it was producing intellectuals who easily matched, and in some disciplines overmatched, their northern counterparts. For example, it may be doubted if any northern political economist equaled Virginia's George Tucker, or if we consider technical sophistication, South Carolina's Jacob Nuñez Cardozo. Among political theorists, Randolph, Calhoun, Bledsoe, and even Beverley Tucker and James Hammond deserve to be read carefully today. In theology, Robert Dabney and Robert Breckenridge are barely remembered, and the great James Henley Thornwell is remembered not at all, although Professor James Farmer in his book *The Metaphysical Confederacy* has just made a splendid effort to resurrect him. Yet Thornwell's writings on theology, ecclesiology, education, and social theory stamp him as a man of wide learning and intellectual depth. Northern theologians like Charles Hodge and William Ellery Channing are still honored, whereas Thornwell, who sometimes rent them polemically, is not. From which we may conclude that if intelletuals wish to be remembered, they had better pick the winning side when war comes.

Here, I should like to focus on the interpretation of history that the southern elite was imbibing at school and that it carried through life, for it informed the elite's politics and world view. Educated southerners read a good deal of ancient, medieval, and modern history in the academies and colleges, and surveys of their private libraries show that they continued to do so afterwards, as is also testified by the jottings in their letters and diaries. To speak of a southern "interpretation" of history requires full awareness that they, like others, weighed competing interpretations and often disagreed among themselves. Yet if we take the vital contributions of the divines, whose books, printed sermons, and frequent journal articles were widely read, and add to them the writings of secular theorists who taught in the colleges and whose writings influenced the social and political elite, we may discern the rough outlines of a distinctly southern and traditionalist way of reading history.

I shall have to resist the temptation to dwell on the work of William H. Trescot of South Carolina, America's first great diplomatic historian, who worked out a coherent theory of historical progress—or better, historical process—at the center of which was the struggle between nations and races for supremacy. Trescot did not leave matters there, for he also argued that the internal progress of nations depended upon the outcome of class struggles. I am not aware that he knew of Karl Marx, but it is as if he had taken up Marx's view and improved upon it in the manner of Benito Mussolini and Giovanni Gentile. But let that pass.

Instead, let us settle for a brief consideration of the thought of Thomas Roderick Dew, the President of the College of William and Mary, whose splendid book, *A Digest of the Laws, Customs, Manners, and Institutions of the Ancient and Modern Nations,* posthumously published in the early 1850s from his college lecture notes, remains a powerful introduction to what we would now call Western Civilization down to the French Revolution, even if virtually no one reads it anymore. By comparing Dew's explicit reading of history with the reading implicit in the theological and social writings of Thornwell and other leading divines, we may glimpse the richness of the historical context in which the southern intellectuals defended slavery, for their context was that of world history and their method was that of sociological comparison. In this they were joined by the luminaries of the bar, including not only first-rate jurists like Thomas Ruffin of North Carolina but legal scholars like George Sawyer and John Fletcher of Louisiana, whose learned proslavery tomes had an enormous

impact on southern thought during the 1850s. Of special note is
Thomas R. R. Cobb of Georgia, who prefaced his impressive book,
The Law of Negro Slavery in the United States, with a long essay—
really a book in itself—on slavery in world history. Cobb applied
the historical and comparative methods to demonstrate that slavery had been ubiquitous in world history among all races, that the
contemporary social systems of Eastern Europe, Asia, and Africa
shared their essentials with the social system of the South, and that
the free-labor system of Western Europe and the North was both a
morally obnoxious form of white slavery and a doomed historical
aberration.

In considering these and other writers—theologians, historians, legal scholars, and social theorists—two common de-
nominators stand out. First, to one extent or another, all grounded
their historical and sociopolitical interpretations in Scripture and
defended their moral claims by a close study of sacred as well as
secular history. And second, all demonstrated serious study of the
presumably scientific political economy of their day—from Adam
Smith to Ricardo, Malthus, and Say. Thornwell proved especially
adept at fusing theology with political economy in a way radically
different from any northern writer, but all of them contributed to
the project. In this way, as in so many ways, their work shows that
the Old South had a vigorous intellectual life intimately in touch
with prevailing transatlantic discourses.

What made Dew an original was his astonishing thesis—astonishing for a proslavery theorist—that Western history constituted the story of moral as well as material progress, and that the
driving force behind that progress, which he extolled, was individual freedom and its attendant freedom of capital, entrepreneurship, and labor. The logic of his thesis drove him to identify
everything he valued in civilization—from ancient Greek to modern bourgeois society—with the progress of human freedom.
Now, so long as he could treat modern slavery as geographically
and racially specific, and as tangential to the course of world
history, he could avoid having his defense of southern slavery stand

in contradiction to his essentially Enlightenment view of progress. Indeed, some of those who only read his famous review of the Virginia debates on emancipation and who ignore the *Digest*, his treatise on political economy, and his essays on women in history and other subjects, have been misled into doubting the depth of his commitment to slavery at all. But Dew was an honest as well as learned and brilliant man, and he could not compartmentalize his thought or proceed in bad faith. Accordingly, he plunged into the so-called social question that was coming to dominate social thought in Europe—*i.e.*, the question of the proper relation of labor to capital, of rich to poor. Invoking the laws of political economy, he foresaw a great class struggle between capitalists and laborers, between rich and poor, and argued that the very material progress he celebrated was condemning the mass of humanity to wretchedness, while the few grew richer and more overbearing. The outcome could only be revolution, anarchy, and the establishment of a new and despotic political order, which would, of course, put an end to the reign of the freedom that had made progress possible in the first place. Hence he prophesied the decline of the glorious progress of the West, and the establishment of military dictatorships, which he abhorred but considered immeasurably preferable to anarchy and perpetual revolutionary lawlessness. Such regimes would be able to master the social question, but only by instituting labor systems akin to that of southern slavery—that is, by reducing their own white workers to slaves or industrial serfs under the command of a master class. In return, needless to say, the workers would be grateful for the cradle-to-grave security and succor that the black slaves of the United States ostensibly were enjoying under their paternalistic masters. Any future progress would have to be slow, sporadic, and limited.

Dew thus ended where George Fitzhugh, Henry Hughes, George Frederick Holmes, Beverley Tucker, J. H. Hammond, James Henley Thornwell, and many others would begin—by celebrating the social system of the South not only as a positive good for black slaves and specific white masters, but as the model for a

future world order for people of all races. That celebration passed
most eloquently into the literary production of novelists like
William Gilmore Simms and Augusta Jane Evans, and of poets like
William Grayson and Henry Timrod.

I here stress the intellectual efforts of the elite without apology
or embarrassment, for, contrary to current academic romance, the
elite played a big and probably decisive role in the tragic history of
the Old South. But it would be a great error to assume that the
leading themes did not resonate among the common slaveholders
and, beyond them, among the yeomen. Andrew Johnson's con-
gressional and local speeches in East Tennessee provide a startling
illustration, especially since they date from the 1840s—that is,
even before he is likely ever to have heard of George Fitzhugh.
Johnson plainly told his yeomen constituents that slavery was
indeed the rock on which all civilized society had been built, and
that the choice they faced was to maintain black slavery or, like the
northern and European workers, prepare to be enslaved themselves.

The southern newspapers kept their readers abreast by publishing excerpts from the British Parliamentary Reports on the condition of the working class and by reporting on the views of
prominent British and European critics, both Tory and Socialist.
Capitalism emerged from these well-documented accounts as a
horror story of unemployment, starvation, child and female labor,
slums, inescapable poverty, and—in a word—misery for the mass
of the population. And wealthy southerners traveled to Europe
every year, bringing back eye-witness accounts with which to
regale the press and the crowded lecture halls that could be found
in almost every town and village.

Most impressively, they demonstrated the sincerity at the horror of what they saw and of the favorable comparisons they made
with southern slavery by expressing their views privately in diaries
and in letters to family and friends. Francis Pickens of South
Carolina, for example, wrote Benjamin Perry from Europe in awe
of the wonders of the wealth, culture, and material achievements

of the new bourgeois civilization. But he added, it made the heart sick to witness the misery of the workers and peasants whose labor makes it all possible. "God save us," he cried out, "from a government based on the free-labor system."

Now, Pickens, Perry, Grayson, Thornwell, Fitzhugh himself, and many others who viewed slavery as the solution to Europe's social question were Unionists, not secessionists, much less fire-eaters. It made sense. For as Pickens wrote Perry from New York during the terrible unemployment and suffering of the late 1850s, slavery would be much safer in, rather than out of, the Union. Bourgeois society was unraveling, and the capitalist countries would have to reinstitute some form of personal servitude to survive. In this perspective, time was on the side of the South.

A great many secessionists—Henry Hughes and Robert Barnwell Rhett for example—shared the analysis of bourgeois society but drew different political conclusions. Both sides, nonetheless, took a global view, analyzed the position of the South through comparison and contrast, and understood that the fate of the South and of slavery depended upon the outcome of a worldwide struggle between competing social systems.

By the late 1840s this defense of slavery in the abstract—*i.e.*, slavery for whites and well as blacks—had become common coin among political leaders as well as ministers and educators. And for immediate purposes, note the assumptions that underlay this line of thought and the methods used to validate it. First, there was universal recourse, in the religiously grounded slave society of the Old South, to divine sanction—to the Bible, which appeared to justify slavery, not merely black slavery, as God-ordained. And there was recourse to the study of ancient history to demonstrate the ubiquity of slavery in all countries and among all races. But the ubiquity of slavery had to be established for subsequent history, if the case was to be made. Hence, the southern intellectuals studied medieval history and the social systems of the modern world to demonstrate that the free-labor system—what we would call capitalism—was a new and dangerous departure, which nicely paralleled the rise of religious heresy, infidelity, and a corrupt liberal theology. Looking at the North's plunge into the religious and secular heresies of radical democracy and Jacobinism, abolitionism, and women's rights, the proslavery southerners denounced the increasing theological and institutional liberalism of the northern churches, sardonically calling their communicants "baptized infidels."

From this perspective the defense of southern slavery turned into a defense of Western Christian Civilization, which the proslavery intellectuals saw as falling prey to moral degeneracy, infidelity, the destruction of the family, social anarchy, and the brutal exploitation of the laboring classes by callous and irresponsible capitalists. It were as if they were crying out, as Allen Tate would do a century later, that American southerners were the only real Europeans left—the last effective opponents of the bourgeois barbarism of the modern world, the last genuine heirs of Christian civilization and a properly stratified and humane social order.

The comparative method reveals, contrary to Larry Tise's assertion in his important book *Proslavery*, that no other slave society generated such a world view. That is, while Cuba, Brazil, Jamaica, and other slave societies produced hard-line defenses of slavery, none produced a broad critique of capitalism as a social system, much less a call for the reinstitution of slavery in the metropolitan countries. The comparative method thereby throws into relief the uniqueness of southern slave society as a hybrid suspended between the premodern and modern worlds. And it provides the basis for an interpretation of southern slavery that could take the full measure of southern distinctiveness while recognizing how much it shared with the bourgeois society it struggled against.

For a second illustration I would like to jump to our own time and focus on the intellectuals who called themselves "Agrarians" during the late 1920s and 1930s and on those who have succeeded them. Let me confess that I do so because I consider them among the outstanding social critics of our time, notwithstanding my reservations about their archconservative world view and sometimes flatly reactionary politics. For above all others, the Agrarians represented a vital continuity with the southern past, and their heirs can legitimately speak of themselves as the bearers of the South's most powerful literary and ideological tradition. Even those who cavil at my estimate of their contributions to social theory would, I hope, acknowledge their enormous contributions to American literature and literary criticism. We are, after all, talking about Allen Tate, John Crowe Ransom, Caroline Gordon, Donald Davidson, John Gould Fletcher, John Peale Bishop, and others of recognized stature.

These were first-rate intellectuals, and it is not my fault that so many of them were politically to the right of Genghis Khan. But beyond that prejudice lies another point. These traditionalists celebrated provincialism of a sort as well as southern distinctiveness. If, therefore, it could be shown that they too saw themselves as heirs of a transatlantic culture, and saw the fate of the South as well as the course of southern history, as bound up with the fate and history of the Western World, then the case would be made.

Certainly, the traditionalist conservatives did not go unchallenged in the Old South, were battered in the New, and have represented a shrinking minority in our own time. We have all been taught about the liberalism of Mr. Jefferson and early-national Virginia, although I may as well admit that I find most of it a myth. No one, however, could fairly dismiss the challenges of the later era—populism and progressivism—as myth. And we need to recognize the nature of the political struggles in the South today, which primarily pit liberalism not against conservatism, but against a free-market older liberalism that calls itself conservative as the result of a misunderstanding. The traditionalists are still with us, partially allied with and often confused with the political current of religious fundamentalism, but the heart of the political right today lies with those who rallied to Ronald Reagan as much for his nineteenth-century free-market economic liberalism as for other and worse reasons. It remains the traditionalists who carry on, however weakly, the struggle for a distinctly southern world

view, which, from antebellum times to the present, has always
been anticapitalist—an anticapitalism that its great theorists from
John Taylor of Caroline to the advanced proslavery writers to Tate
and the Agrarians and on to Richard Weaver and M. E. Bradford
have never made the slightest effort to deny. For better or worse,
to speak of a distinctive southern culture in politically meaningful
terms—not merely a high culture but the cultural mainstream of
society, once we transcend folk culture—means to speak of southern conservatism in its traditionalist formulation, however many
caveats, qualifications, and counterpoints we may wish to file.

One of the largely untold stories about the Agrarian movement
centered in Nashville was its close connection with European
intellectual and political life. Its leading figures either studied
abroad, like John Crowe Ransom, or traveled widely, like Allen
Tate, or at least followed European cultural and political trends
closely. The decision to collaborate with British conservatives on
the book *Who Owns America* in the late 1930s—the book that
served as a sequel to *I'll Take My Stand*—and the Agrarians' close
relation to T. S. Eliot in sociopolitical thought as well as in literary
criticism, should therefore come as no surprise. Indeed, as men-
tioned, Tate proclaimed—sadly, not boastfully—that southerners
were the only real Europeans left anywhere. He should, I believe,
be understood as saying that the South was trying to remain
faithful to the older European Christian tradition and conservative
social order, while the North and Europe itself had embraced the
heresies of liberalism, secularism, and industrial capitalism. He
certainly knew that the South itself was succumbing steadily to
those evils, and he had the wit to recognize that the Old South and
the Confederacy, the demise of which he lamented, had made
their own deep compromises with the bourgeois world he despised.

From the Agrarians to that extraordinary social theorist,
Richard Weaver, and more recently such perceptive critics as M.
E. Bradford, Thomas Fleming, and John Shelton Reed, twentieth-
century southern conservatives have picked up the relay from the

intellectuals of the Old South. Among other things, they have
carried on the attack not only against the Leviathan state and
religious heterodoxy and infidelity, but against capitalism—
against the triumphant social system of the modern world. As
southerners and as traditionalists they could be and have been
ignored. They were, after all, not fated to play well in New York.
Today, they are largely ignored even in the South, where the
universities have passed into the hands of liberals and of free-
market rightwingers who have usurped the conservative label.

The southern tradition, as Weaver called it, remains at bay and
has poor prospects. The intrusion of industrialism, high-tech, and
religious as well as secular liberalism has steadily been sweeping
all before it. The so-called conservatism that rides high in the
South today—the Reaganism, if you prefer—corresponds closely
to the Yankee liberalism of a century ago in its celebration of the
virtues of the marketplace and unbridled capitalism. The participation of the religious fundamentalists in the Reagan coalition
complicates the story, but it does not alter the essentials. The
southern tradition, however, arose and throve on the countryside
and in the villages, which are today being overwhelmed by big
business, high-tech, corporate centralization, the deterioration of
the family, the spread of drugs and pornography, and the rest of the
goodies and wonders of consumerism.

The beleaguered traditionalists fight on as best they can, and for
our immediate purposes their primary significance remains their
insights into the moral and historical origins of the current world
crisis. Far from taking provincial ground, even in their defense of a
version of provincialism, and far from trying to create a traditionalist bunker in the South to shut out and defy the modern
world, they have drawn upon their southern roots to enter the
struggle for a new world order, albeit one that respects a high level
of particularism and regional autonomy.

Here, permit me to restrict myself to outlining some of the
views of Richard Weaver, probably their boldest, most acute, and
most learned modern theorist. Weaver described modern man as

"a moral idiot"—a self-infatuated creature, increasingly alienated from community and family and therefore from his own nature—a man caught up in a frantic and fruitless search for something called identity and for a personal freedom and self-expression indistinguishable from animal license. Now, that may seem like familiar stuff to people who, in recent decades, have been inundated by books on the decline and fall of everything and everyone—by a veritable avalanche of radical popsociology that passes for social theory and, even more ludicrously, for scholarship on the cocktail-party circuit. I could not possibly, in this brief essay, if indeed at all, do justice to Weaver's work—to its depth of learning, its profound insights, its tough-minded critique of both the current world crisis and of the superficial responses to it. I must, I fear, impose upon you, as *obiter dictum,* one man's judgment that, in these matters, his books *Ideas Have Consequences* and *Visions of Order* read like the work of a big man, in contrast to that of whining little boys. I would add, however, that he firmly appreciated the community-based individualism that has characterized the South, and tellingly contrasted it with the bourgeois individualism that has characterized Western Europe and the North. Read with a discerning eye, his essay on "Two Types of Individualism" and his *The Southern Tradition at Bay* are, in their own way, models of a certain kind of comparative history.

Be that as it may, Weaver began a properly epistemological critique of modernity by tracing the current crisis back to the rise of Nominalism in the late Middle Ages, and he carried it through with an attack on the radical features of the Reformation and the Enlightenment. Basically, he attacked the cult of scientism and rationalism—not science *per se* or reason, but the idea that scientific knowledge and secular reasoning are the only methods for understanding the world—that they could substitute for the moral knowledge in God's revealed truth. In effect, he appealed to religion, especially invoking the folk wisdom of what he called "The Older Religiousness of the South," to make a point that could be expressed in secular and universal terms—that man's absurd confidence in his own ability to master Nature was leading to a moral catastrophe and was, more ominously, threatening to destroy the human race itself. Hence his eloquent denunciation of the use of the atomic bomb against Japan and his fierce denunciation of the concept and practice of total war. Weaver knew his antebellum sources and appears to have been especially influenced by the political and theological writing of Albert Taylor Bledsoe. In the end, he, like his antebellum predecessors and most recent followers, viewed bourgeois individualism, egalitarianism and radical democracy as expressions of man's revolt against God and Nature—as man's grand attempt to substitute himself for God at the center of the universe. He saw the outcome in twentieth-century totalitarianisms and the Leviathan state, as well as in the doctrine of total war and mass extermination, all of which he viewed as the logical outcome of massive attempts to remake the human race according to ideological prescriptions and in defiance of all human experience and the fragile, sinful nature of man himself.

In Weaver's hands, this effort exhibited unusual subtlety and erudition. And like his antebellum and Agrarian predecessors, he sought the social origins of a diseased modernity in the rise and expansion of capitalism—in a socioeconomic system that glorified egotism and rejected the truth that all freedom and human dignity are products of community social life anchored by private property. Like the Agrarians before him, he defended private property as a matter of each individual's owning what he himself could work with. He assailed corporate capitalism, along with socialism, as the economic handmaiden of the centralized state that was reducing man to moral idiocy. Conversely, he defended inequality as natural and inevitable and defended political deference, hierarchy, and duly constituted authority.

Whatever one thinks of Weaver's work, which represents an epitome of traditionalist southern thought, two things especially relevant to the essays in this volume emerge clearly. First, twentieth-century southern conservatism carries on the traditionalist thought of the Old South, not in its defense of slavery, which it has firmly repudiated, nor in its defense of segregation and racial stratification, from which it has awkwardly retreated, but in its assertion of a wide range of social and political values that recall those of premodern Europe. And second, traditionalist southern thought, from Randolph and Dew to the present, accepts the fate of the South as indissolubly linked to the fate of the world in general and of Europe in particular. Thus, now as before, the analyses and programs project the southern experience as at least one valuable model for a reconstructed world order. The southern traditionalists, in effect, combine localism with global concern— combine provincialism with a world view that recognizes the South as part of a transatlantic world and yet rejects cosmopolitanism in its various ideological forms. In so doing, they continue a centuries-long struggle against the political and economic consolidationism and personal alienation that have characterized the modern capitalist world. Such a vision necessarily recognizes the defense of southern distinctiveness as requiring the comparative sociological and historical method, while it does battle against the superficial cultural relativism that distinguishes most liberal and left-wing uses of that method.

In short, those who today advocate the comparative method in southern history may fairly claim that they are merely being faithful to the best efforts of the people they are called upon to study, and that there is simply no sound alternative for those who wish to understand the historical development of southern culture. That we have to learn this lesson from the far right, instead of from points on the political spectrum more congenial to the reigning forces in Academia, is just too bad. If we are to do our work honestly and well, we shall have to live with that discomfiture.

Honor and Martialism in the U.S. South and Prussian East Elbia during the Mid-Nineteenth Century

SHEARER DAVIS BOWMAN

Any historian of the United States who attempts to approach the subject of "honor and martialism" in the antebellum South from an international comparative perspective quickly encounters some notable historiographic and semantic detours. In the first place, the international comparativist constantly feels the powerful pull, a pull exerted by much of the most interesting literature on the Old South, to address intranational, interregional questions about the degree to which the white populations of the slave South and free North had similar or different cultures and values. Understandably, these questions have generally held greater interest for most scholars of the Civil War era than have questions about how Southern society differed from or was similar to a society beyond the borders of the United States. After all, it was North and South that went to war in 1861, not the South and South Africa, or the South and Brazil, or the South and Prussia. And I for one hope that the future will bring us many more systematic comparative studies between North and South: careful historical comparisons like *Prison and Plantation,* Michael Hindus's comparison of crime, justice, and authority in South Carolina and Massachusetts from the Revolution to Reconstruction; or *The Web of Progress,* by William and Jane Pease, which juxtaposes Charleston and Boston during the Jacksonian Era.[1]

Accomplished scholars have presented rather different arguments on the issue of cultural differences between free North and slave South. And these differences are readily apparent in studies that deal with the subjects of honor and martialism. On the subject of martial, warlike values, John Hope Franklin, in a 1956 book entitled *The Militant South*, concluded that the region did indeed have "a penchant for militancy which at times assumed excessive proportions," a penchant reflected in the claim of white southerners by 1860 that their region was "the fountainhead of martial spirit in the United States."[2] This claim was largely discounted by Marcus Cunliffe in *Soldiers and Civilians: The Martial Spirit in America, 1775–1865*, first published in 1968. This challenge, from an Englishman no less, to what some southerners saw as a pillar of their regional pride provoked considerable furor; and in his "Foreword" to the book's second edition, Cunliffe responded to his critics by reiterating his contention that North and South "did not differ fundamentally, up to 1865, in their ways of thinking about combat and military display."[3]

Parallel differences of interpretation are obvious in more current studies that focus on the word "honor." For example, according to Bertram Wyatt-Brown's *Honor and Violence in the Old South*, we should recognize a distinction between the antebellum North as "a section devoted to conscience and to secular economic concerns," and the Old South as a section "devoted to honor and persistent community sanctions that eventually compelled the slaveholding states to withdraw" from the Union in 1860–1861.[4] Yet such regional distinctions appear irrelevant in Gerald F. Linderman's *Embattled Courage: the Experience of Combat in the American Civil War*, published in 1987. "Young Americans" North and South, argues Linderman, "would most often cite 'duty' as having prompted them to enlist and 'honor' as having held them to soldiering through their terms of enlistment." Linderman acknowledges that "idealization of the mounted warrior wrapped the cavalry, especially the Confederate horse, within an aura of romance." Nevertheless, he sees the chivalric ideal of knightliness, "an extension and an exaggeration of honor," as having an "intense" impact not only on "the southern upper class, especially the

Virginia gentlemen," but also on the "New England Brahmins."[5] It is within the ranks of this Brahmin elite that one would expect to find Wyatt-Brown's culture of conscience most clearly imprinted. Despite such stark differences in perspective, no student of the antebellum era would dispute that the most "martial" manifestation of personal "honor," the often romanticized phenomenon of duelling, was more prevalent in the slave states than in the free states. At the very least we must agree with Jeannette Hussey, writing in 1980, that "Southern gentlemen viewed the custom of duelling more seriously than did their northern brothers."[6] One student of the subject has gone so far as to suggest that the duel was more deeply rooted in the nineteenth-century South than in any other part of the world. In an entertaining collection of vignettes published in 1951 under the title *Gentlemen, Swords and Pistols*, Harnett Kane declared that "the 1800's witnessed the world's last great stand of formal duelling, in this area below and beyond the old Mason and Dixon line."[7] On the contrary, varieties of formal dueling survived, even flourished, in parts of continental Europe throughout the nineteenth century. Harnett Kane's statement would be more accurate if it read that the South witnessed the English-speaking world's "last great stand of formal duelling." No notable duels took place in England after 1852,[8] while there were notorious if infrequent duels in the South as late as the early 1880s.[9] According to a recent book by V. G. Kiernan entitled *The Duel in European History: Honour and the Reign of Aristocracy*, which is at its best when discussing English history and English writers like Walter Scott and Lord Byron, in mid-century Britain dueling was rapidly being "relegated to the realm of fantasy," its reality fading due to multi-pronged attacks from Utilitarian thinking, from Evangelical religion, and from the critical pressure being exerted by "both middle-class and working-class opinion."[10] In the South, with an enslaved laboring class excluded by caste bondage from any claim to participation in the political arena, there was no "working-class opinion" to promote an antiaristocratic assault on dueling. Nor did the Old South have a self-conscious middle class distinct from the landed gentry, although evangelical Protestantism and classical republican moralism had sufficient clout within all strata of white society to keep state anti-dueling laws on the books. Even in the midst of the secession crisis of 1860–1, so fervently sectional a journal as Richmond's *Southern Literary Messenger* could publish an anonymous essay that attacked dueling as "monarchical in its origins, aristocratic in its maxims, and unchristian, immoral, and irrational in itself," and as based upon a false conception of both honor and the gentleman. This misconception emphasized "rank or position; also good name or reputation," and permitted "fornication, adultery, drunkenness, prodigality, duelling, and revenge in the extreme." (Perhaps the author had in mind the notorious Alexander Keith McClung, a Kentuckian by birth who became known as the "Black Knight of the South," and was, according to one historian, "perhaps the South's best known and most feared duelist."[11]) The *Messenger* essayist proceeded to offer an alternative to the "technical 'gentlemen'" who engaged in dueling and "pass current in the aristocratic circles of society." This alternative was *"the true Christian gentleman,"* "the model of the highest, most honoured, God-sanctioned type on earth," distinguished by "high generosity, scrupulous courtesy, and genuine politeness." This authentic gentleman looked upon the principle of honor as demanding "fidelity to every highest obligation of morality and natural religion."[12] The *Messenger* essay serves to illustrate a point made by Edward L. Ayers in his 1984 study of crime and punishment in the nineteenth-century South: due to the power of evangelical Protestantism in the region, "the most powerful critique" of the duelist's code of honor "came from within the South itself."[13] The *Messenger* essay also points up a fundamental ambiguity that bedevils every attempt to formulate clear-cut definitions of the words honor and gentleman as they were understood in the nineteenth-century Western world; for both honor and gentility (in the sense of that which is characteristic of a gentleman) could serve to denote either one's inner dignity and personal rectitude or one's external status and public repute.[14]

Whereas Ayers has emphasized "the fundamental ambivalence of the antebellum South as a whole towards honor,"[15] I would also stress the fundamental ambivalence inherent in the concept of honor itself.

Let me return briefly to Great Britain. Kiernan suggests that the waning of the duel in England was a prime example of the "tactical retreats" that "conservatism . . . showed itself so adept at in nineteenth-century Britain."[16] Conservatism in the mid-century South, by which I mean here simply the determination to preserve a regional status quo based on slavery as a tripartite system of labor discipline, race control, and capital investment, proved itself far less adept at such "tactical retreats" before the growing power of antislavery opinion in the more populous free states. For many white southerners during the 1850s, dueling could and did become intertwined with their prideful search for a regional cultural identity distinct from and superior to that of the self-righteous and hostile North. This seems particularly true of those southerners who defended Preston Brooks' caning of Charles Sumner in 1856 on the grounds that the South Carolina congressman had been "impelled by the highest motives," to quote the editor of the *Richmond Enquirer,* or on the grounds that the abolitionist senator from Massachusetts had declared himself "not amenable to the code of honor," to quote the author of a letter to the *Enquirer.*[17] As Daniel J. Boorstin has suggested, "'honor' became less an ideal toward which they [Southern gentlemen] strove than an idealization of their actual conduct."[18] To what extent the antebellum South's self-conscious regionalism, or sectionalism, and its glorication of martial manliness, had a plausible nineteenth-century parallel in the British Isles in the form of Scottish or Irish nationalism, I will leave to scholars better versed in British history.

Enough of Great Britain for the moment. My principal goal here is to explore what light another transatlantic regional comparison can shed on the phenomena of honor, martialism, and dueling in the South during the mid-nineteenth century. My comparative standard is a region in north central Europe unsurpassed in its reputation for aristocratic militarism—East Elbian Prussia, which in the mid-1800s comprised those six of the Hohenzollern monarchy's eight provinces that were situated entirely or partly east of the Elbe River: moving roughly from east to west, the six provinces of East and West Prussia (administratively united as provincial Prussia from 1824 to 1878), Posen, Pomerania, Silesia, Brandenburg, and Saxony. This territory encompassed most of present-day East Germany, northern and western Poland, and the Kaliningrad Oblast of the Soviet Union.

What Americans call the duel was known by several different terms in German-speaking central Europe. The German *Duell*, like the English duel, derives from the archaic Latin *duellum*, meaning war. Those of us who, as high school students, toured ancient Gaul with Caesar's *Commentaries* will recall that the later Latin word for war was *bellum*, while the word for two or double was *duo*. The combination *duo-bellum* seems to have generated the later understanding—some would say misunderstanding— that a duel was "a miniature war between two individuals."[19] Another German word for the duel, *Zweikampf*, communicates the same message: a combat or battle between two persons. The word *Zweikampf* encompassed duels with pistols, which became increasingly popular during the nineteenth century in affairs of honor among army officers and political opponents. Another word, *Mensur*, was restricted to the highly stylized fencing contests, with protective gear, that were part of what one historian calls "the 'hidden curriculum' of student subculture" at most German universities.[20] This ritualized and domesticated dueling, engaged in by members of elitist associations or fraternities known as Corps and *Landsmannschaften*, usually drew blood and often left scars, but seldom caused critical or fatal wounds. (In Louisiana during the early decades of the nineteenth century, where French influence prolonged the use of swords in affairs of honor,[21] death was a more likely outcome of dueling swordplay than was the case among fraternity fencers in Prusso-Germany.) East Elbian apologists for dueling offered similar justifications of the practice among both university students and army officers: just as the duel serves as a test of courage for officers and thereby helps prepare them for war, wrote a retired general, so "student duels [*Bestimmungsmensuren*] in the universities are a test of courage, of which we should not rob the youth."[22]

Most serious mid-century dueling in East Elbia seems to have involved army officers, even though an officer making offensive insults that provoked a challenge and led to a duel with a fellow officer could be dismissed from the corps. According to official figures for the Prussian army reported by Karl Demeter, between 1843 and 1856 there was an annual average of 4.6 serious affairs of honor involving regular army officers—serious meaning that at least one person involved in each duel received formal punishment from the military authorities.[23] Albrecht von Boguslawski (1834–1905), a retired Lieutenant General, recalled in the 1890s that during the previous half-century he had been involved, in a variety of ways, in some fifty affairs of honor, five of which had resulted in actual duels.[24] After the Revolution of 1848–9 introduced an elected assembly to the Prussian monarchy, dueling in Prussia spread out from its traditional enclaves, among military officers and university fraternities, and spilled over into political conflicts between conservative monarchists and liberal parliamentarians. In other words, as in the antebellum United States, dueling spread to the arena of party and factional strife. The era of the second party system in the U.S. fomented such famous southern duels as that in 1837 between old friends George Dromgoole, a Virginia Whig, and Democrat Dan Dugger of North Carolina, or the 1845 affair involving North Carolina Whig Thomas L. Clingman and Alabama Democrat William L. Yancey.[25] Yet the duel that aroused the greatest furor during the thirties and forties involved not two southerners, but a Congressman from Maine, Jonathan Cilley, who in 1838 accepted what turned out to be a fatal challenge from Kentucky Congressman William Graves.[26]

One of the best-known duels in mid-nineteenth century Prussia

took place in Berlin, in May of 1861, between General, later Field
Marshall, Edwin von Manteuffel, then head of the royal military
cabinet, and Karl Twesten, a judge and an outspoken anti-govern-
ment deputy in the Lower House of the Prussian parliament. The
duel grew out of the bitter political struggle over the army reorganization bill being pushed by the government of the new king,
William I—a struggle that would soon lead to the king's fateful
appointment of Otto von Bismarck as minister president in 1862.
Karl Twesten had written a brochure entitled "What Can Still Save
Us," in which the head of the military cabinet was referred to as "a
mischievous [unheilvoll] man in a mischievous position." Manteuffel issued a challenge to Twesten, who accepted it even though
he considered the duel a medieval relic. The weapons used were
pistols, and the affair ended when Twesten received a serious
though not fatal wound to his right arm. Although one could cite
this affair as evidence of a traditional culture of honor among
upper-class Prussians, in this instance the duel stood out as a
weapon of political intimidation (a purpose which the duel also
served in the Old South). To quote Erich Eyck, one of the premier
historians of the Bismarckian era: "Everyone understood the sense
of this duel, as Twesten himself understood it: criticism of military
affairs should be made possible."[27] Several years later, in 1865,
Bismarck himself adopted much the same tactic when he issued a
challenge to a duel with pistols to one of the founders of the
Progressive party, the Berlin pathologist and university professor
Rudolf Virchow. Bismarck had contemptuously belittled the arguments contained in a report submitted in favor of increased naval
appropriations by a special commission, whose parliamentary
spokesman was Virchow. The professor responded on the floor of
the chamber of deputies by saying that the minister president had
obviously not read the entire report. "But if he has read it," stated
Virchow, "then I really do not know what I should think of his
veracity."[28] This statement prompted Bismarck's challenge, which
became public, and which created such a furor that the presiding
officer of the Lower House made a formal declaration that Virchow

should feel no compunction to fight on account of anything he had said in his official capacity as a deputy. Elaborate behind-the-scenes negotiations terminated the affair without loss of face to either man,[29] and Virchow remained a member of the Prussian parliament until 1902.

* * *

More than a few people, in response to the idea of comparing the Old South and contemporaneous East Elbia, have asked me, with an understandably skeptical look in their eyes, whether Prussia had any direct influence on the Old South. Very little, I must respond, either in terms of immigration or ideas. There is not even evidence to support the old notion, propagated by such former academic giants as William E. Dodd and Carl Becker, that the early and influential proslavery ideologue Thomas R. Dew (1802–46) of Virginia imbibed his conservative critique of natural-rights political theory while studying at some German universities before joining the faculty at William and Mary College in 1826 (though he did visit the German Confederation as a tourist).[30] Ironically, the best known native of East Elbia to make his home in the antebellum South—Francis Lieber (1807–72) of Berlin, who studied at the Prussian universities of Berlin and Halle before receiving his doctorate from the Saxon University of Jena—had to repress what one biographer has called "a growing distaste for slavery" during his tenure as professor of history and political economy at South Carolina College from 1835 to 1856.[31]

Nonetheless, it does seem that the Prussian nobility and officer corps played a small part in helping to spread the formal duel and aristocratic code of honor from Europe to America during the revolutionary war against England. The best known German-speaking transfer agent was a man whose statue stands in Washington, D.C.: Friedrich Wilhelm Augustus Heinrich Ferdinand, Baron von Steuben (1730–94), born in the city of Magdeburg, located on the west bank of the Elbe River and then part of Hohenzollern Brandenburg. During the Seven Years War of 1756–63

Steuben became a captain and what we would call "a General Staff officer with the troops" [*Quartiermaster Leutnant*].[32] At the war's conclusion he failed to receive the promotion he expected; instead, he was demoted to staff captain with a garrison regiment and soon summarily discharged at the age of thirty-six, perhaps because the king had just discovered that Steuben's noble title was spurious, or perhaps because Steuben had made the "inconsiderate step," as he later termed it,[33] of challenging a senior officer to a duel. After a 1777 meeting in Paris with Benjamin Franklin and Silas Deane, Steuben was able to present himself to the Continental Congress and George Washington as Lieutenant General Baron de Steuben, fresh from service as aide-de-camp to the King of Prussia. The rest of the story, which has Steuben commissioned Inspector General of the Continental Army with the rank of major general, and demonstating his practical genius by adapting Prussian drill techniques to American conditions, is already familiar to many American readers. Less familiar, probably, is the challenge to a duel that Steuben issued in 1778 to Major General Charles Lee of Virginia, a former regular British officer who had become one of Washington's most outspoken critics. Lee, having demanded a court martial to vindicate his conduct at the battle of Monmouth, was in fact convicted of disobeying orders to attack, retreating unnecessarily, and showing disrespect to Washington.[34] Steuben, after reviewing the official Journal of the Court Martial, sent his aide-de-camp, Benjamin Walker, to deliver a written challenge to Lee for having "cast indecent reflections" on Steuben's conduct. "Were I in my own country, where my reputation is long ago established," wrote Steuben with something less than complete candor, "I should put myself above your epigrams and would have despised them. But here I am a stranger. You have offended me; I desire you will give me satisfaction. You will choose the place, time, and arms; but as I do not like to be a distant or slow spectator, I desire to see you as near and as soon as possible." The duel did not materialize, for Steuben accepted Lee's explanation that he "had not the least idea" of disparaging the Prussian's "courage."[35]

A rough equivalent to Steuben in the Confederate Army during the Civil War was Johann August Heinrich Heros von Borcke (1835-95), author of *Memoirs of the Confederate War for Independence,* which recounts his tenure as a staff officer with General J. E. B. Stuart in 1862–63.[36] A second lieutenant with the Second Brandenburg Regiment of Dragoons in 1860, Borcke resigned his commission in order to fight for southern independence,[37] and arrived in Charleston in 1862 on a blockade runner from the Bahamas. His account of the stopover in Nassau shows that a Prussian Junker could be just as racially condescending toward blacks as a southern planter. His *Memoirs* report that he was greatly "amused" by "the negro women" in Nassau. "In all their native hideousness of form and feature, they bedizen their persons with European costumes of every fashion, fabric, and colour, and walk the streets with a solemn dignity that even a Spanish hidalgo might envy."[38] Although von Borcke manifested the same concern with chivalrous conduct and glorious reputation as had Steuben, his noble pedigree was, unlike Steuben's, above reproach.[39] Yet I have found no evidence that Heros von Borcke was ever party to a duel; and I have searched in vain through his *Memoirs* and a later untranslated work, entitled *With Prince Frederick Charles,* for any discussion of dueling and honor. Nonetheless, the latter book contains an interesting account of von Borcke's audience with His Majesty William I in 1866, after the Prussian Confederate had returned home. Borcke, despite having presented himself to Minister of War Albrecht von Roon as "Stuart's Chief of Staff and General Inspector of the Cavalry of the Army of Northern Virginia," was being commissioned a lowly second lieutenant along with a dozen or so other men. During the king's review of his new officers, he reportedly shook von Borcke's hand and said: "I am happy to see you here again, and I thank you for having brought so much honor [*Ehre*] to Prussia in distant lands."[40] Here we see a straightforward royal understanding of honor as glorious reputation. A somewhat analogous but less pretentious use of the word honor by a contemporary Prussian woman is to be found in the autobiography published by Fanny Lewald in the early 1860s. Recounting her adolescent experiences in Berlin, Lewald noted that "While one views it as a matter of honor [*Ehre*] for a young man to earn his bread, one considers it as a kind of disgrace or dishonor [*Schande*], to allow daughters to do the same . . ."[41]

Although the cases of Steuben and von Borcke demonstrate that there were some direct links between the histories of East Elbia and the Old South, the comparability of the two regions does not derive from the influence of one society on the other. Juxtaposing the South and East Elbia circa 1850 does satisfy both of the criteria specified by French historian Marc Bloch in his classic 1928 essay on the comparative method: "a certain similarity or analogy between observed phenomena—that is obvious—and a certain dissimilarity between the environments in which they occur."[42] The analogies between the antebellum South and contemporaneous East Elbia seem to derive from two principal sources: first, similarities between each region's landed elite—the plantation gentry and landed Junkerdom, both of whom included adherents to the duelist's code of honor; and second, structural and functional parallels between plantations and Junker estates [*Rittergüter*, literally "knight's estates"] as at the same time commercial agricultural enterprises and authoritarian political communities. Plantations and knight's estates produced generally profitable cash crops, especially southern cotton and tobacco, East Elbian wheat and wool, for an international capitalist market then centered in England. And the proprietors of knight's estates, like southern planters, farmed their land with laborers who were subject to noneconomic forms of coercion. Junker landowners retained personal and inheritable judicial authority over their laborers until mid-century, and their local police power survived into the early 1870s, even though hereditary bondage was abolished in Prussia, by monarchical fiat, over half a century before Lincoln's Emancipation Proclamation and the Thirteenth Amendment to the Constitution accomplished the same end in the South. Yet plantations and Junker estates existed within very different geographic, political, and racial millieus. To cite obvious dissimilarities, the provinces of Prussian East Elbia had no expansive frontier, no republican constitutions, and no black slaves, while the states of the U.S. South had no hereditary monarchy or nobility, no legacy of serfdom, and no large standing army. Indeed, the differences between the two regions as historical environments were of such magnitude that the logic of comparing them can be expressed by borrowing the words that Robert Brentano used to justify his comparing the English and Italian churches of the thirteenth century: the South and East Elbia are each "meant to be seen, for a change, against what it was not. In this sort of profile it has a different look."[43]

Some obvious differences can be highlighted by surveying emancipation and its aftermath in East Elbia. The liberation of Prussia's privately held serfs came as an early installment in the broad-ranging Prussian Reform Movement of 1807–19, orchestrated by the royal bureaucracy in the aftermath of the humiliating defeat inflicted on the Hohenzollern armies by Napoleonic France in 1806. Despite this military setback, which temporarily discredited the Junker-dominated officer corps, the Junkers received substantial state-mandated compensation in land and money in return for the abolition of their lordship over peasant land and their rights to compulsory labor services. This is the sort of compensation that southern planters did not receive during the abolition of chattel slavery. That East Elbia's landed elite received postemancipation compensation helps explain how many Junkers were able to take aggressive advantage of the profitable opportunities presented by the international capitalist market during the middle decades of the nineteenth century for the agricultural commodities, wool and grain, that could be produced on the cold and dry plains of the Prusso-German northeast—cold and dry relative to the climate of the U.S. South. (Other factors that bolstered Junkerdom's entrepreneurial muscle were the infusion of untitled families and new money after the bureaucratic reformers ended the nobility's legal monopoly on the ownership of knight's estates, plus the direct financial support that the monarchy provided to Junker landowners through the provincial mortgage credit associations [*Landschaften*], first established in the late 1700s.) Junkerdom also proved very successful in maintaining a high degree of political clout on the national level throughout the 1800s—far more successful than did the South's plantation gentry. This can be ascribed to two principal factors. First, whereas the provinces of East Elbia remained the preponderant heartland of the Prussian monarchy, even after the unification of Germany under Hohenzollern authority in 1870–1, the states of the plantation South became more and more of a minority section within the United States during the nineteenth century. Second, what historian Hans-Jürgen Puhle has called the Junkers' "privileged position next to the bureaucracy and the military in the Prussian power syndicate,"[44] made them part and parcel of a formidable and adaptable authoritarian regime that did not exist in the United States.

Given our concern here with the topic of honor and martialism, perhaps the most dramatic difference between the South and East Elbia was the size and influence of the national military establishment, the standing army, a dissimilarity due primarily to the location of the Hohenzollern dominions on the open plains of north central Europe, and the geographic isolation of the American republic from serious external threats. The discrepancy between the size of the Prussian and U.S. armies greatly impressed Virginia's Thomas R. Dew, who observed in 1836 that Prussia, with a population smaller than that of the United States, maintained a peacetime army of 126,000 troops, twenty-one times the number of men (6,000) serving in the U.S. Army.[45] On the eve of the 1848–9 Revolution the Prussian army numbered 9,434 regular officers, of whom seventy-seven percent (7,264) had noble titles.[46] On the eve of the Civil War, the army of the United States numbered 1,080 regular officers, of whom some 300 left with the seceding slave states.[47] Whereas the duelist's code of honor continued very much a part of the officer corps' subculture in mid-century Prussia, by the 1850s, according to Edward Coffman, U.S. Army officers "were rarely confusing dueling with honor anymore."[48] Regardless of how one defines the term "militarism"— whether one sees it as an imbalance between civil and military authorities in favor of the military, or as a function of symbolic relationships between certain socioeconomic structures and the military establishment[49]—East Elbia was clearly a more militaristic society than was the South. However, this does not mean that East Elbian society as a whole manifested a greater propensity for personal, extra-legal violence than did southern society. In fact, the reverse appears true.[50] In seeking to explain why extra-legal personal violence was more widespread in Dixie, I would point on the one hand to the absence of the authoritarian bureaucracy that governed in Prussia, and on the other hand to the combination of the slave plantation and the western frontier, the two interacting phenomena that U. B. Phillips pointed to decades ago as decisive influences on the development of the Old South.[51]

Another dramatic difference between the two regions revolved around the defiantly republican politics of the U.S. South and the pervasively monarchical traditions of Prussian East Elbia. An 1849 pamphlet by Count Adolf Heinrich von Arnim-Boitzenburg helps to illustrate the significance of the dichotomy. "The Prussian army is more accustomed than any other to seeing in its king the one and only commander, its personal leader and highest lord," wrote Arnim-Boitzenburg. Requiring the officer corps to pledge abstract allegiance to a constitutional document rather than personal loyalty to their king, as the revolutionaries of 1848 demanded, would sap "the spirit of the army," insisted the Count; and this martial spirit was absolutely necessary to protect Prussia's relatively small population against the other great powers of Europe.[52] In contrast, the antebellum southern elite inherited from their revolutionary forebears an abiding distrust of standing armies as engines of tyranny. In the South the concept of personal honor was intimately wrapped up with ideas about the manly republican independence and liberty of free citizens, as opposed to the submission and

degradation associated with slavery.[53] In monarchical and militaristic Prussia the crown energetically promoted throughout the
nineteenth century the idea that an officer's honor consisted first
and foremost in the punctual and precise execution of express
commands.[54] Since the Hohenzollerns had been trying to curtail
dueling among their army officers since the seventeenth century,
on the grounds that fighting among military as well as civilian
officials detracted both materially and philosophically from monarchical power and authority, the officer corps found itself torn in two
directions: between, on the one hand, its traditional view of itself
as a privileged warrior caste, which looked upon dueling as "a
symbol of courage, of honorableness;"[55] and, on the other hand, its
unquestioned loyalty to the crown as the font of authority and
honor. A compromise of sorts between king and officer corps was
implemented by royal regulations issued in 1843. Their chief
architect was General and Minister of War Hermann von Boyen
(1771–1848), who believed that dueling could constitute a valid test
of courage and character, but who also saw the officer corps as
having the obligation and the right to intervene in affairs of honor
so as to prevent frivolous duels.[56] According to the 1843 regulations, regimental councils of honor and Tribunals of Honor had
jurisdiction over all personal quarrels and affronts among officers
that could lead to dueling, and unauthorized duels were subject to
punishment after the fact.[57] The Old South had some faint civilian
variations on this theme in the form of committees established by
local and state antidueling associations to rein in affairs of honor.
Harriet Martineau observed that one such committee, "A Court of
Honor" instituted during the 1830s by an antidueling society in
New Orleans, "ended by sanctioning, instead of repressing, duelling."[58] Much the same can be said of Prussia's 1843 regulations,[59]
which remained in force for three decades, until new regulations
issued in 1874 preserved the councils and tribunals of honor but
placed greater authority in the hands of regimental commanders.[60]

Although East Elbia's monarchical militarism was absent from the Old South, both regions had evolved as colonial lands. The Elbe River had constituted the eastern frontier of the medieval German empire ruled by the Hohenstaufen dynasty. Hence, East Elbia and the South were settled largely by immigrants from western Europe who crossed the Elbe River to the east, or the Atlantic Ocean to the west, in search of land and opportunity. Hereditary bondage began to take hold in East Elbia and the South, during the sixteenth and seventeenth centuries respectively, as the result of complex processes that served the needs of substantial landowners for bound, coerced labor forces to raise cash crops for export to northwest Europe. As Georg Friedrich Knapp pointed out in 1891, "The modern large-scale business concern of the Junker estate [*Rittergut*] began with the forced labor of the unfree, just as the modern plantation business in the colonies began with the forced labor of the unfree; but the planter obtained Negroes in Africa and made them slaves; the *Rittergut* owner did not reach so far, for he took his peasants and made them serfs."[61]

There is considerable dispute in recent scholarship about how much agricultural capitalism should be ascribed to these serfholding Junkers and slaveholding planters. I am not going to risk here an extended voyage on the stormy seas of political economy, except to note that the dispute usually reflects the differences between a perspective on "capitalism" that focuses on markets and profitability and one that views "capitalism" as a discrete mode of production and system of social relations under which a wage-earning proletariat shares with its employers formal equality before the law, and under which purely economic considerations, as distinct from hereditary legal and group distinctions, dictate class relations.[62] Nevertheless, it is important to emphasize that the historical records of both colonial planters and contemporaneous Junkers indicate that what we might label entrepreneurial behavior and aristocratic values are not mutually exclusive. As Hans Rosenberg wrote in 1978 with regard to sixteenth-century Junkers, "The historical evidence demonstrates very clearly that . . . a rational, economically acquisitive mentality and conduct of life was quite compatible with the ethics and customs of an aristocratic class."[63] More recently Jack P. Greene, while discussing eighteenth-century Chesapeake society, has concluded in comparable fashion that "The 'market mentality' so powerfully exhibited" by the seventeenth-century founders of the plantation gentry "by no means dissipated but coexisted—easily—with rising aspirations for the establishment of a traditional patriarchy."[64] When we look toward nineteenth-century planters and Junkers, we need to remember that aristocratic valuations of personal honor and dueling could coexist—again easily—with a market-oriented and entrepreneurial acquisitiveness.

Although the U.S. South and Prussian East Elbia both originated as colonial lands, the historical timing and the cultural legacy of colonization were quite different for the two regions. Germanic colonization of the Slavic lands east of the Elbe peaked from the twelfth to the fourteenth centuries, and had effectively ended before English colonization of North America even began. After the seaboard colonies won their independence from England in the 1780s, voluntary immigrants of predominantly English and Scotch-Irish ancestry, and involuntary immigrants of African ancestry, streamed into the trans-Appalachian West. Thus, James Westphall Thompson could suggest in 1915 that "What the Trans-Allegheny country was to the United States in 1800, that the Trans-Elban country was to the Germans in 1200."[65]

Yet the process of colonization left the nineteenth-century South and East Elbia with very different racial legacies. Whereas Germanic colonists and indigenous Slavs became thoroughly intermixed in most of East Elbia within a couple of centuries, the European and African settlers in the South continued to live under a caste system even after the abolition of racial slavery for blacks. The ranks of landed Junkerdom in the mid-1800s, even in the older provinces of Brandenburg and Pomerania and East Prussia, included a large number of Slavic names like von Kleist; and the extended von Kleist family owned a total of fifty-three knight's estates in 1856. Hans Hugo von Kleist-Retzow of Pomerania, who became a member of the House of Lords, told his peers in 1866 that "I, my family, of Slavic stock, became German."[66] To be sure, the Prussian government feared the enduring strength of Polish national sentiment among the Polish aristocracy [szlachta] in Prussian Poland, the province of Posen especially. But in the Old South a man of known black ancestry could never hope to be accepted in the public arena on equal terms with whites, although there were occasional and anomalous African–American planters: men like the very fair-skinned Andrew Durnford of St. Rosalie sugar plantation in Louisiana's Plaquemines Parish,[67] or the darker-skinned mulatto William Ellison of Wisdom Hall cotton plantation in the Sumter District of South Carolina.[68]

Whereas southern culture and politics on the eve of the Civil War were actually bifurcated between black bondage and white freedom, contemporaneous East Elbia was heir to a more consistently hierarchical, corporatist view of society as composed of "organic," legally distinct classes, or estates [Stände]. This difference is fundamental to understanding some important differences between honor and dueling in the two regions. In Protestant states such as Prussia the Reformation had deprived the clergy of its medieval status atop of the corporatist pyramid, leaving the landed nobility as the premier social group in the land. In 1847, when King Frederick William IV opened the gates to political revolution by summoning the representatives of his realm to meet in Berlin as a United Diet, the delegates were divided into four distinct groups: the higher nobility, the lower nobility, the residents of cities, and the population in the countryside.[69] These traditional corporatist divisions, already incongruous in a society where noblemen and commoners intermingled occupationally and professionally as bureaucrats, army officers, owners of knight's estates, and university students, became more and more anachronistic after the Revolution of 1848–9 brought manhood suffrage and quasiconstitutional, quasiarliamentary government to Prussia. Nonetheless, the notion that honor was estate-specific, that each

each social group had its own particular claim to dignity and public respect, retained much of its cultural sway. And dueling, with its notion that only one's peers had "capacity to give satisfaction," had been traditionally viewed as an prerogative of noblemen, who were supposed to have a monopoly on martial courage and chivalrous conduct, and who carried the practice of dueling with them into those activities thought to be appropriate for aristocrats: university studies, the officer corps, and the higher bureaucracy. During the second half of the nineteenth century such upper-class activities became identified by German writers as appropriate to the status of gentlemen. Thus historical sociologist Karl Demeter, writing in the early 1960s, could conclude that "the one central feature to be found in the private social conduct of the German officer-corps in modern times," is "the social ideal of the *chevalier*, of the gentleman."[70] The irony in this statement is that German authors had to borrow both the concept of gentleman and the word itself directly from England; for the German language had no comparable word, since German history had no social group like the English gentry, in the sense of a class of gentlemen situated beneath the hereditary nobility but above the ordinary mass of commoners.

The situation was very different in the antebellum South, where the free white population admitted of no formally aristocratic, group-specific distinctions. To be sure, there was a perception among self-consciously upper-class southerners in the older plantation areas that the code duello, as detailed by former South Carolina governor John Lyde Wilson's oft-cited 1838 pamphlet *The Code of Honor*, applied only to altercations between men of distinction who qualified as proper, "high-toned" gentlemen. Yet in practice dueling was hardly limited to the ranks of what some observers have euphemistically termed the southern "aristocracy." Consider the following announcement, entitled "Fatal Duel," that appeared in a small-town Whig newspaper in West Tennessee in April of 1842, and concerned an affair in a small south Louisiana river town: "A duel was fought on Wednesday, ult. [ultimo, i.e., the month before the present one] between a Mr. Clark, clerk in the land office, and a Mr. Isriel, sugar broker, in which the latter was killed at the first fire.—Weapons pistols."[71] If land office clerks qualified as gentlemen, then the word was fast losing its elitist connotation and becoming applicable to all respectable citizens. This is precisely what happened in the antebellum South as property qualifications for voting were removed by the various states and as white manhood suffrage became the rule, coming even to Virginia and North Carolina in the 1850s. Accordingly, all white adult males could lay claim to the same privileges of full citizenship, and therefore to an equal share in gentility and honor. This was precisely the argument made in 1849 by the *Richmond Whig* in an article entitled "Abuses in the English Government." The English were condemned for being unable to separate "the idea of a gentleman from a certain degree of wealth and splendor, and certain aristocratical pretensions on the score of birth." In contrast, stated the *Whig*, "in America, every man, let his birth or station be what it may, who is distinguished by honorable and upright conduct, is understood to be a gentleman."[72] Moreover, this process—we might call it, after Max Weber, the "social de-mocratization" of gentility and honor[73]—was encouraged by the widely perceived necessity to promote the unity of white south-erners in support of black bondage, even though less than one-third of the white population in the eleven states that eventually joined the Confederacy belonged to slaveholding families. Consider the statement of Alabama Governor and Black Belt planter John A. Winston in 1855, during his second inaugural address, when he argued that "the existence of a race among us—inferior by nature to ourselves, in a state of servitude, necessarily adds to the tone of manliness and character of the superior race." Consequently, nonslaveholding whites in the South were "higher in the scale of intelligence" than lower-class whites in the free states, and "above those menial acts of servitude" which the latter performed. Furthermore, the nonslaveholding white was distin-guished by his high degree of patriotism, his elevated regard for duty, and "his polite bearing to, and his chivalrous defense of the fairer and better portion of creation." Such admirable sentiments, insisted Governor Winston, were "not peculiar to the educated and accomplished gentleman only. They belong to the Southern man without regard to his rank or position in life."[74] In other words, the traditional prerogatives of a superior class in Europe had become those of the superior race in the American South.

Ironically, conditions in the Old South bring to mind some of the conditions that prevailed in western Europe during the several centuries following the collapse of the Roman Empire, as a feudal social order of free nobles and enserfed masses took shape. Kiernan analyzes that feudal society in words which anticipate the slave South: "Despite great inequalities among the free, their freedom was a badge to be cherished by all alike, and an ideal which could in time be linked with the Roman republican virtue of liberty."[75]

Commentary / Edward L. Ayers

Without a second and unarmed, I have no inclination to offer a fundamental challenge to Professor Bowman's argument or his character. In fact, he has served us well by focusing on honor, martialism, and dueling as indices of comparison between the antebellum planters and the pre-1848 Junkers. I would like to build on the wealth of detail he has provided to help clarify the larger comparison between the South and Prussia, a comparison that has consumed so much of our energies over the last decade.

We might begin by distinguishing more carefully among the three related phenomena Professor Bowman discusses, for each tells us something different about the two societies we are trying to understand. Better than most things we could examine, dueling assumed recognizably similar forms in both the South and Prussia, was considered a signal institution of both regions, elicited considerable contemporary comment, and evolved in ways that allow us to use it as a barometer of the planters' and Junkers' sense of themselves. On the other hand, while martialism provided much of the impetus and context for dueling in Prussia, the southern attraction for martial values had only a brief opportunity to attach itself to a powerful military establishment. As a result, southern martialism necessarily remained more a cultural predisposition than an entrenched way of life. Honor, the larger culture in which both dueling and militarism were embedded, was more than the sum of its parts; it remains, after many studies, an elusive, complex, and problematic concept.

Besides breaking the topic down into distinct components, I would also like to set it in motion in a way that Professor Bowman did not attempt. One of the most challenging things about comparative history is that our targets are more likely than not moving at different speeds and maybe even in different directions. I would like to use that challenge as an opportunity to examine change rather than merely to freeze two societies in time in order to compare some essence they may or may not have shared over several decades.

Let me begin with a brief sketch of the evolution of the Junkers that will take us somewhat beyond Professor Bowman's focus. The landowners of Prussia experienced many hard times from the fifteenth century on, as they were buffeted by the vicissitudes of commercial agriculture, by an unstable political environment, by devastating military defeats, by a restive peasantry. Fortunately for the Junkers, though, in the eighteenth century they joined in a tight alliance with the state, which they served as officials and as officers. They survived as a class through all the vicissitudes of the nineteenth century, in fact, largely because they were so deeply attached to the state, an attachment that grew stronger in the face of the challenges of the new century.

After the defeat of the Prussian-led army by Napoleon at Jena in 1806 and the attendant end of serfdom and beginning of free trade in land and estates, the Junkers maintained their strategic position in the military. As increasing numbers of civil positions went to better-educated commoners, the Junkers of Prussia channeled their poorly educated sons into the military in astonishing proportions. Even as the Junkers' economic power dwindled in the early decades of the nineteenth century, their sons found proud sanctuary in the army. As one observer wrote in 1846, "when he gets a small beard, when the epaulettes for the first time flourish on his shoulders, when the plume for the first time waves from his head, when the soldiers in all corners present arms, how should he not feel that he is predestined to represent a 'higher being' in this world?"[1]

After 1848 the Prussian nobility saw further erosion of their ancient power over the rural folk among whom they lived and held on to their position in the army even more tenaciously. In the turmoil, the Junkers championed the army as the only true guarantor of order and justice; because the revolution left much of the old order intact the Prussians were able to dominate the powerful army in the 1860s and 1870s as they had in the 1830s and 1840s. Moreover, when the Junkers made an economic comeback in the last third of the nineteenth century they cultivated their self-consciously archaic ways, aided by the weight and privilege of their noble titles. Even as young noblemen took middle-class wives, they assimilated the commoners into the ethos of the military, "feudalized" them (creating a topic of much discussion in the society pages of American newspapers along the way, who were outraged that so many of our best young women were opting for marriages to dessicated European noblemen). The military schools of Prussia, meanwhile, dwelt on honor and military virtues at the expenses of other teaching.

History, in other words, seemed to be running backward east of the Elbe: industrialists were becoming ennobled and the ideals of the Enlightenment eroded even as the Junkers were becoming ever more deeply engaged in the international capitalist market. Perhaps the greatest testimony to the growing gap between an eroded personalism on the estates and a continued tradition of personal honor came late in the century; in those years, nearly two million rural laborers left the Prussian provinces and the Junkers turned to distinctly non-feudal, transitory, imported labor—yet the landlords preserved their traditional place in the Prussian bureaucracy and in the military. In 1900, 61 percent of its officers were noblemen, and the higher the officer the more likely he was to be of the oldest and most honorable families. In other words, honor seemed to inhere far more in modern bureaucratic and military structures than in archaic relationships between estate owners and their workers.

The contrasts with the history of the southern planters are striking. The well-known analogies between the postwar planters and the Junkers have been drawn because of their reactionary domination over an agricultural region during an era when the larger society was undergoing rapid industrialization. This brief sketch makes it clear that the Junkers had far greater success in adapting the new social order to their ideals and purposes than the postwar planters could even have hoped. After emancipation, the planters saw no further concerted attack on their plantations, but in every other facet of life they saw a precipitous and steady erosion of their power and influence. Once southern lawmakers granted planters the power of the lien in the 1870s, the landlords asked for little else from their state and national governments other than to be left alone. They were. Despite a few sentimental and overtly nostalgic novels and songs, the cultural power of the planters evaporated in the New South; the tides of change were on the side of the town dwellers, with their attachment to the emerging mass culture and mass economy of Gilded Age America. The sons and daughters of the planters married into the families of merchants and professionals and moved to town—not the other way around. The tiny professional army of the United States, the army that southerners still associated with their defeat, offered small refuge. The churches saw a new differentiation by class as well as by race, as common people created their own congregations, out of the reach of the planters.

The evolution of the planters and the Junkers across the nineteenth century shows, in other words, how intimately the planter class's power and identity were tied to slavery, not merely the plantation or even to race. The planters, unlike the Junkers, enjoyed no important role in the national government or military, no hereditary nobility, no ties of sentiment to a monarch. When slavery was gone, the planters had no other institution in which they could find refuge.

The history of dueling is the clearest example of this cultural dimension of class domination and testifies to the deep differences between the two landholding classes. Let me briefly trace the evolution of dueling in their societies. It seems that the heyday of the southern duel came in the 1830s and 1840s, here on the cotton frontier. Yet the practice fell under steady and increasing attack, and the 1850s may well have seen a decline in the practice. We see relatively little evidence of dueling in the Confederacy, as the elective officer corps undermined some of the rationale for dueling and as Christian soldiers such as Lee and Jackson clearly stood above the practice. The postwar years saw a steady diminution of dueling, even though a few famous conflicts appeared among the other kinds of violence that quickly became synonymous with the New South. Within a generation after Appomattox, the southern duel was a thing of the past.

Not so in Prussia. There, the duel flourished during the same decades it flourished in the antebellum South—and then continued to flourish, even as Germany experienced some of the most rapid industrial growth in Europe. In fact, as Bowman points out, dueling actually spread from the military and the university to politics after the reforms of 1848, when an elected assembly was established. As a recent account observes, "duelling continued to be practiced on quite a substantial scale in Protestant Prussia, not only among students but also among army officers, officers of the reserve, civilian aristocrats and impeccably bourgeois professionals such as doctors, dentists and apothecaries well into the twentieth century."[2] The mention of students in this passage is significant, for the universities of the South had nothing like the dueling societies of Germany. As the century drew to a close, as ritualized dueling and scarred cheeks proliferated in German universities and as the universities overtook the army as the major disseminator of dueling in Prussia, southern universities rushed instead to adopt football, with its more diffuse and flamboyant (and in the early years of the sport in what was to become the SEC, deadly) use of the violent impulse and quest for collective honor.

Why the difference? Why the persistence of the duel in Prussia and its atrophy in the South? It seems clear that, as the Prussian Road analogy argues, both the planters and the Junkers were in some ways anomalous classes, taking their identity from their local privilege and power while remaining in tension with the larger structures of their nation states. Early in their histories, both relied on the whip and the gun to control their subalterns, even as both spoke in a language of paternalism and noblesse oblige. Both subsequently had to contend with upheavals of labor and politics, and both found their values challenged by the spokesmen of liberal democracy. Both had to trim their ambitions to fit national political realities over which they had limited control.

The major difference is that the more extreme Prussians, with all their heavy baggage of manners and power, were better able to adapt to change than the planters, with their carry-on bag of tradition (a bag that contained evangelical Protestantism and ideals of representative government as well as traditions of domination). The death of the duel in the South reveals how little integrity and weight the planters had outside of slavery. While antebellum politics had in many ways turned around slavery, the planters had no special body in the national government—as did the Prussians—they could use to harness or soften the change that swept over them. Southerners hardly dominated the United States Army in the decades after their defeat, and even if they had the army was of little cultural importance in America.

Such institutions were vital—and this is the key—for in both the South and in Prussia honor was not some naive holdover from a "traditional" culture. Instead, it was something that had to be self-

consciously constructed and maintained. That it could be maintained even in the face of industrial capitalism is made clear by the
German experience; modernity was not some unitary substance,
some all-encompassing and internally consistent ethos that triumphed over everything in its path. But without the sense of
confidence and common identity fostered by some institution
morȅ exclusive and ennobling than sharecropping or a motley
Democratic party, the planters could not muster the energy for
dueling, could not maintain a proud and bristling honor. And could
not dominate the New South culturally or ideologically.

Which brings us to a final twist. The Junkers managed to lend
the ancient values of honor a new, if temporary, lease on life,
leading the dentists and pharmacists of Prussia to the dueling
ground. That would seem to suggest that the Junkers were a
dominant reactionary class in modern Germany, a class that lent
much of its style and many of its values to the Germany of the
twentieth century. Indeed, the notion that Germany followed a
unique, and tragic, path to industrial capitalism, a path tortuously
winding through authoritarianism and archaic militarism, a path
that began in Prussia, has become an article of faith—and the
foundation of a whole genre of southern history. The notion of that
Prussian Road was part of a critical wave of historiography emerging after World War II that sought to counteract the conservative
tradition of modern German history that dissociated the Third
Reich from earlier eras of German history. As such, it served a
salutary and noble purpose. But in the 1980s a new and influential
revisionist school in German history has expressed skepticism
about applying an implicit model of "modernization" drawn from
American social science and an idealized version of British and
French history to every other country in the world. As a leader in
this revision puts it, "I have become more skeptical over the years
about the version of continuity in modern German history that
relentlessly catalogues the malign role played by pre-industrial
elites and institutions. . . . We hear too much about the Germany
of the spiked helmet and too little about top-hatted Germany, . . .

too much about the power of a pre-industrial elite and too little about the effects of capitalism in structuring German society and politics."[3] This revisionist school seeks a broader vision of Germany's path to Hitler, one that does not allow the easy solution of blaming it on the Junkers, one that does not stop large parts of history. We do not have to accept all its arguments and implications (and I do not) to see that it throws the concept of the Prussian Road into doubt even as it applied to Germany.

Just as revisionists want to stress the role of groups other than Junkers in modern German history, so do I think our focus on the power of the planters obscures how much else was going on in the postwar South, how many other groups played their role in making the New South what it was, good and bad. Our fixation on the postwar planters obscures, most importantly for the discussion at hand, the recognition that honor was not the planters' exclusive preserve. Honor was not merely "ambivalent," as Bowman would stress, it was multivalent, highly inflected. It had powerful meaning to groups other than those at the top of the social order. In fact, as I have argued elsewhere, honor died from the top down in the New South—where druggists and dentists never thought of dueling (the very idea sounds like one of Faulkner's satires). Honor apparently stayed alive, though, among the black communities of the urban South and among the mountain communities of Appalachia. Both these groups lived in a world increasingly integrated into America's state and economy, but in the late nineteenth century took many of their values and actions from one another rather than from the mass society. And part of those values included the honor-driven but less stylized violence that was always far more common in the South than in militaristic Prussia. I believe honor was created anew in segregated Southern neighborhoods and in mountain hollows as well as in the Prussian military and fraternities. By the end of the nineteenth century, the planters and Junkers were among the least likely groups in their societies to be engaged in personal violence.

In sum, the comparison of the Prussian and Southern experi-

ence with honor and dueling suggests that we abandon some of the
snug teleological conceptions of economy, class, and culture that
so often distort comparative history. Neither the planters nor the
Junkers were simple preindustrial classes, but constantly negoti-
ated among contradictory demands and aspirations, modern and
archaic; more than this, neither the New South nor post-1848
Prussia were mere holdovers from an older age, drifting through
history. As unfortunate as it may be, it seems that the violence of
honor was not merely the product of some discredited fragment
within otherwise progressive societies, but changed its form and
substance with dismaying ease in societies deep in the change of
the nineteenth century. When we set comparative history into
motion, the enterprise becomes even more challenging and dis-
concerting—and maybe that is the way comparative history can
serve us best.

Social Order and the Female Self: The Conservatism of Southern Women in Comparative Perspective

ELIZABETH FOX-GENOVESE

Modern conservatism arguably begins with Edmund Burke, or, more to the point, with the great French Revolution that prompted Burke to his celebrated *Reflections*. For the French Revolution, in radically repudiating inherited notions of hierarchy and particularism, enormously accelerated the political implementation and ideological maturation of capitalism and bourgeois individualism, accelerated, that is, the revolutionary and self-revolutionizing social system that has, however unevenly, conquered the Western world and is irreversibly imposing itself on the rest.

Modern conservatism, in this perspective, emerged as the attempt to slow, soften, and sometimes even oppose outright the effects of those momentous changes.[1] But—and this is the main point—modern conservatism always has been, as it remains, deeply implicated in the social and ideological systems it mistrusts. Itself the product of bourgeois individualism, it cannot profitably be understood as a simple continuation of "traditional" thought and practice. Nothing more clearly reveals this complicity of modern conservatism with individualism and the capitalism it articulates than the difficulties that those most "traditional" of conservatives, the southern conservatives, confront in their heroic, if ultimately unavailing, attempts to stave off the worst incursions of both without decisively breaking with them.

Antebellum southern conservatives, most flamboyantly but by no means exclusively George Fitzhugh, had a firmer grasp of the issues—or, better, wrote from the marrow of a social system that

49

could lay some claims to holding capitalism and individualism at arm's length.[2] Their proslavery ideology defied the full implications of individualism by openly proclaiming the virtues of hierarchy and particularism. From Fitzhugh, who favored a complete break with the capitalist market and flirted with the appeal of Catholicism, to Henry Hughes, who promoted a secular "warranteeism" that in many respects foreshadowed modern fascism, proslavery ideologues resolutely insisted that civilization required the enslavement of some and, on that basis, perpetuated aspects of preindividualist thought, notably a sharp, particularist distinction among conditions. To a man—and woman—they grounded the justification of particularistic conditions in the "natural" and Biblically sanctioned subordination of woman to man.

Because of its grounding in slavery as a social system, antebellum southern conservatism departed in significant respects from the emerging Western conservative mainstream in Great Britain and France, although because of its intimate ties to transatlantic culture and thought, it also never entirely broke with it. Notwithstanding promising beginnings, notably by Richard Weaver and Louis P. Simpson, the full story of southern conservatism remains to be told, but will, inevitably, be a story of the tensions that characterized the slaveholding intelligentsia's attempt to adapt the bourgeois conservatism of their British and French colleagues to their own distinct social relations.[3] In this respect, southern ideology faithfully captured the complexities of a southern slave society torn between its commitment to the most advanced developments of its time and its determination to protect and justify slavery as the foundation of a just social order.

The repudiation of slavery as a just condition lay at the core of bourgeois individualism, which, in transforming Christian thought into a systematic, propertied individualism, defined slavery as the antithesis of freedom rather than following traditional thought in regarding it as one form of unfree labor among many.[4] Although initially the implications of this line of thought eluded many of its proponents, they were inescapable and, increasingly, divided southern slaveholders from their northeastern and western European counterparts. From 1820 to 1860, southern intellectuals gradually found themselves alienated from the leading currents of bourgeois thought from political economy and law to religion.[5] During the same period, southern literati increasingly called for regional journals to represent the South's distinct literary culture. Especially during the 1840s and 1850s, with the rise of northern antislavery and abolition, not to mention the beginnings of the women's movement, southerners ever more insistently proclaimed the distinctiveness and integrity of their own values. But even as they defined those values as fundamentally different from bourgeois values, they continued to admire and draw upon conservative bourgeois intellectuals whom they were happy to enlist in the service of their cause.

In essential respects, the conservatism of slaveholding women remains barely distinguishable from the conservatism of the men of their class and region, whose values and premises they overwhelmingly shared. As I have argued elsewhere, most slaveholding women prided themselves on participating in the literate culture of their region, including its transatlantic antecedents.[6] They assuredly participated in the elitist social attitudes of their class, and may fairly be said to have, if anything, more sharply emphasized the distinctions between themselves and those whom they viewed as their social inferiors than the men. Of their commitment to slavery, there are no reasonable grounds to doubt, occasional private mutterings about abuses notwithstanding. Their devotion to the Bible-based Christianity of their region permeated their most private writings, which it frequently structured.[7] One after another wrote in her journal of the quality and content of the preaching she had heard, noted her own Bible reading, and agonized about her progress toward worthiness as defined by scripture and interpreted by the southern clergy.

The conservatism of slaveholding women developed apace with the conservatism of their region, gaining in definition and resolution at least partially in response to the progressive unfolding of the more radical implications of bourgeois individualism elsewhere. Slaveholding women of the late eighteenth and early nineteenth centuries, like Mary Campbell of Virginia, tended to express their conservatism almost unthinkingly as an acceptance of their own privileged position.[8] For them, the foundations of that position in slavery did not necessarily differentiate it from that of elite women in bourgeois societies, whether in the North or in Europe. They comfortably accepted early bourgeois values—notably the emerging ideology of domesticity—as fully compatible with, and indeed the proper realization of, a modernized aristocratic ethos, such as that embodied by the Whig aristocracy in Britain. Revering George Washington and celebrating the legacy of the Revolution, they never doubted that their peculiar institution perfectly embodied true revolutionary values.[9] In this respect, they indeed resembled Burke in celebrating the American Revolution while deploring the French.

The Second Great Awakening, or what has been called the "rechristianization" of the South, drew many slaveholding women to a renewed preoccupation with religion, thus tempering their sense of self as derived from social position with a sense of self as grounded in religious observance and commitment.[10] In the late 1830s, Mary Moragne, who was determining to marry the minister of her choice, reflected on her mother's response to the news. "Her countenance grew heavy with apprehension:—she could not smile—they had been looking for *wealth & rank & fame* for me; but pride cannot now influence my resolves; the first duty I owe in this respect, is to my own heart."[11] Yet after her marriage, Mary Moragne, out of respect for her husband's wishes, forsook the writing for publication that had given her so much pleasure, thus confirming that her sense of obligation to her own heart did not extend to self-determination in the full sense of individualism. She also, as best we can tell, remained firm in the elitist social and racial attitudes of her parents and class.

By the 1850s, slaveholding women were intervening more frequently and openly in the politics of their region and, enjoying enhanced opportunities for education, were, in ever greater if still small numbers, expressing themselves on the salient issues of the day in print. The ardently proslavery Louisa McCord, who admittedly published under her initials rather than her full name, remained anomalous in directly engaging debates in politics, political economy, and theory, but hardly unique in entering the proslavery lists broadly defined. Caroline Lee Hentz, Julia Gardiner Tyler, Mrs. Henry Schoolcraft, and Augusta Jane Evans—to name but the more visible—all took up their pens to defend the values and institutions of their region, notably slavery to which they credited innumerable beneficent effects. All of these women drew upon the proslavery ideology that was being elaborated by southern men. Writing of slavery itself, of the condition of labor in general, of woman's position, or of religion, they followed the general structure and tenor of the dominant proslavery discourse. In so doing, they were faithfully articulating the values of the many other women of their class who, in journals, letters, and private conversations, defended the same positions.[12]

Commitment to proslavery effectively guaranteed the fundamental conservatism of slaveholding women's general world view and specific positions. With respect to the politics of secession in particular, many of them proved as tough as—in some instances tougher than—their men in pushing for an intransigent prosouthern stance, although they normally did so in private rather than in public.[13] As Julia Gardiner Tyler, the wealthy northern wife of former president and Virginia slaveholder John Tyler, argued in an angry response to an antislavery polemic by the Duchess of Sutherland, southern women were especially well positioned to become informed about public concerns. In the South, "politics is almost universally the theme of conversation among the men, in all their coteries and social gatherings, and the women would be stupid indeed, if they did not gather much information from this abundant source."[14]

In her response, Julia Tyler especially berated the Duchess of Sutherland for having invited the women of the so-called free states to intervene directly in the slavery question. The women of the South, she insisted, regarded any such appeal as an unmiti-

gated affront to themselves. Julia Tyler was simultaneously chastis-
ing the Duchess for her attack on slavery and for inviting women to
participate directly in politics. The American woman, she lec-
tured, "with but few exceptions," appropriately confines her life to
the "sphere for which God who created her seems to have designed
her." Within that sphere, she exercises her influence "as wife,
mother, mistress—and as she discharges the duty of one or all of
these relations, so is she respected or otherwise."[15] The women of
the southern states have as their particular province "to preside
over the domestic economy of the estates and plantations of their
husbands" and they hardly take as a compliment the proposal to
"introduce other superintendence than their own over the condition of their dependents and servants."[16] Southern women recognize a political insult to their persons and dignity when they
receive it. They are, "for the most part, well educated; indeed they
yield not in this respect to any females on earth."[17]

    And to demonstrate that she had not wasted her opportunities,
Julia Tyler launched into an informed and polemically astute discussion of southern and English social relations, picking up the
common proslavery theme that the English should begin by looking to their own forms of social oppression before criticizing those
of others. Specifically, the English would do well to consider their
own "aristocratic establishments" of primogeniture and entail and
to contemplate how they would feel should well-meaning southerners take it upon themselves to enlighten the impoverished
English rural classes about their oppressed condition. Slavery,
Tyler insisted, constituted a simple case of "individual property
rights," in which no respectable southerner would intrude at home
or abroad.[18]

    Julia Tyler's insistence on slavery as a form of property rights
subtly called attention to the mutual respect that ruling classes
owed to each others' institutions, and even suggested that southerners were more democratic and faithful to the principles of
individual liberty than their English counterparts. Caroline Lee
Hentz, in *The Planter's Northern Bride*, used fiction to develop

similar themes, although she, more than Julia Tyler, insisted upon
the benefits of slavery to the slaves. For Hentz, free labor itself
constituted the primary culprit. After painting a heart-rending
picture of the impoverished condition of white workers in northern
states, she followed up by depicting a free black servant who
begged for reenslavement on the grounds that she could not
possibly provide for herself as well as slaveholders would provide
for her.[19]

Mrs. Henry Schoolcraft, in *The Black Gauntlet*, yet more explicitly argued the proslavery case from the perspective of both
masters and slaves. In her view, historical example demonstrated
that slavery "has been the efficient cause of civilization and refinement among nations."[20] For South Carolinians in particular the
"exemption from *manual* labor" afforded by slaves "is at the foundation of a class of elevation and refinement, which could not,
under any other system, have been created."[21] That same system,
she held, had also provided for the slaves with a care and instruc-
tion that far exceeded anything provided to northern workers. Let
the abolitionists look to "perfecting the morals of those poor,
degraded pale-faces, that surround the doors of their own State."
And she invoked in support of her assertion a denunciation of
white slavery drafted by operatives of the Pemberton Mills in
Massachusetts according to whom the oppression they suffered
was so tyrannical and their wages so low "that negro slavery is far
preferable."[22]

Writing in the midst of mounting sectional crisis, Mrs. Schoolcraft, like Julia Tyler and Caroline Lee Hentz, was in part respond-
ing to the abolitionists whom she regularly charged with irresponsible meddling. But more than the others, she also directly challenged the abolitionists' world view. South Carolinians, she ap-
provingly avowed, were "'old fogies,'" in contrast, for, unlike the
abolitionists they do not believe "that *God* is a progressive being;
but that throughout eternity *He* has been the same; perfect in
wisdom, perfect in justice, perfect in love to all his creatures."
From this perspective, she found it impossible to comprehend

"the new-light doctrine, 'That slavery is a sin.'"[23] Mrs. Stowe's
vision of a world in which "all are born equal" was nothing but a
millennial fantasy. Even Thomas Jefferson's "All men are born free
and equal" defied six thousand years of historical experience and
has caused nothing but mischief.[24]

Augusta Jane Evans, arguably Louisa McCord's only intellectual equal among antebellum southern women, fully grasped the
challenge of formulating a conservatism appropriate to a modern
slave society. In *Beulah*, her second novel, published in 1859, she
explored a young woman's crisis of faith as a paradigm for the crisis
that confronted southern society as a whole.[25] Impressively
learned and gifted with an acute theoretical mind (strange
qualifications for a successful woman novelist), she modeled her
protagonist's travail on Coleridge's "The Rime of the Ancient
Mariner" and her own philosophy on Carlyle's *Sartor Resartus*.
Perhaps no antebellum woman's novel more firmly identified a
woman's struggle for identity with the main intellectual currents of
the age, certainly none engaged in such a thorough investigation of
contemporary metaphysics. Evans did not, in *Beulah*, specifically
attend to the problem of slavery, although her proslavery conviction cannot be doubted. Her concerns focused on the state of mind
of the master class, on its fitness to rule. Her having chosen a
woman to embody that challenge testifies as fully as one could wish
to the seriousness with which she took women's minds and their
obligation to account for themselves.

Beulah offers an intellectual woman's dense and sustained argument for woman's subordination to man, but, above all, for her
subordination to God. Evans never suggests, however, that subordination should be equated with inferiority. Herself a devout
Methodist, Evans never succumbed to the temptation of Catholicism, which she had, in her first novel, *Inez*, blisteringly attacked.[26] Nor did she participate in the individualist temptation to
argue for subordination on the grounds of natural inferiority. She
unmistakably intended to claim individual agency and account-
ability for women. But she emphatically rejected what she saw as

the disastrous implications of Emersonian individualism, insisting, like McCord, that woman could only realize her individual potential in her particular condition as woman. Evans, like many other slaveholding women, perfectly grasped the connections among individualism, abolitionism, and the dawning defense of women's rights. Louisa McCord, for example, scornfully dismissed women's claims to independence and equality as an open invitation to turn the world into a "wrangling dog kennel."[27] For McCord, women's protests amounted to nothing more than childish railing against the human condition—an unwillingness to accept the laws of nature. In invoking nature in general and women's physical weakness in particular, McCord was, in fact, betraying her own flirtation with bourgeois thought, notably bourgeois science. Just as her interest in Josiah Nott's theories about the separate origins of the races, which many of the leading southern clergy resolutely opposed, pointed toward postbellum racism, so did her willingness to justify women's subordination on the basis of biological difference point toward "scientific" sexism. After the war, Evans herself began to move in the same direction, but before it she continued to struggle to develop a particularist theory of the female self that would simultaneously guarantee social order and permit women the full development of their talents. Her wrestling with the problem of how best to justify women's subordination to men cuts to the heart of southern women's conservatism in comparative perspective.

The core of slaveholding women's conservatism lay in their acceptance of slavery as the necessary foundation of their families' property and the social order of their region. Many, like Mrs. Henry Schoolcraft, also followed such proslavery ideologues as Thomas Roderick Dew in viewing slavery as the necessary foundation of any civilization worthy of the name.[28] The men who fashioned the modern proslavery argument, notwithstanding differences in tone and emphasis, readily insisted that the subordination of slaves and the subordination of women constituted inseparable aspects of a unified world view and social system. Yet the differences among them, which superficially concerned different ways of presenting a single argument, masked divergent tendencies in southern conservatism. If a Dew or a Fitzhugh, like many of the divines, adopted an essentially historical and particularistic argument, a Henry Hughes unquestionably pointed toward a modern corporatism. The differences, if insignificant in time and place, carried important implications for women and illuminate the complex ways in which proslavery thought intersected with emerging bourgeois conservatism. And, given the sad history of postbellum racism, they especially reveal the ways in which slavery, notwithstanding its horrors, contained the full implications of bourgeois conservatism.

The argument for women's subordination to men on grounds of physical weakness was hardly unique to the South and proved eminently compatible with bourgeois individualism. Most bourgeois intellectuals warmly embraced women's subordination, without closely investigating the way in which it contradicted the central principles of individualism. In fact, the bourgeois ideology of womanhood, which developed in the eighteenth century and matured in the nineteenth, broke with previous views of women by simultaneously universalizing the principle of all women's subordination independent of class and by promoting a newly favorable image of women as innately good, gentle, and nurturing.[29] During the early nineteenth century, the subordination of women within the family thus emerged as the main bastion of corporatism within individualist ideology. The debates over women's independent political participation and the property rights of married women challenged the denizens of individualism to follow the logic of their ideology to its inexorable conclusion by acknowledging the equality of all individuals—or, to put it differently, by acknowledging women as individuals. Most resisted that logic. But increasingly, the deep hostility to hierarchy and particularism that informed individualism encouraged political and social theories to justify women's subordination on biological rather than social grounds.

Initially, the bourgeois ideology of womanhood had represented
an important element in the attack on social hierarchy, if only by
implicitly asserting that women, like men, shared an identity that
transcended class lines. But gradually during the first half of the
nineteenth century, it began to reveal its inherently conservative
character.[30] For the exclusion of women from individualism permitted the perpetuation of illusions of community and harmony in
a world that was increasingly governed by the capitalist market. At
the dawn of bourgeois individualism many women were themselves drawn to their newly enhanced prescribed roles. But, as the
intensification of the capitalist market began to erode the economic independence of households, as demographic trends confronted
more women with permanent spinsterhood, and as education
introduced some women to the lure of rewarding accomplishment,
some women began to chafe under their enforced dependence on
men. Economics and ideology combined, as they so often do, to
introduce women to the possibilities of individualism for themselves. Bourgeois societies responded to these changes and ambitions in contradictory ways, frequently by improving women's
access to education, sometimes by recognizing the property rights
of married women, and eventually by granting women the vote.
But in all of these societies women's halting advance toward individualism was accompanied by a panoply of formal and informal
restrictions on their equal opportunities. Bourgeois conservatism
thus moved from an unquestioning acceptance of the natural
subordination of women to the adoption of increasingly arbitrary
sexist values and practices.

Not surprisingly, antebellum Southerners found much to admire and accept in the bourgeois rhetoric of womanhood. They
wrote as sentimentally as any of woman's sphere, of the sacred
character of motherhood, of the harmony of the domestic circle.
From their perspective, they were proving themselves the true
custodians of the fundamental values of western civilization. Nor
were they significantly more self-critical than their bourgeois
counterparts in adopting the bourgeois rhetoric of womanhood to

refer to women's nature and mission since the dawn of time. During the postbellum period, moreover, they too turned to the arbitrary and restrictive practices of bourgeois conservatism. But during the antebellum period, they grounded their version of bourgeois domesticity in the discrete character of a modern slave society. Thus even when they most enthusiastically embraced bourgeois rhetoric, they used it to describe and legitimate a different reality.

The differences are not always obvious. On the one hand southern women from McCord to Hentz to Evans emphasized the roles as wives and mothers for which women were naturally suited, thus suggesting that women's subordination derived from natural frailty and need for protection. On the other hand, they also stretched the understanding of female individualism by supporting women's education, intelligence, and ability to form valuable independent judgments. In both respects, their conservatism did not self-evidently differ from that of other elite women of their age or, for that matter, from that of conservative slaveholding and bourgeois men. Yet most slaveholding women did differ from their conservative bourgeois counterparts in their commitment to a legally defined hierarchical social system and in accepting without serious question the particularistic character of their own condition as an integral part of it. The difference, in other words, lies not so much in rhetoric or in everyday practice as in the ideology and social relations that informed rhetoric and practice.

In the absence of any systematic study of the conservatism of bourgeois women, the comparisons necessarily remain tentative, but some suggestions are possible. As Marilyn Butler has argued, Jane Austen, for example, unmistakably espoused conservative social views, and resolutely opposed the sentimental view that "subjective experience is the individual's whole truth."[31] In Butler's view, Austen, by having heroines accept marriage as the fitting conclusion for their aspirations as individuals, carried "her partisan meaning further than it could be carried in reasoned argument, even by Burke."[32] Not all Austen critics, to be sure, accept Butler's view. Feminists in particular frequently credit Austen with a much deeper commitment to female agency and independence than Butler would allow. But these debates, in essential respects, miss the main points. First, the tension in Austen's novels between women's independent agency and their willing acceptance of a social fate that muffles it precisely captures the tensions of conservative individualism. Austen's heroines must choose what is good for society and, accordingly, good for them. They enjoy considerable latitude to make the wrong choices and suffer the consequences. Second, and for our purposes more important, Austen's representation of the social system within which they make their choices indisputably privileges bourgeois over aristocratic values. Thus, in *Persuasion,* the mobility of navy people is invoked to redress the bankruptcy of the traditional aristocracy.[33]

The case of Hannah More, the best known of early nineteenth-century female apostles of conservatism, reinforces the point. An Evangelical and a member of the Clapham Sect, More promulgated a kind of religious paternalism as the proper relation between social classes and grounded her social vision in the domestic subordination of woman. Women, whom she viewed as naturally more delicate, frail, and morally weak than men, required the protection and retirement of the domestic sphere in which they found their highest destiny in assuring the happiness of men who were naturally fitted for the contests of the public world.[34] Southern women read More with great admiration, embracing her writings as a convincing articulation of their own situation and values. But More opposed slavery and devoted much of her energy to the education of the rural poor for whose edification she wrote innumerable homiletic tracts. Much like Austen, More, in other words, sought to persuade women willingly to accept their own subordination as the most effective way of stabilizing an inherently unstable capitalist world.

Whatever More's popularity among southern women, her career and interests demonstrate that her conservatism differed from theirs in essential respects, notably in her fundamental acceptance

of individualism. She was, to her very core, a reformer who sought
to make the world a better place by promoting worthy causes. That
she also sought to guard it against too rapid upheaval—sought,
that is, to keep various groups willingly in their appropriate
places—in no way belies that acceptance. For southern women, as
McCord acerbically noted, reform betokened Yankee meddling. It
would be hard to imagine southern women writing tracts of any
variety to educate the white rural poor, much less the black. Many
did seek to introduce their slaves to the benefits of Christianity,
some even taught favorite slaves to read, but the kind of reform that
envisioned other members of society as individuals who must be
brought willingly to accept their condition did not figure among
their desiderata. Not least, most intuitively understood what Mc-
Cord explicitly stated: Any serious movement to reform would,
sooner or later, point toward the abolition of slavery. At most,
accordingly, southern women supported their clergy's advocacy of
reforming slavery in the interests of strengthening it—of making
the South a genuinely Christian slave society.

Never immune to the rhetoric of bourgeois individualism, never
unilaterally opposed to individualism itself, southern women frequently assimilated aspects of bourgeois thought to their own
commitments. It is, for example, possible to read Evans's *Beulah*
as an extended allegory for the reform of southern society. But the
reforms that Evans proposed, including a turning away from the
corruptions of fashion and a turning towards the virtues of tem-
perance, were all mobilized in the interests of consolidating slave
society and delineating a world in which individualism could be
contained within particular conditions rather than overriding
them. If proslavery southern men anchored the legitimacy of
slavery in the subordination of woman to man, slaveholding women were more likely, in their heart of hearts, to anchor the
subordination of woman to man in the exigencies of slavery—more
likely, that is, to accept their own subordination as necessitated by
that slavery which they firmly believed essential to any acceptable
social order.

Commentary / Barbara Jeanne Fields

In days gone by, when the excitement of campaigning for civil rights, black nationalism, and pan-Africanism, and the search for worthy antecedents in the campaign, launched politically engaged scholars into the study of history, the phrase *rebellious slave* seemed to many a redundancy. When fervor for economic democracy, and the search for worthy antecedents in that struggle, launched others into the study of the working class, the phrase *revolutionary worker* seemed to many a redundancy. Today, as the quest for equality for women propels scholars into studying the history of women, many similarly regard *feminist woman* as redundant. The passage of time, the accumulation of research, and the growing maturity of new specialties finally arrived in the academic mainstream eventually brought recognition that not every slave was a rebel nor every worker a revolutionary. Then came recognition that asking whether they were or were not, and why or why not, was not the only or even necessarily the most important question to ask about slaves or about workers. Finally—the beginning of real wisdom—came recognition that the respect we as historians owe to human beings of the past, by virtue of their humanity and their wrestling with the human condition, neither increases nor diminishes according to whether or not they ratify our own current political preferences by appearing to have anticipated or shared them.

In her paper, as in her recently published book,[1] Professor Fox-Genovese reminds us that *feminist woman* is not redundant either; that asking whether slaveholding women were or were not feminists is not the most pertinent way to set about understanding them; and that the respect historians owe them, like the respect historians owe to all human beings of the past, does not depend on how well they serve as preceptors for modern feminism. The slaveholding plantation women of the Old South were not feminists, any more than they were abolitionists. Nor should that

surprise anyone. As Professor Fox-Genovese makes clear, it would
be surprising if they had been, occupying as they did a privileged
position in a slave society. Women who belonged to the plantation
aristocracy of the Old South were thoroughly, profoundly, and
authentically conservative.

Rather than try, in vain, to provide them a forged pedigree as
abolitionists and feminists, Professor Fox-Genovese has chosen to
explore the content and source of their conservative pedigree
and to distinguish their conservatism from that of their bourgeois counterparts. Exploring the content and source of slaveholding women's conservatism requires distinguishing theirs from
the bourgeois conservatism of their time as well as our own. That is
a task as vital for coming to terms with our own world as for
understanding the slave South. It is also a task fraught with com-
plication.

To begin with, our accustomed language sometimes complicates
the task, because we are so apt to take for granted that the same
words mean the same thing. The language of domesticity and
woman's sphere is a case in point. In celebrating the value of
domesticity, plantation women sounded not so different from their
northern bourgeois counterparts. Like the garden of pastoral
literature, the domestic sphere may appear at first glance to be a
generic entity, interchangeable between North and South, slave
and free society. But Louis P. Simpson has demonstrated how
profoundly the garden changes when the gardener is a slave.
Professor Fox-Genovese demonstrates, in turn, how profoundly
hearth and home inevitably change when she who tends them is a
slave. They are no longer even in the same place. As Professor Fox-
Genovese mischievously—and accurately—observes: "Northern
bourgeois literature featured the kitchen as the heart of the household, the mother's empire. . . . southern literature, like southern
architecture, honored the kitchen by expelling it from the house."
The kitchen was an outbuilding, in which the mistress tarried no
longer than she had to. Meanwhile the slaves, who were forced to
tarry there, did not have kitchens for the preparation of their own

families' food. For them, the kitchen symbolized labor for others, the opposite of its meaning in the northern language of domesticity.[2]

Further complicating the task of distinguishing the slaveholders' conservatism from the bourgeois variety is the fact that southern slave society, particularly at its most mature—that is, during the antebellum years—developed in the midst of an expanding bourgeois world and in response to the needs of that world. Moreover, the slaveholders aspired to take from the bourgeois world whatever they found serviceable in the construction of their own. And yet, such borrowings were bound to undergo remodeling before they would fit comfortably in slave society. For example, despite some feints in that direction, slaveholders generally did not require biology to explain social inequality, whether that of women or that of Afro-American slaves: the particulars of history and, behind them, the ordination of God served the purpose that science increasingly had to serve in the northern states, where bourgeois individualism was a datum of daily life. The heyday of scientific racism and sexism for the South came after, not during, slavery.

Racial ideology, in the sense of a conviction of the innate biological inferiority of people of African descent, found its natural habitat where people of African descent constituted an obvious exception to a radically defined individual liberty, an individual liberty so commonplace in everyday life that no great astuteness or imagination was necessary to take it for granted: in other words, the natural habitat of racial ideology is in the free states, where both slavery and the presence of Afro-Americans became increasingly minor exceptions in the wake of the American Revolution. An ideology that explains why some people are exceptions to a rule of individual autonomy has no real work to do in a society in which individual autonomy is not the rule—in which it is not even, as in bourgeois society, a widely entertained illusion.[3]

Southern conservatives, men and women, recognized bourgeois conservatives as their kin. But they also understood that the fundamental premises of bourgeois society contradicted the fundamental premises of their world—starting with the bourgeois assumption that the free-standing, autonomous individual is the center, the essential building block, and the ultimate end of social life; and southern conservatives insisted on the moral superiority of their premises over those of bourgeois society.

The point warrants a bit of elaboration, because we go through our world so thoroughly saturated with the ideology of individualism that we easily forget that there really is no such thing as a free-standing, autonomous individual; that, however paradoxical it may sound, nothing is more profoundly a product of the group than the identity of the individual. Human eggs have been fertilized in test tubes, but no human being has ever yet grown to maturity in a laboratory. A human being is a human being only in the context of a human society; that is, in cooperation with other human beings. Who we are depends on who the other human beings are, what they do, and what we do with them. Most important of all, it depends on where we draw the boundary line between ourselves and them. That boundary line is what defines an individual and none of us can draw that line purely at will.

No matter who or where we are, we understand the shape and limits of our individuality only with reference to the community. For example, if someone who already knew a person's name asked that person who he or she was, most Americans would probably respond by giving their occupation or the name of their employer: I am a clerk, a cab driver, a student, a lawyer, a college professor; I work for International Harvester, for National Public Radio, the Social Security Administration, Columbia University. Most people probably would not even stop to think about it. It goes virtually without saying in our society that we are what we do for a living. But that does not go without saying in every society; perhaps, indeed, not here in Faulkner's country. Certainly if someone asked the same question of a southern slaveholder during the nineteenth century—let us say in Virginia—the answer would have been I am so-and-so's child, so-and-so's great-grandchild, so-and-so's wife or mother, so-and-so's niece, nephew, aunt, uncle, or cousin.

That spirit lived on in Virginia, as in most of the South, long after slavery. Virginia Durr's father scandalized a group of very proper Virginia ladies during the 1930s by telling a story that he considered funny and they did not. According to his story, the school board in a very rough mining district in Walker County, Alabama, got together to hire a schoolteacher. An old man among them, just barely literate, took tablet and pencil and wrote asking the University of Virginia in Charlottesville to recommend an appropriate young man for the job. In time, the old man

> got this beautifully written letter back, beautiful handwriting and addressed properly: 'Dear Sirs, My Name is St. John Washington Jefferson Randolph, or whatever—a very old Virginia name. On my mother's side I am connected to the Jeffersons, and on my grandmother's side I'm connected to the Lees, and on my great-grandmother's side I'm connected to the Fairfaxes.' He gave them about four pages of his genealogy. And then he ended by saying he would like to apply to teach at the school in Walker County. Well, the writing was very delicate, beautiful, very legible, but very fine. So the school board got together and read the letter. They figured out page by page. And they discussed what to reply. Then the old man got out his tablet again and wet his pencil and wrote: 'University of Virginia. Dear Sir, We have read your letter. N'er mind. You needn' come. We weren't lookin' for no man down here for breedin' purposes, jus' one to teach school.'[4]

Let me put it this way. Immersed in a world dominated by a bourgeois concept of the individual, we readily assume that you are what you do. Slaveholders, rejecting bourgeois individualism, were more likely to assume that you do who you are. Slaves did who they were, men of the planter class did who they were, and women of the planter class did who they were. "Who they were," as women, was subordinates of the men who headed the households to which they belonged.

Subordinate did not mean *inferior* to them, nor did it necessarily mean *oppressed.* The conservatism of planter-class women, like that of planter-class men, rested on their acceptance of slave society as the only just, decent, humane, and Christian order; and on the women's acceptance of their own subordination as essential to that society. The women assuredly grumbled upon occasion about the nuisance of living surrounded by "a negro village" as one put it, or denounced the philandering and abusive behavior of overbearing fathers, husbands, and brothers. Some scholars have been seduced by this and other evidence into mistakenly supposing that slaveholding white women were a "subversive influence" on slavery[5] or even that they were closet abolitionists. But when slavery was at its most vulnerable to subversion—during the Civil War—slaveholding women proved to be its die-hard supporters and the slaves—especially the slave soldiers—its bitterest and most implacable enemy. They called for help from both armies in propping slavery back up, even when their men had reluctantly concluded that the game was over. As for the grumbling and complaints of slaveholding women, these merely identified inconveniences incidental to the system that sustained their privilege and anchored their identity. Those loudest in complaint, moreover, differed from real abolitionists in basing their criticism of slavery, not on the suffering of the slaves, but on the burden and inconvenience to themselves.[6]

"Doing who they were" meant, for slaveholding women, accepting certain responsibilities and certain inconveniences as attaching to the position they occupied, not voluntarily, but by decree of Providence. I am reminded of a moment in the movie "The Mission" when the Jesuit superior tells his subordinates: "Remember. This is not a democracy, it's an order." For slaveholders, a godly society was not a democracy, but an order. Slaveholding women played a large role in seeing to it that others kept their places in that order. Professor Fox-Genovese has informed us that the women "more sharply emphasized the distinctions between themselves and those whom they viewed as their social inferiors than the men." It is very often women's work, especially the work of women belonging to the privileged classes, to preside over the rituals that embody hierarchy and domination: to teach table manners; to censure bad language; to set and judge fashion; to issue and withhold invitations; to snub social trangressors, upstarts, and outsiders; to administer those delicately honed social insults that form such a staple of Victorian novels. Thus, however distasteful the truth may be to those who expect women to be natural allies of the oppressed, it is not surprising that southern plantation women tended to be more overt and explicit racists and snobs than their men. After all, that was their job. Or perhaps I should better say "their duty." Even better, it was who they were.

For slaveholding men and women, "doing who they were" also meant accepting a discipline and rationale for their activity in the social order that presupposed a higher purpose than the egoistic gratification of the free-standing, bourgeois individual. As Mrs. Henry Schoolcraft insisted, in the excerpt that Professor Fox-Genovese quoted: "[E]xemption from *manual* labor is at the foundation of a class of elevation and refinement, which could not, under any other system, have been created." In other words Mrs. Schoolcraft, like other members of her class, believed slavery essential to progress and civilization. That is what gave slaveholders such confidence that their social order was morally superior to that of bourgeois individualism.

Needless to say, the slaves took a different view concerning the moral quality of slave society. But it was not in the name of bourgeois individualism and the untrammeled sway of the so-called free market that they condemned slavery. And, for any of us here who think that our moral standpoint is automatically superior to that of the slaveholding conservatives, that raises the question: what higher purpose does our own society recognize as a suitable discipline and rationale for our social activity? For all the slaveholders' self-congratulatory cant about the favors they were doing for the slaves, for all the unrealistic and self-serving estimates of what the slaves received from their owners compared to what their labor produced, the most thoughtful slaveholders knew and candidly admitted that they lived on the proceeds of their slaves' labor and that the slaves suffered in order to make possible for others a life of ease and cultivation. The advance of progress and civilization was the duty attached to that privilege.

I cannot help contrasting the slaveholders' view with the one that prevails in our own society, in which egoistic gratification does not require a justification or the discipline of a higher purpose. Where slaveholders frankly affirmed that slaves must occasionally suffer for the good of civilization, a recent self-styled conservative President of the United States declared that people live on the streets in our country because they want to. A well-known conservative columnist, commenting on criticism of Malcolm Forbes's multi-million-dollar birthday party, merely remarked that Forbes has a right to spend his money any way he likes. In our society, the free market enjoys a degree of religious veneration that slaveholders might have thought more appropriately reserved for the Deity. Limousines, luxury condominiums, cocaine, assault rifles, pornography, nuclear weapons: all are equal in the sight of the Free Market.

Needless to say, the slaveholders did not live up to the ideals they held out for themselves. Nor were their ideals such as most of us—not to speak of the slaves—would share. But I wonder if some of the slaveholding conservatives might not say, if they could come back to behold the spectacle of our society, that at least they were getting thrown out of a higher-class joint.

Emancipation and the Development of Capitalist Agriculture: The South in Comparative Perspective

STEVEN HAHN

The relationship between emancipation and the development of capitalist agriculture is at once very basic and exceptionally complex. It is very basic because the development of capitalist agriculture would have been unimaginable without the abolition of a wide array of customary and compulsory ties, obligations, and claims that variously bound rural producers to the land and to their betters while, in many instances, also providing them with recognized rights over and access to productive resources. Capitalist agriculture, that is, depended upon the destruction of servility and of the complex grid of use rights which had long prevailed in the countryside, and upon the fashioning of new relations of property and power which made possible the production and circulation of commodities in a self-sustaining and ever-expanding manner.[1]

At the same time, emancipation and the development of capitalist agriculture by no means constituted an easily discernible, direct, or linear process. Servile emancipations took place over several centuries; they gave way to an assortment of social formations, only some of which could be deemed nascently capitalist; and the erosion of servility in certain areas was soon accompanied by the rise or intensification of servility in others. Indeed, the roughly coincidental emergence of slavery in the Western Hemisphere and of serfdom in Eastern Europe and Russia owed, in part, to the success of large numbers of peasants in Western Europe at preventing their hard won emancipation from servile domination from passing quickly into an unwelcome emancipation from their control over means of production and subsistence.[2]

Nonetheless, it was the late eighteenth and nineteenth centuries that witnessed the great age of emancipation and the great age of advance in capitalist agriculture as integrated phenomena of worldwide proportions. This is not to say that slavery and other servile relations were toppled chiefly for economic reasons or to suit the narrow interests of an agrarian and industrial bourgeoisie: Emancipations were preeminently political struggles, and capitalist reorganization was neither a necessary nor, in many cases, even a desired outcome. It is to say that the growth of world markets and colonial empires—themselves the fruits of both earlier emancipations and the deployment of newly bound labor— had, by the nineteenth century, created a context in which struggles over social relations on the land reached unprecedented and steadily reinforcing international dimensions. The transition to capitalist agriculture took a good many forms, however tempting (and I might add misleading) it has been to use England as the case against which all other experiences are measured; and it convulsed the countryside over broad sections of the globe, generating massive migrations and some of the most threatening popular movements of the period.[3] In these regards, the South offers a remarkably useful example of the diversity and intersections of the transition, while demonstrating the limitations of addressing the problem from anything but an international and comparative perspective.

To place emancipation at the center of the development of capitalist agriculture implies a decisive, if not an altogether neat, break—though the break proved to be neater in some areas, such as the South, than in others. Like many societies of the time based on slavery and bound labor, the Old South long depended upon the sale of its staples on the world market, and thus boasted an economy with a pronounced commercial character. And like those societies, too, it had important sectors in which relations other than slavery or servility—including free wage labor—had or were coming to establish a real foothold: sections of the Upper South making the transition from tobacco to grain; hilly, mountainous, and generally infertile stretches of the countryside; and coastal cities, especially in the 1840s and 1850s, chief among them.[4] A substantial white majority with large numbers of nonslaveholders may have set the South apart in the hemisphere, but it is worth noting that in the South, as well as in Cuba and Brazil, the expansion of slavery into rapidly developing territories during the early to mid-nineteenth century produced a demographic shift that simultaneously chipped at the base of the institution elsewhere.[5]

Still, the cotton boom and the political aggressiveness of the first planter class to have wrested its independence from colonial rule gave slavery in the Old South a strength and resiliency unmatched even among those slave and servile societies experiencing economic booms of their own. Prussian Junkers seeking to avail themselves of improved market conditions during the last third of the eighteenth century found it difficult to increase seigneurial obligations on the peasantry and therefore began to employ wage labor. Cuban sugar planters started, as early as the 1840s, to import Chinese coolies, who came to join salaried employees, day laborers, task workers, and sharecroppers, as well as slaves, on their expanding estates. And some Brazilian *fazendeiros* conducted labor experiments with European immigrants for several decades before the large-scale recruitment of Italian workers commenced in the final years of the slave regime.[6]

No such experimentation with alternatives to slave labor was to be found in the staple-growing areas of the Old South. If anything, planters and their allies looked to enlarge the domain of slavery and further restrict the emergence of a free or quasifree labor force by demanding federal protection for their chattel in the western territories and by taking the offensive against the already small and vulnerable free black population. Agricultural reformers and bourgeois entrepreneurs who hoped to promote diversification, improved farming methods, and economic development made limited headway and, for the most part, ultimately bowed to the primacy of the slave-based plantation system.[7] As a consequence, even amidst the flush times of the 1850s when the market economy touched more of the South than ever before, the organization of production largely resisted the incursion of market relations. Whether on plantations or on far more numerous farms, the household remained the dominant unit of production, consumption, and reproduction, embracing, as it were, the prevailing social division of labor. Legal and customary dependency of various sorts—slavery being the extreme and absolute representation—thereby continued to mediate basic relations. Indeed, in a variety of ways, the vitality of slavery not only enabled nonslaveholding farmers to sustain a considerable degree of market participation without succumbing to the market's logic; it may also have provided a hedge against the full expansion of market relations in the free states.[8]

The prosperity and relative stability of southern slave society helps explain why the slaveholders, when faced with an external challenge to their designs, chose to fight rather than switch: chose, that is, the course of rebellion instead of the course of compensated compromise favored, however reluctantly, by their counterparts in the Americas and Eastern Europe.[9] Although slavery collapsed nearly as rapidly in the British Caribbean, neither there nor anywhere else (save for St. Domingue) did slavery or serfdom end amidst the conflagration and shift in political power that marked the South. Yet, the distinctiveness of the southern transition from slavery did not end with emancipation or even with Reconstruction. For while the abolition of slavery and servile labor ended up accelerating the development of capitalist agriculture most everywhere abolition took place, it propelled the South most quickly and most fully down that road.

An argument such as this does, to be sure, fly in the face of many recent assessments of the postbellum South which emphasize the persistence of extra-economic compulsions and the very protracted route the region followed to capitalist relations—a route that some believe was effectively blocked until the massive disruptions and federal interventions of the 1930s. Indeed, although the dramatic character of emancipation and Reconstruction may have distinguished the South from most other servile societies, the fastening of new forms of coercion making for a gradual transition to free labor seemed the firmest basis for strong comparisons between them.[10] I would suggest, however, that these views tend to adopt an ideal-type notion of freedom and free labor that would be difficult to locate even in advanced capitalist economies, let alone in the agricultural sector where the compulsions of necessity alone rarely proved sufficient to attract and discipline a labor force; that they tend to focus almost exclusively on the plantation districts; and that they tend to confuse the relics of the old order with the essence of the new. Important resemblances in the experiences of postemancipation societies there certainly were, and those resemblances did involve the implementation of coercive mechanisms. But the patterns of change which ultimately differentiated the South owed to the particular ways in which widely significant and intersecting developments took shape: the struggles between landowners and laborers; the ebbs and flows of the world economy; and the ability of the landed classes to mobilize the resources of the state.

The fate of postemancipation societies rested first and foremost on the resolution of the "labor question." Once the personal dominion of masters and lords had been terminated new relations of property and power had to be constructed. Estate owners normally sought to limit the alternatives available to their liberated workers and to exercise as much control as circumstances would allow, believing that compulsions of some sort were requisite to the viability of their enterprises. Estate laborers, for their part, normally sought to establish relative economic independence if possible, or at least to define terms compatible with enlarging their spheres of freedom and autonomy. The contest was especially intense in areas, like the British Caribbean, where slavery ended abruptly and attempts at a structured gradualism (apprenticeship in this instance) failed miserably and in short order. The planters, who retained local political authority and increasingly won the sympathies and support of the metropolitan government, resorted to the now familiar devices of vagrancy and police ordinances, tax and land policies, rental charges, and a highly circumscribed franchise in an effort to enforce the freed-people's dependence on the sugar estates and bolster their own bargaining position. And on the smaller islands with little unculti-vated land, the planters largely succeeded, paying low wages and increasing staple exports.[11]

In those Carribbean territories with more substantial hinter-lands, the planters had a tougher row to hoe, as the freedpeople initially managed to boost wages, establish free villages, and lay the foundations for a black peasantry. Jamaica saw dramatic de-clines in sugar production and the abandonment of many smaller plantations; the newer and more dynamic sugar colonies (Trinidad and Guyana being prominent examples) looked to a different solution. Benefitting from government financial support, the planters there began to import growing numbers of East Indian contract laborers—themselves the products of British imperialism and the concomitant commercialization of agriculture. Nearly 400,000 eventually arrived, to be supplemented by migrants from Africa, China, and other West Indian islands, and helped to buffer the path to capitalist relations. By the turn of the twentieth cen-tury, East Indians whose indentures had expired and who worked for wages predominated on Guyanese plantations. Thus, as the corporate reorganization of export agriculture commenced and market conditions improved, the British West Indies generally combined forms of wage labor on the estates with quasi-indepen-dent peasantries.[12]

In Brazil, unlike the British Caribbean or the American South, the transition to free labor was well underway in both of the major plantation regions before final abolition was decreed in 1888. The northeastern sugar economy had been in prolonged decline and, owing to private manumissions, interregional slave traffic, and seasonal migrations of poor peasants and squatters from the *sertão*, free workers outnumbered slaves on the *engenhos* by the early 1870s. The south-central coffee economy, especially the western districts of São Paulo, though experiencing rapid growth and receiving thousands of slaves from the northeast, embarked upon a program of European immigration of sufficient scale in the mid 1880s that Paulista estates soon boasted a majority of contract laborers.[13]

Emancipation thereby hastened the already established trajectories of agricultural reorganization, while the formation of the planter-dominated First Republic the very next year reinforced regionally variegated patterns of social relations and economic change. With Paulista *fazendeiros* at the helm, state subsidies promoted the continued influx of Portuguese, Spanish, and, above all, Italian immigrants, most of whom were peasants and agricultural laborers victimized by rural commercialization in their countries of origin. Working for wages under *colono* contracts, they comprised, by the first decade of the twentieth century, about two-thirds (and often as much as nine-tenths) of the agricultural labor force in São Paulo's burgeoning western plateau, displacing ex-slaves who were left, for the most part, with low-paying seasonal employment there or sharecropping arrangements in the moribund Paraíba Valley. The taxation of exports furthered economic growth, and a federal-state valorization scheme helped planters weather the crisis of slumping coffee prices in the late 1890s, and may have contributed to the eventual rise of a good many rural immigrants into the ranks of landed proprietors.[14]

Northeastern sugar planters also found advantages from the political changes that attended emancipation. Administrative decentralization confirmed their control over a long dependent laboring population, which despite ex-slave flight from the estates proved more than adequate to the level of demand, while government aid of several sorts provided incentives and resources for the construction of mechanized central mills (*usinas*). But the planters and millowners took a backseat to the wealthier and more powerful *fazendeiros* to the south, and the northeast continued to suffer from capital shortages and unfavorable market conditions. Technological modernization proceeded slowly, few immigrants arrived, and sugar growers relied upon a mix of squatters, sharecroppers, steadily impoverished wage laborers, and the various services of a hard-pressed peasantry. The region thereby assumed its unenviable status as a classic example of Third World underdevelopment.[15]

The Cuban case, by contrast, showed different possibilities for cane producing areas. A propitious combination of fertile land, scarcer labor, and proximity to the North American market enabled resident planters to accumulate capital and lead the way in technological modernization despite the rising challenge of European beet sugars. By the 1860s, most mills ultilized steam power, and they exploited the labor of Chinese coolies (thanks to state support), convicts, and free wage laborers as well as of numerically dominant slaves. The tide of abolitionism thus seemed less threatening, though the planters used their political power to prolong the transition and minimize disruptions.[16]

Nevertheless, when it came in the 1880s, emancipation did not simply speed the advance of previous trends; it was decisive to the reorganization of the entire industry and, in the words of one scholarly authority, to "rationalizing the confused labor system efficiently." For in the 1880s and 1890s the old integrated *ingenios* fell by the wayside and a new social division of labor based on the separation of production and processing came to the fore. The large, heavily capitalized *centrales*, as they were known—and rarely owned by old planter families—employed wage labor and established many of the institutions associated with company towns; in turn, they found supplies of cane from among an assortment of cultivators (*colonos*) who primarily included white tenants, petty proprietors, and former planters. The ex-slaves who remained in the sugar districts largely joined a swelling pool of seasonal laborers, some of whom migrated from other Caribbean islands and some of whom made excursions of short duration from Spain. Those ex-slaves who sought greater independence moved to the less developed eastern provinces, where prospects were best for renting or purchasing parcels of land. Postemancipation Cuba thereby saw an advanced form of capitalist agriculture in the sugar sector coexisting with a long established and more recently replenished colored peasantry that mixed market and subsistence farming and managed to withstand the later encroachments of the cane economy.[17]

The peasant emancipations of Eastern Europe necessarily had quite distinctive features when compared to the slave emancipations of the Americas. Yet, it was hardly accidental that they came in roughly the same period; and those on the European continent played an equally, if not more, important role in the development of capitalist agriculture. In Prussia, for example, the heavy servile obligations that Junkers were able to impose on rural producers in the fifteenth and sixteenth centuries began to unravel in the last third of the eighteenth century as prices for agricultural goods rose and peasants fended off new seigneurial demands. In response, some of the Prussian estate owners enclosed demesnes, commuted labor services, adopted improved rotations, and hired labor.[18]

But there is little doubt that the pivotal moment came with the reforms of the early nineteenth century that abolished hereditary serfdom and proclaimed land a free commodity. Like most other emancipations, this one came by administrative fiat, left the landed classes in direct command over the countryside, and involved compensation for them: in fact, the process of indemnification served to increase Junker landholdings and available capital, while maintaining a range of servile dues for the next few decades. For a time, the estates relied heavily upon the labor of cottagers (*Insten*), who received houses, subsistence plots, and other in-kind payments in return for their toil. Increasingly, however, and influenced by the rapid expansion of sugar beet production in the years after 1848—itself very much dependent upon the end of servility and the consolidation of holdings—the Junkers paid wages and employed growing numbers of seasonal migrants, mostly from Poland but also from Italy, Scandanavia, and Russia. In short, with the assistance of the Prussian state, the Junkers transformed themselves into an agrarian bourgeoisie.[19]

At the same time, the Junkers' success in maintaining substantial political power in a unified Germany lent a special character to capitalist development in the nation as a whole. Access to the apparatus and resources of the state not only secured the local authority of the landed elite and made needed credit available, but also buttressed much of the agricultural sector against deteriorating conditions in the world market that wrought havoc elsewhere. Under the auspices of Bismarck, the Junkers were able to win a significant tariff trade-off in 1879 (the famed "marriage of iron and rye") that protected the domestic market from the avalanche of cheaper grains produced chiefly in the United States and Russia and helped promote an alliance between the estate owners of the east and the peasant proprietors of the south and west, who had freed themselves from servile ties long before and stood to benefit. The Agrarian League, founded in the 1890s to resist the Caprivi government's assault on protectionism, embodied the institutional expression.[20]

Thus, if emancipations were essential to the development of capitalist agriculture, they also gave rise to a variety of patterns which were, in turn, shaped by the worldwide flow of goods as well as by the worldwide circulation of laborers who had been cut loose from their traditional moorings. Indeed, the emancipation of slaves and peasants could hardly have fueled the progress of capitalist relations (nor would it likely have occurred) were emancipation not an integral part of the larger transformation of the countryside and of a dawning new age of imperialism. Even so, the outcome remained in doubt; in those rare cases when slavery and seigneurialism ended in the midst of revolutionary struggles that tipped the balances to the exploited (as in St. Domingue and

France) the road to capitalist relations witnessed retreat or much slower advance.[21]

That estate owners for the most part avoided such unpleasantries and retained, or in some instances enlarged, their political power proved decisive to the trajectories of postemancipation societies, for they were then able to preserve the economic sector most fully linked to commodity markets and to accumulate a labor force under conditions in which the laborers now owned their persons. The persistence of extra-economic compulsions testified to the sensibilities and maneuvering room of planters and seigneurs who scarcely wished to negotiate with their former charges, and to the aspirations of freedpeople who scarcely wished to remain subject to their former owners. It should also remind us that the creation of a labor market is a political, much as an economic, process, usually accompanied by great contention and violence, and that all work relations in which workers lack full claim to the net product involve submission to authority.[22]

Where the landed classes had access to capital together with considerable political and economic leverage there could be a relatively rapid appearance of a classic, wage-earning, rural proletariat. Yet, it was far more likely that postemancipation societies would see the rise of complex and interwoven "packages" of social relations that combined—in one of several ways, due in part to the nature of the crop—a core of proletarianized workers; a reconstituted, sponsored, or previously established peasantry that nonetheless was dependent upon the production of market crops and stints of labor on the estates; a pool of seasonal migrants from near and far; and, where political networks and resources would allow, a sizable number of contract laborers who provided a semblance of stability for several transitional decades. In some places, like Germany, those "packages" could also include a substantial group of petty proprietors who relied on household labor and forged an interregional coalition with the landed elite in defense of the agricultural sector as a whole. Which is to say that while capitalist relations came to rest at the heart of the new productive systems—necessity increasingly brought freed persons to the estates and the sack increasingly drove them off—those relations spread in an uneven and, at times, contradictory fashion.

The South certainly shared many of the experiences common to other postemancipation societies, especially in the plantation districts. Although the abolition of slavery came amidst the convulsions of war and the military defeat of the Confederacy, the general structure of landownership largely remained intact, the planters attempted to tie the freedpeople to the estates through both legal and extra-legal means while the freedpeople attempted to crawl out from under their thumbs, immigrant labor schemes were widely discussed, and the staple economy soon rebounded, at least in terms of levels of production. Yet, what is striking in comparative perspective is the speed and extent to which capitalist relations came to prevail in the countryside. Not only did a reconstituted peasantry fail to surface in any significant form, but the very substantial sector of white family farmers, which had rested chiefly on the periphery or utterly outside the market economy before the war, steadily succumbed to the market's advances thereafter, as the postbellum South ultimately evinced a remarkable degree of economic integration. Infusions of capital from the North and abroad played a role; far more important, however, was the declining power of the South and its landed classes in the national poilitical economy created by the character of emancipation itself.

The transition to capitalist relations in the postwar South was neither unitary nor one-dimensional. As elsewhere, it was shaped by the crop cultures and organization of production under slavery and by the specific ways in which slavery crumbled during the Civil War. The most rapid and direct movements toward wage labor came in those areas in which operations were highly capitalized to begin with or in which labor requirements were highly seasonal. Thus, Louisiana sugar planters, despite suffering from wartime devastation, preserved gang labor, paid wages, and experimented with Chinese, native white, and Italian workers before strikes and general labor instability led them—like their Cuban counterparts—to build central mills that employed blacks and obtained cane primarily from white renters, some of whom leased large tracts and hired on black field hands.[23] Wealthy rice planters along the coast of South Carolina and Georgia, who also had substantial capital investments, did not fare so well. The early occupation of Union forces during the War set in motion a train of events—including land distribution and restoration, a complex of cash and share agreements, and bitter labor struggles—that headed toward the irreversible decline of the export sector along with the emergence of one of the largest enclaves of black petty proprietors to be found in the South. But when the rice industry resurfaced on the prairies of Louisiana, Texas, and Arkansas, it did so on the basis of outside capital, extensive mechanization, the rental of big parcels, and seasonal wage labor.[24]

In those areas of the Upper South increasingly devoted to wheat, livestock, truck, and general farming, the need for year-round labor was limited and, especially in those states that did not leave the Union, credit was more available than in the ex-Confederacy. So it was that a core of black farm hands, tenants, and croppers was complemented by impoverished and irregularly employed wage laborers who either circulated in the countryside or came there from cities and towns during harvest. In some places, like Louisa County, Virginia, a very high proportion of black household heads succeeded in acquiring plots of land; but the plots were far too small to provide subsistence or a livelihood, and they were usually sold off by substantial farmers looking to raise liquid capital and secure the services of seasonal workers—a pattern quite common to the development of capitalist agriculture, as Lenin observed long ago.[25]

It was, of course, in the cotton heartland—the region most closely studied and at the center of recent scholarly debate—that the transition from slavery seemed most protracted and problematic. There the hard-fisted vestiges of coercion survived most tenaciously as planters and freedpeople struggled their way toward a system marked by strong doses of personal domination and dependency, of extra-economic compulsion and repression, and of forced labor in various incarnations. We have, perhaps, underestimated the early importance of wage labor, as Lawanda Cox suggested in a pioneering essay now forty years old: By 1870, for example, three of the cotton states ranked among the top ten states nationally in the value of wages paid to farm labor, and half of the 226 counties nationwide that recorded expenditures for farm wages tripling the national average were located in the cotton areas of Georgia, Alabama, north Florida, and the Mississippi Delta. Still, there can be little doubt that, for the most part, capital-starved planters used what familiar means remained at their disposal to squeeze surplus out of a labor force whose own resistance helped plot a tangled route to sharecropping.[26]

The vagrancy ordinances, anti-enticement statutes, lien laws, and bonds of indebtedness that went into the vital workings of the postwar plantation system would seem to make a mockery of the concept of free labor. And, after all, there is England, the "paradigm of agrarian capitalism," to consider. But that "paradigm of agrarian capitalism," stretching from the sixteenth to the nineteenth centuries, was encased by the harsh Elizabethan codes on the one end and the Poor Law on the other. As late as the 1860s, rural laborers in Britain who broke their contracts were regarded as felons and those who disobeyed orders were subject to imprisonment at hard labor. Social relations in agriculture, even in developed capitalist economies, quite simply have fed upon methods of coercion long since abandoned in other sectors. More to the point, the offensive against the freedpeople, fortified as it was by legislative sanction, had the effect, not of formally binding them as individuals to the estates or to the direct authority of propertyholders (though there were well-known examples of this) but of creating a class bereft of the means to produce or subsist on their own account. Southern courts, by the 1870s, began to confirm the results: sharecroppers occupied the legal status of wage laborers.[27]

small producers: in particular, a market in labor-power with attendant devices to limit an independent subsistence base, and the predatory advances of merchant capital. Yeoman households did their best to fend off the worst, which in part meant greater self-exploitation; but it was a losing battle—all the more so given the steady decline of cotton prices and the inability of cotton growers to obtain relief. By the end of the century, most of the South's cotton was raised by white labor, tenancy and sharecropping were rampant, and growing numbers looked to textile factories and other sorts of regular and seasonal employment.[29]

As a consequence, the alliance of big and small landed property, which had boosted secession and doomed Radical Reconstruction, began to come unhinged. A shared interest in disciplining free black labor, embodied in the shrill cries of white supremacy, may have prevented dissolution. Yet, the failure of large landowners adequately to defend cotton agriculture, and their developing accommodation with merchants and industrialists, added to the burdens of smallholders and led many to break ranks. The fuse was thereby lit for the explosion that shook the southern countryside in the 1890s: an explosion that detonated variously in Italy, Spain, Ireland, India, and China as capitalist agriculture spread relentlessly during the second half of the nineteenth century. By then, developers had already made inroads into Appalachia, though too late for the explosion to have been louder still.[30]

That the Populist explosion rocked the West as well as the South should draw our attention to the effects of emancipation on the course of agricultural development nationwide. While this subject is too large and complex to consider here, I should like to conclude with some suggestions. For in ways that deserve far more study and appreciation, emancipations may have promoted, at once, the expansion of capitalist agriculture in the North and West and the dominance of industry over agriculture nationally.

Most dramatically, the unfolding of emancipation and Reconstruction contributed to the rapid settlement and ruthless exploitation of the trans-Mississippi regions, owing principally to railroad and land policies that gave the edge to big capital. And there, as elsewhere in the country, the advanced sections of the rural economy came to depend on the wage labor of immigrants from countries that were emancipating their peasantries through the abolition of servile ties, the commodification of land and labor, or both. The role of Chinese, Mexican, and Japanese workers in the growth of California agriculture is probably best known, but to these may be added Basques in sheep ranching and Italians in viticulture. On the east coast, the pattern was similar. From the 1870s on, over two-thirds of the Irish, Scandanavians, and southern and eastern Europeans—as well as half of the Germans—who arrived on the shores of the United States described themselves as farmers, farm laborers, or common laborers; and while a great many of them ended up in industrializing cities and towns, more than a few toiled in the countryside, notably on the truck and dairy farms of the Northeast and Middle Atlantic. In Massachusetts, for example, as early as the 1870s, eight of ten farm laborers were foreign born.[31]

The great wheat farms of the upper plains and of eastern Washington and Oregon were less reliant on immigrants. The ranks of their labor force included large numbers of poor farmers and homesteaders who followed the harvest over hundreds of miles and whose presence reflected the deepening vulnerabilities of smallholders during the last decades of the nineteenth century.[32] To be sure, it is easy to dissociate events on the plains and in the West generally from those in the South. But if we consider the course of emancipation and Reconstruction in broader perspective and as part of wide ranging struggles for power within the nation— and if we venture some counterfactual possibilities—the connections may prove a bit clearer. It has been most tempting to think about the results of a more radical emancipation and Reconstruction, bringing significant land confiscation and redistribution. Of greater plausibility, especially in comparative context, however, would have been a far less radical emancipation and Reconstruction, one that left the South and its planters with substantial bargaining power and influence over national policy. Under such circumstances, the political axis linking the South and the West, committed as it was to easier credit and better terms for agricultural proprietors, would likely have been stronger and the trajectory of economic development would likely have been altered.[33] The national political economy might then more closely have resembled that of Germany, with even more disastrous consequences for black workers. Thus, we may be presented with one of the supreme ironies in the vaunted notion of American exceptionalism: At a time when the concept of bourgeois revolution has come under such intense attack that many Marxist historians have jettisoned or drastically qualified their use of it, the distinctive dynamics of emancipation and Reconstruction in the United States may in fact offer a classic example.

Commentary / Peter Kolchin

Steven Hahn offers bold—and I believe generally persuasive—challenges to dominant historical interpretations of both the antebellum and postbellum South. I would like to put his argument in the context of existing historical literature, and to offer some brief observations of my own about the nature and significance of his thesis.

Hahn begins by asserting that before the Civil War southern agricultural relations, dominated by the slave-based plantation system, were fundamentally noncapitalist. In doing so, he follows the lead of a number of recent scholars, most notably Eugene D. Genovese, who have stressed the degree to which slavery set the South apart from the rest of the United States.[1] At the same time he takes issue with the still more widely held view, expressed by a broad range of historians from Kenneth M. Stampp to Robert W. Fogel and Stanley Engerman, that slavery was simply another business and that southern planters were profit-maximizing capitalists par excellence.[2] As James Oakes, one of the most forceful recent exponents of this viewpoint, puts it in his book *The Ruling Race*, the essential point is "the profound impact of the market economy on the nature of slavery."[3]

Hahn and Oakes are, of course, talking about very different things that revolve around different understandings of the meaning of capitalism. Those who have stressed the capitalist nature of the slave economy correctly point to the commercial orientation of southern agriculture—slaveowners grew cotton, tobacco, rice, sugar, and other products for market sale—and conclude that slavery was fundamentally capitalist. To Hahn, however, following Genovese—and ultimately Karl Marx—the relations of *production* are of more central importance than those of exchange: although the antebellum South had a highly commercialized economy, it was fundamentally noncapitalist because of the limited presence of the key element of capitalism—sale of labor-power on the open market (that is, the free hiring of labor). In other words, although relations between slaveowners and the outside world were pervasively shaped by the market, those between masters and slaves were not.

On one level, this debate over whether or not the slave South was capitalistic is essentially semantic, revolving around different definitions of capitalism. It is more than that, however, because it involves very different understandings of how slavery affected southern society. One can, of course, define a term however one wishes; it is the *utility* of the definition that is at issue. Those who stress the market orientation that planters shared with northern businessmen and see plantation slavery as merely a variant of a prototypical American entrepreneurialism of necessity minimize the overall impact of slavery on the antebellum South, while those who stress the distinctive nature of master-slave relations perforce proceed to elaborate on how those relations helped shape a South that was also distinctive. Given the abundant evidence we now have on this subject, I believe that the approach taken by Hahn is the more useful of the two.[4]

After establishing the noncapitalist nature of antebellum southern agriculure, Hahn then proceeds to argue that emancipation served as a major watershed in southern history, one that ushered in the spread of capitalist agriculture. Indeed, he suggests, although emancipation everywhere went hand-in-hand with the tortuous triumph of capitalist relations in the countryside, the overthrow of slavery produced a more far-reaching transformation in the southern United States than anywhere else, and came closer to constituting a "classic example" of a "bourgeois revolution."

Here again Hahn boldly takes on a variety of weighty opponents. In maintaining that emancipation propelled a capitalist revolution in the South, albeit one accompanied by widespread use of extra-economic compulsion, he challenges two major competing schools of historians. One group, prominent among whom are Jonathan Wiener, Jay Mandle, and Crandall Shifflett, sees basic continuity between the antebellum and postbellum South, insisting that the continued existence of a class-based, exploitative labor system meant that little had changed. As Shifflett puts the argument in his careful study of Louisa county, Virginia, "After the war . . . the social structure remained essentially unchanged. . . . The story of Louisa is one of a missing revolution."[5] The other group, consisting primarily of economic historians such as Robert Higgs and Stephen J. Decanio, denies the coercive nature of postbellum agricultural relations and maintains that the market acted to allocate resources in the most equitable and efficient manner possible.[6]

Hahn is correct, I believe, in rejecting both of these positions.[7] To say that one must decide whether postbellum southern agricultural relations were characterized by coercion *or* competition, continued exploitation *or* the sway of the market, is to set up a false dichotomy, to imply that market competition of necessity precludes coercion and exploitation. In fact, as Hahn points out, the spread of capitalism was virtually always accompanied by heavy doses of extra-economic compulsion—certainly this was so in the so-called classical case of seventeenth-, eighteenth-, and nineteenth-century England. What is more, given the unequal distribution of resources that prevailed in the postemancipation South, the market could hardly act as an impartial arbiter of economic relations. On the other hand, the continued existence of exploitative labor relations and "class rule" hardly prove that nothing changed, for throughout human history these have been features of widely varying social orders; if continued exploitation means that nothing changed, then one might well question whether any change is ever possible. Such a position—that all oppression and exploitation are interchangeable—is profoundly ahistorical.

Hahn's position that emancipation prompted the spread of rural capitalism is logical, and yet—because it is based on a particular understanding of capitalism—it runs the risk unless phrased carefully of amounting to little more than a truism or tautology. If capitalism by definition requires the sale of labor-power by free workers, then slavery by definition is incompatible with capitalism and the abolition of slavery automatically makes possible capitalism's spread. Hahn does not, of course, see emancipation producing an immediate, across-the-board establishment of rural capitalism; he notes the persistence of old, precapitalist ways that combined in varying degrees with wage labor in what he terms "complex and interwoven 'packages' of social relations"; the triumph of true capitalist agriculture was thus protracted even after the overthrow of slavery.

This formulation, however, produces some complex problems of its own with which I am not sure Hahn fully comes to grips. First, it requires one to make what I think are questionable distinctions among types of agricultural labor, with wage labor representing a more "advanced" or "progressive"—that is, more capitalistic— form of relation than sharecropping. Certainly, this was not the view of the freedpeople themselves, who in the immediate postwar years generally expressed a clear preference for cropping (which seemed to provide them with at least a limited measure of independence) over wage labor (the dependent nature of which struck many as only superficially removed from slavery). Nor, unless one simply defines it as such, is it clear why wage labor should be regarded as *objectively* more advanced than sharecropping. Rather than seeing sharecropping as a remnant of the old order, I think one might better view it as one variant of free-labor productive relations, a variant that within the context of a generally capitalist economy was compatible with the overall development of that economy.

Second, and related, Hahn does not entirely make clear how or why he considers the capitalist revolution to have been more thoroughly successful in the southern United States than elsewhere. Indeed, he seems to suggest that only where the power of the landowners vis-à-vis the freedpeople was greatest could "true" capitalism—based on wage labor—prevail; where the former slaves had access to economic or political resources, they resisted being turned into dependent wage laborers and opted for independent peasant proprietorship, extreme examples of which, he notes, are offered by Haiti and France. This assumption that the so-called "Prussian" road was the only route from bondage to capitalism strikes me as problematical. It implies the interesting paradox that things changed most where they changed the least (that is, the capitalist revolution was most pronounced where landowners maintained the bulk of their economic and political prerogatives). But this thesis is belied by Hahn's own example of agricultural change in the South, where fundamental change occurred in part precisely because landowners lacked the power to impose a Prussian-style settlement and were forced instead to accept a series of compromises. In other words, there seems to be a conflict between the model Hahn implicitly adopts for the transition to capitalism, and his argument that this transition was especially sweeping in the United States South.

I think that Hahn's case for emancipation as a bourgeois revolution can be strengthened by abandoning a narrow focus on the triumph of agricultural wage labor and talking instead about the transformation of society. As Eric Foner notes in his recent book *Reconstruction: America's Unfinished Revolution*, after many

years of emphasizing how little things changed in the postemancipation South, historians have once again begun to use the word
"revolution" to characterize the Civil War and Reconstruction;
"Like a massive earthquake, the Civil War and the destruction of
slavery permanently altered the landscape of Southern life," Foner
writes. This notion of emancipation as representing a fundamental
point of discontinuity, which owes much to the pioneering work of
C. Vann Woodward and has been propounded by other contributors to this volume, including Barbara Fields and now Edward
Ayers, meant far more than the triumph of wage labor, important
as that was; the postemancipation reconstruction of the South
touched the section's economy, social structure, politics, class
relations, and race relations and fundamentally altered the social
order.[8]

Hahn is on target, I believe, both in insisting on the political
nature of this transformation and in proposing to evaluate it in
comparative perspective. The transformation of the postemancipation South was especially far-reaching because southern planters—who under slavery had dominated society to a degree
unmatched elsewhere—faced an unparallelled challenge to their
authority with the defeat of the Confederacy. Widely perceived as
traitors to their country, the former masters were allowed to play a
much smaller role in shaping the new order than those in most
other countries. The assault on the power of the planter class was of
course only partially successful, but it did result in a postemancipation settlement that was "radical" by the standards of most
other societies where bondage was overthrown: not only did the
former masters receive no compensation for the loss of their
human property, but the South entered the new era under more
sweeping political restructuring—so-called radical Reconstruction—than occurred elsewhere. In short, establishment of the
new order in the South took place within the context of a political
framework that was unusually conducive to a far-reaching social
transformation.

Nevertheless, despite the changes brought by emancipation,

within a few years the South experienced pervasive disillusionment, as one group after another concluded that things had gone
dreadfully wrong. Former slaveowners, of course, resented the
loss of their prerogatives; but supporters of emancipation, too—
whether freedpeople, radical Republicans, free-labor reformers,
or poor whites—expressed increasing dismay over the course of
events. The ex-slaves deplored the failure to provide "real" freedom (a view shared by an increasing number of historians today),
while many of their erstwhile northern supporters came to question whether blacks were ready for full citizenship and concluded
that the Reconstruction effort was a tragic mistake. Meanwhile,
yeoman farmers, many of whom had at first seen real promise in
Reconstruction, saw their precarious independence undermined
by the spread of commercial agriculture. The South of the 1870s
and 1880s appeared to be caught up in what was much less than a
zero-sum game, with no winners, only diverse groups of losers.

This pervasive disillusionment is a subject in which I have
recently become interested, and I would like to ask your indul-
gence for a few moments to explore its relationship to emancipation and the ensuing social changes. On the surface, the widespread perception among contemporaries that everything was
going wrong would seem to support the position of those historians
who maintain that little had changed with emancipation, that
continued oppression and exploitation marked a basic continuity
between the Old South and the New. I would suggest, however, a
very different thesis: that the pervasive sense of disillusionment
and failure was in part a function of the very transformation that
accompanied emancipation, and that this sense was strongest
precisely where the postemancipation effort to restructure society
was greatest, including preeminently the southern United States
and Russia. For like the South, Russia experienced what can be
termed a "Reconstruction" following emancipation during which a
series of so-called "great reforms" were instituted, and during
which the former bondsmen—unlike those in, say, Brazil—were
at the center of national attention. As in the South, however, the

sense of hope engendered by these developments was soon replaced by political reaction accompanied by bitter disappointment and feelings of betrayal.

Of course, there was much hardship, exploitation, and suffering in Russia and the United States South following emancipation; in both, these conditions were exacerbated by the unfortunate historical accident that emancipation preceded the onset of a generation-long period of agricultural deflation and depression that engulfed the Western world. But I believe that much of the disillusionment stemmed from dashed hopes raised by emancipation, hopes that were greatest where the postemancipation transformation was most sweeping. During his travels through Russia in the 1870s, British journalist Sir Donald MacKenzie Wallace was struck by the overwhelmingly negative view of emancipation's consequences expressed by educated Russians. "Very soon," he wrote, "I came to see that my authorities . . . were suffering from shattered illusions. They had expected that the Emancipation would produce instantaneously a wonderful improvement in the life and character of the rural population, and that the peasant would at once become a sober, industrious, model agriculturist. These expectations were not realized."[9]

As Mikhail Gorbachev is now discovering, revolutionary change tends to be unsettling because it produces diverse, indeed often contradictory expectations that are almost impossible to fulfill completely. This was certainly true with emancipation. Victorious northerners, freedmen, and poor whites all expected a basic transformation of the South, just as peasants, revolutionaries, liberal reformers, and government bureaucrats did in Russia; the problem is that they had very different expectations of what the transformation should entail. In general, the former bondsmen sought to maximize their independence and autonomy, whereas many of their "benefactors" sought to turn them into model nineteenth-century citizens by instilling in them the "bourgeois" values of sobriety, punctuality, initiative, and self-discipline. With such divergent goals, the bondsmen and their benefactors were bound not only to be disappointed, but to be disappointed in each other. In short, I would suggest that rather than viewing this pervasive disillusionment as evidence that emancipation brought few changes to the South, we should see it at least in part as an ironic consequence of the kind of revolutionary change Hahn outlines.

I have perhaps tried to touch too many bases in the short span allotted to me. Let me conclude by reiterating that I agree with Hahn's basic thesis, although I have questions about some of the details of its application, and I find the comparative framework that he uses to explore his topic appropriate and fruitful. As someone who is also using a comparative approach to investigate some of the same questions, I very much look forward to seeing the further results of this research.

Economics or Culture? The Development of the U.S. South and Brazil in the Days of Slavery

RICHARD GRAHAM

By the middle of the nineteenth century two slave "powers" had emerged to prominence in the Western hemisphere: the United States with roughly four million slaves and Brazil with two million—far more than any other single nation.[1] The fact that the United States was also fast becoming a leading industrial economy has naturally impelled many comparisons between the U.S. North and South. Eugene Genovese and Elizabeth Fox-Genovese, among others, have argued that slavery was the single most important cause of the difference between the two regions.[2] I accept much of their argument. Yet other factors besides slavery need to be taken into account. The South was too progressive and even too industrialized by comparison with other slave societies for slavery to be considered the single or major dividing line distinguishing nineteenth-century economies from each other world-wide; granted that the South was not as industrialized as the North, but few areas of the world were. At the very least, therefore, other comparisons can enhance precision in describing and evaluating slave economies and measuring their dynamism—or lack thereof. Here I argue that by comparing the South to Brazil we can significantly extend our understanding of the institution of slavery and its relationship to economic performance. Only by making this and other comparisons can historians free themselves from the all-too-easy fallacy of concluding that what was, was bound to be.

Lest there be some misunderstanding regarding my argument, let me note at the outset that I do not mean to minimize the importance for world history of changes in labor relations and in the nature of property holding. Making labor-power into a commodity to be traded in a market is a valid definition of industrial capitalism. But then we must be careful to avoid the tautology of finding the cause for the rise of capitalism in the presence of those very qualities by which we have defined it in the first place. Still, my intention here is not to challenge that overarching understanding of the nature of capitalism or engage in futile debates over its proper definition, but to explore in more detail the variations among slave economies (by definition, noncapitalist) and the mesh between slavery and economic growth. This will not, of course, satisfy those who think the relations of production are the only variable worth studying and that, therefore, the only meaningful comparison is between societies that differed in this respect.

We can begin by drawing attention to some obvious similarities between the U.S. South and Brazil. Besides the plantation system based on the labor of slaves on large estates, we may note: the production for an international market of a single major staple, a tropical or semitropical crop; the steady geographical shift of that crop associated with (allegedly) worn-out soils and impelled by surging prices; the presence of a large and relatively forgotten segment of the population that was neither slave nor planter; low investment in human capital; few large cities; a small local market for industrial goods; the relative lack of industrialization; and the location outside its borders of both the principal sources of capital and the controlling centers of its commercial life, insurance business, and carrying trade. In short, both areas were technically backward, rural, nonindustrial, socially retrograde, and characterized by a paternalistic ethos.

Despite these similarities, marked differences are also notable. And it is in accounting for these differences that we can begin to understand the relative weight of economic and cultural factors in history.

First, then, let us examine the differences. Some of these spring entirely from the fact that we must compare two areas at slightly different times, with somewhat different kinds of boundaries.

Cotton began to increase rapidly as a southern product in the last decade of the eighteenth century; its planters hit their full stride when they moved into the lower South in the 1820s from which time cotton accounted for half of all United States exports; and planters faced the end of slavery in the 1860s. In Brazil the first real growth of coffee production did not occur until the 1820s, and it did not account for half of Brazil's exports until the 1850s. Coffee planters did not have to deal with the end of slavery until the 1880s. Meanwhile, conditions in the world market changed, ideologies changed, and the Civil War in the United States itself affected Brazilians. And the choice one makes of comparable periods implies choices of areas to be compared. Both Brazilians and North Americans had used slaves to produce export products since colonial times, most notably sugar in Pernambuco and Bahia, tobacco in Virginia and Maryland. Cotton first gained importance in South Carolina and Georgia, while later its production centered in Alabama, Mississippi, and Louisiana. Coffee became initially prominent in the valley of the Paraíba do Sul River in the area feeding the port of Rio de Janeiro. Its cultivation gradually spread southwestward up the river and, finally, in the 1880s, into new regions of west-central São Paulo province, moving further west and south later on. A good part of this movement occurred only after the abolition of slavery in 1888.[3] At any rate in both cases we encounter two post-independence economies focused on the export of crops produced with slave labor.

Turning to more substantive points of difference, we may identify three areas that in the nineteenth century were considered preeminent measures of economic progress: transportation, agricultural technology, and manufacturing industry. The South, aided by its geography, possessed a far superior transportation system. The coastal escarpment in Brazil runs much closer to the sea than in North America and cuts off the kind of rivers that penetrate the tidewater regions of South Carolina and Georgia. In any case the coffee region lies beyond it in the highlands. Brazil has an extensive and navigable river system, but it drains a region—the Amazon Valley—that is only today yielding to man's effort, however misguided, to bring it into commercial production. In contrast, the Mississippi and its tributaries, besides linking today's Midwest to the South, could not have been better placed to carry southern cotton to a port (New Orleans). To be sure, the major early coffee region occupied a river valley, but rapids break this river along most of its course and waterfalls separate it from the sea, so that planters could use it to ship coffee, if they were lucky, only for a few miles from plantation to local commercial center. In the coffee area of west-central São Paulo that came into later development, rapids also interrupt the rivers and these flow, in any case, westward away from the nearby ports and toward the Río de la Plata, over a thousand miles away.[4]

The road system of the American South easily surpassed that of Brazil, partly because of the more favorable topography, partly because of greater capital resources, and partly because of institutions more suited to the mobilization of energies toward road building. Although travellers in the South complained bitterly about the muddy tracks that passed for roads, these nevertheless did form a network which spanned the cotton South and upon which wagons and stagecoaches traversed regularly. Even if many roads led only as far as the nearest point on a navigable river or, later, to a railhead, even so they carried the cotton to gins and to market. Community effort, frequently impelled by a local tax, built these roads and elected local officials to oversee them; landowners supplied the labor, that is, that of their slaves.[5] In Brazil's coffee region, hairpinning trails plunged precipitously from the upland valley to the coast. Mule trains or slave caravans traversed them, but not, generally speaking, wheeled vehicles. Roughly laid flat stones on the steepest curves provided an occasional firm footing, but elsewhere roads became quagmires when it rained, and rainfall along the escarpment averages 147 inches per year. Central or provincial governments financed the construction and maintenance of these trails; planters and county governments on the one side and higher authorities on the other constantly clashed

over assignment of responsibility for their poor state. Individual
local planters, without cooperative effort, sometimes built private
roads that led from plantation to rivers or (later) to railroad, but
county governments remained helpless to command the efforts of
the planters for community needs. A private toll-collecting company built the first macadamized road in Brazil in the 1840s, but
not until 1861 did it complete an extension into the coffee region.[6]

Yet for all the inadequacy of these roads, Brazilians still relied
entirely on them long after American southerners had turned to
railroads. Here again, most of what has been written about southern railways compares them to those of the North, behind which
the South sadly lagged.[7] But when contrasted with Brazil, that
picture radically alters and becomes even more startling when we
consider that the South also enjoyed excellent river transportation
through the new cotton areas.[8] In 1860 the cotton states encompassed almost 6000 kilometers of railways, whereas the coffee
regions of Brazil had only 112, although the figures became more
similar if we consider the extent of lines in Brazil by the time of the
end of slavery there. Still, Brazil as a whole in 1890 enjoyed only
half as many kilometers per person as had the South thirty years
earlier.[9]

Another marked dissimilarity between these two slave economies is to be found in agricultural technology. Those who debate
the backwardness or efficiency of southern agriculture most often
compare it with the North.[10] But in Brazil, even the common plow
was rarely seen. Granted that in the older coffee areas the exceed-
ingly steep hills could not be plowed even "up and down on slopes"
as was done in Georgia,[11] and that coffee cultivation had special
requirements. Granted also that Brazilians used some plows, and
that more investigation of the history of Brazilian agricultural
technology must be done before we can speak confidently about
the differences. However, Brazilians made virtually no use of
scrapers, cultivators, harrows, or mechanical seeders until the
twentieth century. The hoe remained the principal instrument of
farm labor in Brazil and, in general, oxen never gave way to mules,

remaining in use in coffee regions until tractors began to take their place after 1950.[12] Even a hasty reading of the agricultural history of the South makes ludicrous the claim by some Brazilian historians that planters in the Paraíba Valley did not use modern agricultural equipment because of the incompatibility between mechanization and "slave relations of production" or that slaves were "incapable of productively managing techniques which require the use of machines." In the United States South slaves managed sophisticated tools and machines.[13]

In Brazil as in the South, planters cleared the forest with slash-and-burn techniques and principally ensured the fertility of the soil they used by moving onto new lands.[14] The comparative advantage of new areas and the profitability of extensive rather than intensive land use proved a major obstacle to the use of modern agricultural technology.[15] Brazilian historians, as was once the case for those of the South, still ascribe this alleged tendency to the "routine" spirit of the planters in the older area and to their supposed irrationality in holding onto outdated practices, but in making that argument they ignore the relative costs of land, capital, and labor that may have made such decisions highly rational.[16] In any case, planters in both regions preferred to put newly cleared lands into production, rather than improving older lands.

Despite these similarities, planters in the United States also took many measures—unknown in Brazil—to maintain soil quality. They sometimes applied cow manure, no doubt less difficult to do on open cotton fields than under semi-permanent rows of coffee bushes. Chemical fertilizer, guano, potash, and lime—all used to some degree in the South—remained virtually unknown in Brazil. Similar contrasts can be noted regarding the practices of contour plowing, crop rotation, terracing, and draining. Although Brazilian planters used labor profligately, I am not aware of their undertaking such backbreaking tasks as digging swamp mud to spread on fields. Coffee planters did some mulching of the bushes with dead leaves or the sweepings after the harvest, and slaves cultivated around the bushes twice a year. But Lewis Cecil Gray describes the much more systematic practice in the South by the 1820s and 1830s of cutting up the cotton stalks and plowing them under.[17] True, Brazilians did try out new seeds, but relatively few planters read agricultural journals; indeed many of them were totally illiterate. Within the few Brazilian publications, agricultural improvements received some attention to be sure, and reformers sometimes published tracts on agricultural techniques, but planters and journalists carried on no extended debates regarding agricultural methods nor did they express widespread concern with these matters. Brazilians hardly ever formed specifically agricultural societies, except to withstand the onslaught of abolitionists in the 1880s; not until the end of the century did they hold fairs to stimulate adoption of better agricultural methods.[18] In short, Brazil lagged far behind the South in every aspect of agricultural technology.

The South was also far more industrialized than Brazil. So far I have noted differences in the agricultural sector and in transportation facilities; contemporaries, however, despite some hesitations, usually saw industrialization as the final measure of progress.[19] Textile factories, shoe manufactures, flour mills, and iron foundries thickly peppered the South by comparison with Brazil.[20] Much more systematic examination of industrial progress is required before the exact dimensions of the gap can be stated, but its overall nature is clear. The South in 1860 had three times as many cotton mills and millworkers as did Brazil twenty-five years later, and four times as many spindles.[21] Although Brazil can claim superb iron ore resources, the few iron foundries of Brazil worked principally with imported pig.[22]

At this point let me pause to make an historiographical comparison. In both Brazil and the United States historians have explained industrial backwardness by the presence of slavery. In Brazilian historiography it has become almost a truism that industrialization and slavery were mutually antagonistic, whereas in the United States only some have made that argument. Even the end

of the slave system in Brazil is generally explained by citing
internal contradictions that became more intense as slave labor
itself produced the wealth that undid the foundations of slavery.
The argument goes this way: Increased exports finally stimulated
the rise of a few cities and enlarged the consuming market while
also earning foreign exchange that could pay for more and more
capital goods. Eventually, Brazilians or foreigners set up some
textile plants, flour mills, shoe factories, and other industries.
Rails laid to carry away the product of slave-worked plantations also
made industrial goods accessible to formerly isolated plantations.
On the plantations themselves increased prosperity enabled
planters to invest in coffee processing machinery. All these developments, it is argued, lessened the attractiveness of slave labor,
which could best be used at rough and repetitive agricultural tasks,
rather than at skilled industrial ones. The complete alienation of
the slave from his labor dampened his initiative and reduced his
interest in caring for equipment. He responded weakly to incentives. Furthermore, the high capital investment in the slave himself slowed the turnover of profit from his labor; encouraged the
owner to maintain him constantly at work and thus weakened the
impetus toward investment in labor-saving machinery; and ham-
pered the fledgling industrialist in times of retrenchment, since he
could not dismiss workers in order to cut costs. In addition, the
attitudes of slave-owning planters remained "premodern" and patriarchal, status-conscious and inclined to costly display of wealth
and position rather than to entrepreneurship and investment.
Drawing both on Weber and Marx, several authors have elaborated on these themes.[23]

The North American experience casts doubt on most of these
generalizations and suggests a more ambiguous historical reality.
Southern industrialists did not hesitate to use slave workers. Five
percent of the entire slave population—around 200,000 persons
—worked in some sort of industry. Skills were systematically
taught the industrial slaves, and many of them performed highly
technical jobs, as well as exercising managerial functions. Rail-

roads relied on slave labor extensively, not only for construction but in such responsible positions as that of brakemen.[24]

The hiring-out system obviated some of the obstacles to industrialization alleged to be inherent in the slave system. Owners rented their slaves to others, in the United States often industrialists, who, if financial conditions worsened, could return them to their masters. These would then put the slaves to other employment. About one-fifth of all slaves working in industry in the South were hired from someone else. In Brazil also it was a common practice to own slaves in order to rent them out. We know some industries there relied on hired slaves; but many more could have. Instead, most of the hired slaves performed domestic duties or worked as porters and stevedores carrying and loading coffee. We do not know whether the practice of hiring out was more or less widespread in Brazil than in the South, but the flexibility it engendered in the United States was presumably as possible in Brazil.[25]

In nineteenth-century Brazil, perhaps even more than in the South, slaves often hired themselves out, finding their own work to do for a wage and returning a fixed sum to their masters. These slaves, like those of southern cities, acted virtually as free persons, arranged their own work and wages, often secured their own housing, and sometimes acted as contractors, hiring free laborers or employing other slaves. Although the practice was widespread in both southern and Brazilian cities, it was eventually outlawed in the South, whereas it was licensed in Brazil. Surely the relationship between employer and employee is qualitatively different from that between owner and owned; but in the hiring-out system, both relationships existed simultaneously, with wide implications for the growth of capitalism.[26]

Even rural slaves in Brazil sometimes received cash in much the way free men did. First, because many planters allowed slaves to use provision grounds on which to raise foodstuffs,[27] and slaves sometimes sold their excess production, either—as ordered—to the master or—perhaps more commonly—clandestinely to the owner of a country store who did not hesitate as well to purchase small amounts of "stolen" coffee. Second, some planters used cash as an incentive for extra work, paying a monetary reward, for instance, for any basket of coffee harvested beyond a certain minimum.[28] Thus chattel slaves themselves came to own some property, often in cash, and to become accustomed to receiving some sort of wage in exchange for their work. In this way the distinction between slave labor and wage labor tended to blur as far as their role in the economy goes, although certainly not in other ways.

If the prosperity and industrial strength of the antislavery North rested, to some degree, on the profits derived from commerce in and manufacturing of slave-grown cotton,[29] did such contradictions appear within the South itself, as Brazilian historians argue happened in Brazil? Did the very prosperity built on slavery lead to the erosion of the slave system? Richard Wade lends support to the Brazilians' point of view and argues that slaves were systematically driven from southern cities by those whose values found encouragement in the growth of urban centers and industrial prosperity. Yet, here, ironically, he could have profited by considering the Brazilian case, since a similar decline in the number of urban slaves in Brazil has long been understood to spring from the increasing demand for their labor in the countryside and to have preceded the rise of urban abolitionism. Barbara Fields argues that, if slaves were in greater demand on agricultural estates than in the cities, this fact in itself demonstrates the incompatibility of slavery and urban life.[30] Some planters of the South actively opposed industrialization because it would lead, they feared, to immigration of white workers who might threaten the continuation of slavery. Although Brazilian planters opposed protective tariffs and may have been cool to industrial impulses, they did not consider immigration a threat; some eventually even joined the abolitionists and decreed the end of slavery in order, as they saw it, to be able to get more immigrants for their fields—not their factories.[31] Insofar as slavery produced or encouraged those forces opposed to industry, the results were very different in these two slave regions.

Therefore, although historians may have correctly identified slavery as a contributing factor in slowing industrialization, preventing self-sustained development, and keeping industry from becoming the predominant form of economic activity, much more needs to be specified in order to explain why one slave region was so much more successful at industrializing than was another. The causative link is at least not direct. The South possessed more slaves than Brazil and they formed a larger proportion of the population. In the five principal cotton states of the South almost half the population was enslaved in 1860; in the three principal coffee states of Brazil only a quarter of the population was slave in 1872.[32] Yet the South surged far ahead in industrialization, in transportation, and in agricultural technology. No one would argue that the higher number of slaves explains the difference. Nor can it be said that even though the South had more slaves, the institution itself was not as strong as in Brazil; on the contrary, the strength of the slave system in the United States was so great that it may be said to have required a civil war to end it.[33]

What other factors, then, could explain the difference? For heuristic reasons we may begin by separating the causes of those differences into economic and cultural categories, although they are intimately linked one to the other. We may begin by dismissing an allegation often made by historians about Brazil, namely that its failure to industrialize resulted from its dependence on international trade and capital. It supposedly relied too heavily on the export of one crop; the profits from merchandising the crop went into the hands of foreign merchant houses, foreign shipping firms, foreign insurance companies (especially British); and these profits were therefore not available for domestic reinvestment.[34] Yet the proportion of cotton and coffee in each nation's exports is roughly comparable. Cotton accounted for more than half the total exports of the United States from 1830 to 1860, reaching 63 percent in the late 1830s. In Brazil coffee accounted for over 40 percent of the

country's exports from 1830 to 1870, more than 50 percent in the
early 1870s, and about 60 percent from 1875 to 1890.[35] The United
States, furthermore, exported over two-thirds of its cotton production in every year except two from 1820 to 1860, and as much as 80
percent in all but three years from 1825 to 1845.[36] And cotton not
destined for Britain was mainly exported from the South to the
North. Moreover, British firms financed most of the merchandising of cotton; insofar as they did not, the profits of cotton commerce fell primarily into the hands of northern ones.[37] The
interest of Great Britain in the United States South was intense
and direct: witness the diplomacy of the American Civil War.[38] So
southerners, just as Brazilians, produced an export crop and depended on others for its commercialization. It is not the fact that
Brazil was thus dependent that explains its lagging economic
development vis à vis the South.

On the contrary, it is the extremely close ties between the South
and the world capitalist system that may more logically explain
some of the higher levels of agricultural, transportational, and
industrial technology the South enjoyed. For to say technology is
to say capital, and the South attracted more capital than did Brazil.

The South may not have attracted enough capital or as much as
southerners wished. Like Brazil, for instance, it encountered
difficulty in raising capital for railroad building. Although planters
and local merchants in both areas often took the initiative in
creating railroad companies, sometimes investing their own resources, they also needed outside investors and found they had to
attract them with special stimuli. In both places, government
authorities played an important role in this effort. In Brazil, the
national and provincial governments, acting together, guaranteed
a return of 7 percent on capital invested in approved rail lines. In
addition, the Brazilian central government bought a substantial
share of stock in one major railroad that served the coffee region
and eventually took over direct ownership and operation; later in
the century provincial governments also owned and operated
railroads directly. In the South, government support of railroad

building consisted both of indirect assistance through provision of free land surveys by state employees, tax exemptions, monopoly franchises, and grants of public land, and also much direct aid such as cash subsidies and loans, guarantees of railroad bonds, and even outright ownership. Southern counties and cities employed public funds further to aid railroad building. Both Brazilian and American southern governments borrowed money to finance this aid, frequently from England. In short, governments in both regions felt the need to apply the resources of the state because capitalists in England and in the North had other, more profitable or less risky investments to make.[39]

Yet from the data I have already presented it is clear that despite similar obstacles more capital found its way into southern railways than into Brazilian ones, to take just one example. The same was true for agricultural technology which, by definition, meant greater capital investment.

Both Brazilians and U.S. southerners paid for these capital goods with their exports. So which area was better equipped by the value of its exports to do so? The South, by far; and here is a major key to the puzzle. In every year except three of the last twenty-five years of slavery, the value of cotton exports from the South exceeded the value of coffee exports from Brazil, in most years by two-to-one and often by a considerably higher ratio. Moreover, the difference is cumulative. Now, not all export earnings went to purchase technology for the South: United States imports from abroad—paid for with cotton—went to the North as well.[40] But clearly cotton provided a much greater potential for capital-goods purchases by the United States as a whole than coffee did for Brazil, and cotton planters had substantially more wealth for investment in railroads, industry, and agricultural tools and machinery than did coffee planters. This material fact is of major importance in distinguishing these two slave economies from each other.

Besides using its current exports to pay for capital goods, a region may also be able to count on foreign investments and loans.

Which of these two areas—the American South or Brazil—most attracted international investors?[41] We know that in both areas planters received most of their credit from their factors. It was with that money that they mechanized their operations, applied new fertilizing techniques, or bought slaves and land. The factors, in turn, borrowed from banks, often British banks.[42] But comparing the amount of credit offered by factors in Brazil and in the United States will probably be impossible because of their large number and varied interests. Somewhat more solid ground, but still only symptomatic, is the much greater prevalence of banking institutions in the South than in Brazil. The dividing lines between merchants who sold on credit, merchant-bankers, and full-fledged banking institutions, of course, is not always clear. But the number of formally constituted banks in Brazil lagged far behind that of the American South even if the South trailed the North. The difference may be accounted for partly by legislation: Each state in the U.S. wrote its own bank laws and, especially before 1835, banking legislation imposed few restrictions on banks' rights to issue currency, lend a high proportion of their deposits, or virtually abandon liquidity. In Brazil firm centralized control was usually operable, and policymakers were very conservative. Banks proliferated in the South whereas banks did not operate significantly in Brazil at all until after 1850.[43]

The local banker in both regions was tied into a vast chain of credit relationships that did not respect national boundaries. And capital resources were always greater in London, and later in New York, than they were in New Orleans or Rio de Janeiro. So it is in those centers—London and New York—that we must look for explanations for the greater flow of capital to the U.S. South than to Brazil.[44]

A political consideration may be important here: The greater ease with which industrial enterprise spread into the South may have resulted from the very lack of national boundaries between it and the North. Political unity and a common currency, together with geographical proximity and cultural affinities, surely encouraged northern investors to place some of their funds in southern enterprises rather than, say, in France. What we do know is that, despite the draining of southern financial resources to northern cities, at least some of these resources eventually returned to the South as investment to a degree far greater than in Brazil where the industrial and commercial center was in an entirely different country.

But a more powerful explanation for the relative paucity of agricultural credit in Brazil springs from the greater willingness of lenders to finance the production and merchandising of cotton than of coffee. Cotton was a surer bet. And that conclusion is not surprising when one considers the place of each crop within the rising industrial system of Europe or the North. Cotton was central as a raw material. If coffee supplies had been cut off, the progress of industrial capitalism would not have been affected, but a threat to cotton production, such as the one posed by the American Civil War, sent ripples through the entire world economy.[45] Although financing cotton production ran the short-run risks of over-supply and falling prices, in the end cotton easily secured its place as an essential raw material while coffee remained primarily a dessert, albeit also a slightly addictive stimulant.

But capital was not invested only in the production, transport, or marketing of cotton. Planters and merchants in both areas shifted some of their borrowed or accumulated capital into industrial enterprise. The estates of deceased coffee planters in Brazil normally included stocks in banks, cotton mills, and railways, as well as government bonds.[46] But southerners invested in industry to a much greater degree than did Brazilians. Why was this so?

Here we come to another set of contrasts: differing social structures among the free, despite the fact that both societies held so many in bondage. Even with equivalent export earnings and equal access to international credit, Brazil would likely not have invested as much in industry as did the American South. Strictly economic—or, better, financial—explanations for the differences between the U.S. South and Brazil are not sufficient. The social structure must also be considered.

First, the size of the market crucially affects industrial development, and the better distribution of the South's wealth among the free meant a larger demand for industrial goods.[47] Then, the South enjoyed other benefits of a more equitable social system— in a word, human development—and profited as well from the greater social mobility which fostered entrepreneurship. So a significant amount of its export earnings were invested in production rather than consumed. These differences need to be explored and explained.

Land tenure is one measure of the distribution of wealth in an agricultural society. The image of the large estate with the plantation house dominating a vast acreage of cotton or endless fields of coffee typifies the traditional view in both areas. Frank Owsley launched a vigorous debate in the 1940s when he argued that men of middling wealth, with few or no slaves and moderate landholdings, predominated in much of the South. Although romanticizing them as the "plain folk of the Old South," he convincingly showed that the social categories of the South were more numerous and complex than the three groups—planters, poor whites, and slaves—portrayed earlier. Most heads of agricultural families (with the important exception of the slaves) owned their land; landowners comprised 80 to 85 percent of the free rural population. Owsley compiled statistical tables for sample counties in various agricultural regions of the South and showed that, even in the richest black belt areas, half the slaveowners held fewer than twenty slaves. And of the farmers who owned no slaves, only about a fifth were landless.[48]

Owsley failed to consider, however, what proportion of the land fell into the hands of that small percentage who owned, say, more than 5,000 acres. So when he said that he was determining with "reasonable accuracy the social structure of the rural South," one can only question his definition of "social structure."[49] In a devastating critique, Fabian Linden showed that in the black belt, for instance, the wealthiest 5 percent of the farm population owned 33 percent of the land.[50] Furthermore, Owsley paid insufficient attention to the quality of the land held by different classes of landowners and the tendency toward more concentration over time. Even more important, he did not compute the distribution of slaves.[51] There is no doubt that wealth concentrated in the hands of the few in the South.

Whether the concentration was "extreme" or "normal" depends entirely on the basis of comparison, whether agricultural regions of the American Midwest, industrial cities of the northeastern United States, or Brazilian coffee regions. Since by implication historians have always linked this concentration of wealth with the owning of slaves, it seems reasonable to compare the South with another slaveowning society.

But the debate on the concentration of wealth cannot yet be transferred to Brazil for lack of concrete and specific information there on land tenure and the distribution of slaves.[52] The exact nature of land distribution in Brazil still remains unknown,[53] as historians have so far presented only isolated data which defy generalization. A standard measure that allows for comparisons of inequality is the Gini Index (where zero represents perfect equality and 1.0 percent inequality). Alice Cannabrava, in the most comprehensive study done in Brazil, has shown that in 1818—when production of subsistence crops was still widespread in the province of São Paulo and coffee was far from predominant—the Gini Index there for land distribution among landowners reached 0.86. This compares with an index of 0.60 among landowners in the South in 1860.[54] But if very few agricultural workers in Brazil owned land, even Cannabrava's figure would fall far short of representing the extent of the inequality. For instance, using the 1890 figures from two parishes in a coffee-rich county, I calculated the Gini Index number for the distribution of land among landowners as 0.65; but if all men over age twenty are considered as potential landowners, the index number rises to 0.98.[55] That is why Owsley's study still remains so important: in the South there were far more small landowners than in Brazil and far fewer free landless. Access to the legal ownership of land had always been steeply more difficult in Brazil than in the American South and already in colonial days the size of land grants in Brazil dwarfed those of the South. In Portuguese America, the king had granted huge tracts of land called *sesmarias* to his favorites; sometimes these grants were measured in many square leagues. In colonial times in the U.S. South, it became a common practice to limit grants to fifty acres for every person a settler brought with him. Although large properties were subsequently engrossed by a few individuals, the general southern pattern seems to have been one of much smaller holdings than in Brazil.[56]

In Brazil overlapping royal land grants dating from the colonial period and the traditional rights of squatters combined with a virtual absence of systematic surveys or land registries to create a chaotic system of conflicting land claims that victimized the weak and placed a premium on strength, whether measured in wealth, armed men, or political influence. Few surveyed their land because each large landowner saw in the vagueness of his property's borders an opportunity for later aggrandizement. They knew that fuzziness in land titles strengthened their authority, for law can be the recourse of the weak even when originally drawn up by the strong. When export agriculture spread into a new area, subsistence farmers quickly found their claims disputed by the more powerful and wealthy planters. A land law in 1850 called for systematic surveys of existing holdings to be paid for by all who wished their titles confirmed. But, although many landowners did make formal initial depositions as called for by the law, these claims consisted of listing the names of their bordering neighbors; they made no measurements, did not resolve their conflicting claims, and soon forgot further provisions of the law.[57]

Information on slaveholdings in Brazil is even sketchier than the land tenure data. Government officials destroyed the bulk of slave registers—begun in 1871—soon after slavery was abolished in 1888, in order to rob planters of any basis for claims to compensation. We cannot say whether slaveholdings were more or less concentrated in Brazil than in the South, although the lower cost of slaves in Brazil have made them easier to acquire and there is some evidence of widespread slaveownership.[58]

What we can conclude with unquestionable certainty is that better records regarding land tenure and slave ownership exist for the United States than for Brazil, and that is in itself an important symptom of larger differences. The absence of so many of these records in Brazil indicates the sharp differences between the two areas, differences with deep roots in the social history, political economy, and cultural heritage of each one. No national census at all was taken in Brazil until 1872, it did not include land ownership, and its manuscript schedules (which would have shown slave ownership) have since been lost, perhaps deliberately destroyed. Tax records, so useful to Owsley, presume a land tax, a bureaucracy prepared to collect it, and a population prepared to pay it, at least most of the time.[59]

Now the financial condition of that great number of persons who were neither slaves nor wealthy planters impinges directly on any consideration of the size of the market for manufactures.[60] Were free agricultural workers better off in the South than in Brazil? Yes: Most of those in the South, as noted above, owned some land, a condition absent in Brazil. The tradition of the yeoman farmer had no equivalent in Luso-Brazilian experience. Assuredly, the truly poor whites lived similarly: outside the market economy, in abject poverty, barefoot, sick, and malnourished.[61] But the average free person in the South had a much bigger share of the area's buying power than did his Brazilian counterpart. Among the free in Brazil, for instance, there was a common social type known as the *agregado*. He or she depended upon someone else, especially for housing or at least a space in which to live. Most often the *agregado* was a poverty-stricken agricultural worker, sometimes a freed slave, to whom the landowners granted the right to raise subsistence crops on some outlying patch of the large estate. In exchange the *agregado* proffered occasional services, including labor, but especially loyalty. For men, that could frequently mean armed struggle in electoral disputes or fights over land. The *agregados'* claim upon security remained tenuous, and landowners could eject them without hesitation.[62] When combined with the lesser wealth of the region as a whole, it is clear that the purchasing power of Brazilian consumers in rural areas was easily outstripped by that of southerners.

Immigration did not help Brazil increase the number of consumers. In the 1880s, even before the end of slavery, thousands of European immigrants moved onto the Brazilian plantations to work alongside slaves. This phenomenon contrasts with the experience in North America where immigrants avoided the rural slave areas. The fact can be explained not by the Brazilian planters' effort to recruit European immigrants—which they did with some vigor—but by the changing circumstances of Europe, the diminished opportunities for acquiring land in the United States (where they might otherwise have gone), and the widespread and justified belief that Brazilian slavery was about to end. By working under conditions that approached those of slavery, however, the immigrants did not by their presence immediately increase the number of consumers in Brazil. On the contrary, their availability probably slowed the growth of real wages.[63] So the relative poverty of the nonslaveowning, non-slave rural class in Brazil continued despite immigration. This poverty limited the market for industrial goods in the countryside.

The towns and cities of the American South also offered a larger market for industrial goods than did Brazil's urban areas. Estimating the extent of urbanization in Brazil is difficult because the Brazilian census presented population figures by parishes within counties, usually without differentiating between urban and rural areas. Since the territory of parishes varied greatly (and no one has yet calculated the area of each one), even the density of population cannot be known at this time. Yet in all Brazil—an area larger than the forty-eight contiguous United States today—there were only seven counties with more than 10,000 people in 1872. In 1860 Virginia alone had five cities of more than 10,000 each.[64] To be sure, neither Brazil nor the U.S. South had what could be called a city system. Outside visitors to both Brazil and the South described sleepy small towns and the absence of bustling commercial centers; but my own reading of travellers' accounts and secondary sources leads me to believe that the South enjoyed a much more active town life, with more local merchants and more exchanging of goods, than did Brazil.[65] Joaquim Nabuco, the Brazilian abolitionist, described the effect of slavery upon Brazilian towns in this way:

> With the exceptions of Santos and Campinas in São Paulo province, Petrópolis and Campos in Rio de Janeiro, Pelotas in Rio Grande do Sul, and a scattering of other towns, there are no commercial houses outside the [provincial] capital cities where anything can be found beyond a small stock of items essential to life, and even these are crude or adulterated. . . . For this reason, whatever is not ordered directly from the capital reaches the consumer through the peddler alone.[66]

A few Brazilian landowners, who preferred to transact business at the capital, could not provide employment for the storekeepers, smithies, liverymen, lawyers, doctors, bankers, clerks, and others about whom one reads in the descriptions of southern American towns. The towns of Brazil were less numerous, smaller, with a slower pace of commercial activity. The explanation may be sought both in the smaller value of the principal commodity of trade and in the more skewed distribution of wealth.

Towns in the South bustled especially on election day, and politics forms another area of contrasting experience. By 1860 it was not just the men of means who could vote, but almost every free white adult male. True, some historians argue convincingly that the political, social, and cultural predominance of the rich planter gave the South its distinct quality as compared to the North; everyone aspired to be such a planter, and as a kind of seigneur he continued to exercise patronage and influence.[67] Nonetheless, Michael Johnson argues that fear among large planters that the rising democratic pressures from less wealthy southerners threatened their political dominance impelled—at least in part—the secession movement in Georgia.[68]

This contrasts markedly with Brazil. Participation in voting there was extensive; but voting was indirect and voters chose only local electors, usually their patrons the planters, who then wielded all genuine political power. The strength of landowners—or of any group—eludes precise measurement, but it would be hard to believe that in the coffee regions of Brazil any real political power ever rested among small landowners or poor whites.[69] Typically the men who ruled locally derived their ability to attract a clientele in the first instance from their control of property, even if not all the propertied had an equal hand in district politics. As a planter-delegate to a congress of agriculturalists perceptively put it in 1878, it was "necessary to respect the social and economic fact, which we witness in this country, that a great part of the rural population—the preponderant part of the population of the Empire—in one form or another is subject to the big landowners who possess the more productive enterprises."[70]

A squireocracy clearly controlled the polity. Among the coffee-planting families in one county in the Paraíba Valley, these six towered in wealth: Ribeiro de Avellar, Souza Werneck, Lacerda Werneck, Santos Werneck, Correia de Castro, and Paes Leme. Two others, the Miranda Jordão and Teixeira Leite families, owned local businesses, especially lending money to planters and serving as factors or commission agents for them, although they also held some land.[71] These eight families together controlled county politics. In 1842, when parish electoral boards were organized by a triumvirate of priest, police commissioner, and justice of the peace, Paulo Gomes Ribeiro de Avellar, as justice of the peace, and José Pinheiro de Souza Werneck, as police commissioner, joined the priest on one board. Among the other three board members was Francisco Peixoto de Lacerda Werneck, the wealthiest of them all. When the voting took place, eight of the ten victorious electors bore familiar names:

Joaquim Ribeiro de Avellar

Claudio Gomes Ribeiro de Avellar
Manoel Gomes Ribeiro de Avellar
Paulo Gomes Ribeiro de Avellar
José Gomes Ribeiro de Avellar
José Pinheiro de Souza Werneck
Francisco Werneck[72]

Thirteen years later, in 1855 these families still monopolized county and parish offices: among the county councilmen and their
substitutes, we find the names Teixeira Leite, Souza Werneck,
Paes Leme, and Miranda Jordão. In the central parish of the
county, Pedro Correia de Castro served as a justice of the peace, as
did three Teixeira Leites. In the parish of Paty do Alferes, the
deputy police commissioner belonged to the Ribeiro de Avellar
family; his substitute was Augusto Soares de Miranda Jordão who
simultaneously held the position of county councilman. Three of
the four justices of the peace in this parish bore the family name
Ribeiro de Avellar, including the family head.[73]

Everywhere in Brazil men of wealth and substance, especially
planters, controlled the positions of local power.[74] They were the
judges, the local police officials, and the officers in the militia. But
as all these positions were appointive rather than elective, their
success at gaining them meant they had influence at the national
capital as well, and here is a point worth noting. In the U.S. South
the large planter was also likely to exert much local influence, but
did not predominate (at least by 1860) over the central government.

In the process of establishing Brazil's independence from Portugal planters had toyed with provincial autonomy, but concluded
that their class position was safest under a firmly centralized
regime. They themselves created its institutions and took an active
part in central administration. A parliamentary system in Brazil
meant that the prime minister and his cabinet could only emerge
from the legislature, even though the emperor had the authority to
dismiss him and summon a rival to form a government. Members
of parliament were beholden to the local bigwigs whose influence

or presence on local electoral colleges insured their election. Although a law-school education usually characterized legislators (and for that matter most educated people, since it was the typical form of higher education), officials at both the local and central level responded with special sensitivity to the landed interest, if they were not themselves landowners. No historian has undertaken a systematic search through local records to establish the property of cabinet members; but one scholar, relying primarily on biographical dictionaries, has shown that at least 57 percent of them had links to the land, either directly or through family.[75] When slavery was abolished in 1888 it was not against the will of the most powerful sector of slaveowners, for they had concluded that the increasing cost of maintaining slave discipline along with the need to attract additional free workers from Europe outweighed the advantages of maintaining the system. But, by the same token, their disillusionment with the political structures of the empire meant that a year later the emperor slid from the throne without a blow.[76] All this contrasts sharply with the position of southern planters in the United States as they confronted federal power. Their only option, they concluded, was secession.[77]

The greater distribution of wealth among the free also meant that the ordinary free southerner had more political clout than his Brazilian counterpart. And free men evidently used that power to improve their lot: It is remarkable to note, for instance, the amount of public money invested in human development in the South. On this score it far outdistanced Brazil no matter how much it may have lagged behind the North. Only 21 percent of the free persons in Brazil in 1872 could read (22.7 percent in the coffee provinces), while the equivalent figure in the South in 1850 was 80 percent.[78] Whereas in 1860 there were 512 persons in the South for every physician or surgeon (572 in the 5 leading cotton states), there were 5,048 potential patients for each doctor in Brazil in 1872 (and 9,026 within the coffee provinces).[79] The greater amount of attention paid to such human needs in North America surely led to a better-fed, healthier, more energetic work force and entrepreneurial cadre among the free. It reflects a belief, furthermore, shared even by the southern planters, that over-all benefits derived from such investments. Questions of social structure and of politics lead finally to culture or ideology. In those areas of the world ruled by the bourgeoisie, individualism, entrepreneurship, hard work, and social mobility have been emphasized and rewarded, almost by definition; in contrast, a landed aristocracy may be expected to value status, deference, and leisure more highly.[80] The problem here is to account for the difference between two areas both of which, at first glance, seem to have been ruled by a patriarchal, almost seigneurial class. Robert Fogel, Stanley Engerman, and James Oakes are, I think, mistaken when they insist the South was *just* as "capitalistic" as the North, even if we accept their definition of the word; but the South was much more dominated by the values of the bourgeoisie than was Brazil. Although some Brazilian planters invested in railways and cotton mills, many more refused even to contribute to community road-building programs, unmoved by the possibility of greater profits through improved transportation. They did not insist on clear property boundaries and did not clear their titles from conflicting claims, measures that could have facilitated the use of their land as security on loans. They opposed the freedom of banks to lend everything they received as deposits. Many of them long resisted efforts to reform the mortgage laws—even though this would have increased the flow of credit to agriculture—because, more than the southerners, they saw land as a source of power as well as profit. And they especially valued elaborate social ranking. They took for granted that people could generally be distinguished, as one planter put it, "according to the order, scale, or category into which [they were] placed within society."[81] No one thought himself equal to anyone else; all met within a hierarchy and found themselves either above or below all others. The accoutrements of status proved effective devices for maintaining the proper relationship among those of diverse social place: through the defense of honor and rank—sometimes requir-

ing lavish expenditure or displays of openhanded generosity,
sometimes impelling haughty contempt for the poor—the wealthy
sought to validate the deference they received from others.[82]

Now the efforts made by the Brazilian planter to bolster and
maintain his authority within the self-contained system of the
plantation have sometimes misled observers into totally discount-
ing his economic rationality. They understood very well the complex structure of Brazil's export economy, were aware of Brazil's
role in the international division of labor, kept a sharp eye on world
commodity prices, and worried over their profit and loss. They
were businessmen on one side—but lords on another. Most Brazilian planters, like southern ones, probably felt no tension between the role of seigneur and entrepreneur. Like their counterparts in the U.S. South—but more so—they were, as Fox-Genovese puts it, "in but not of the bourgeoisie." A consideration of
comparative ideology among planters points not to black-and-
white contrasts but to varying shades of gray.

At this point, the historian cannot point only to slave relations of
production. Granted that the labor system of the South militated
against the full formulation of a bourgeois ideology, the South still
moved further along that road than did Brazil. The fact that the
U.S. South was politically part of the North is a first step in
understanding why this was so. James Oakes has shown how
widespread among the lesser sort were values and attitudes that
are normally associated with the North.[83] But that is merely a
superficial phenomenon, and we must look much further into the
past. For even the independence movements of Brazil and the
U.S. South had sharply divergent social meanings. Whereas students of North-American history debate whether or not the American Revolution enhanced the country's social democracy and
eased the rise of new social groups to political power,[84] historians
of Brazil today agree that the slow process of independence, which
only ended there in 1831, signified the unquestioned preeminence
of the wealthy in the halls of power. Although landowners on the
frontier clashed with those in older settled areas, and merchants

and bureaucrats vied for position too, the small landowners and
urban petit bourgeoisie played only a small role and profited little
if at all; and the many landless were practically voiceless. The
movement for Brazilian independence was never inspired by the
rhetoric of equal rights.[85]

Further, the social structures of Brazil and of the South in
colonial times had been as dissimilar as were their societies later
on. All evidence suggests that colonial Brazil had a lesser degree of
social equality and mobility than the southern colonies, little as
the latter may have had of either.[86] Even the social structures of the
mother countries from which these two areas emerged as colonies
were significantly different. Nothing symbolizes that difference
more clearly than the contrasting nature of the English and Portuguese revolutions of 1640. Although there is much controversy
over the meaning of the Puritan Revolution, one need only consider the social groups of contemporaneous Portugal and the conservative nature there of the anti-Spanish revolt of 1640 to realize how
different were the structures from which the two colonies originated and how divergent were their dominant ideologies.[87] Social
changes taking place in England long before 1700 will require as
much attention from the historian who attempts to understand the
South's economic and cultural history as does slavery.

Put more directly, part of the explanation for contrasting situations in Brazil and the South will be found in the seigneurial values
and hierarchically structured society more firmly present in Portugal than in England and imported to Brazil with less erosion;
differences, in other words, that run deeper and endured longer
than the institution of slavery. Although merchant capitalism was
vigorous in Portugal even before it triumphed in England, its fruits
were quite different in Brazil. And by the time cotton was king in
the South, more than a century of industrial capitalism had characterized England, whereas Portugal has only now (in the late
twentieth century) begun to enter the ranks of industrial nations.

Such differences left their mark and helped shape the life and
thought of succeeding generations. The larger consuming market

and the greater propensity to invest rather than consume among mid-nineteenth-century southern planters as compared to Brazilians owe much to that heritage. Differences in the respective pasts of Brazil and the American South led to the concentration of wealth in fewer hands in the case of Brazil and the smaller investment there in human development. The more limited market in Brazil did not result from slavery, but derived from an inequality in the distribution of wealth among the free, a condition that dates back to the very settlement of Brazil. The South, like the American North, emerged out of a society where a bourgeois revolution had already begun even before colonization. This fact helps explain the relative clarity of land titles, the smaller size of original land grants, the prevalence of yeoman farmers, the presence of rising middle groups, and the ideology of liberalism.

The contrasts in social structures and in the roles of each area's export crop within industrial capitalism—cotton as an essential raw material, coffee as a dessert—when combined with the greater value of the South's exports, can explain the other differences examined here: The South drew on richer capital resources, applied a higher level of agricultural technology, lived with better transportation services, and witnessed more industrial growth. Comparing Brazil and the South also suggests that in order to understand the causative relationships between any two phenomena—say, slavery and economic development—a look at experiences elsewhere will both illuminate and confuse; old verities will then seem untenable, but new insights can also accrue. And what we at first separated—the economic from the cultural— end up being differing facets of the same reality.

Commentary / Richard H. King

Comparative history involves a kind of higher-order intellectual juggling act in which balls of many sizes and colors are kept in perpetual motion and in relationship to one another. In skillful hands such as Professor Graham's, the comparative method with its ultimate focus on differences offers a subtle, sophisticated and nuanced way of doing history, from which intellectual historians, among whom I count myself, could well learn.

Graham's basic concern in his paper is with why, given the fact that both Brazil and the South were nineteenth-century slave societies, the latter was so much "further along the road" to bourgeois ideology and reality than the former. To advert to one of the earlier conference papers: compared to Junker society east of the Elbe the South seems "backward," institutionally underdeveloped and prebourgeois. Yet when set alongside Brazil, the slave society of the southern part of the United States appears much more "advanced." But Graham is not content to make only a general claim; rather he suggests that three crucial indices of "economic progress: transportation, agricultural technology and manufacturing industry" make clear how far ahead of Brazil the nineteenth-century South was.

The bulk of Graham's paper is concerned, however, not with a description but with an explanation of these differing rates of development. His explanations fall into two categories–economic and cultural, while he chooses to focus on four areas of concern. First, cotton was a more valuable and necessary commodity than coffee on the world market. As a result in international trade, exchange of capital and rates of investment the South outstripped Brazil. Second, the white social structure of the South was relatively more "open" than Brazil's. The masses of whites were better educated; entrepeneurial opportunities were more readily available; and land distribution was more widespread.

Moreover, the political institutions and cultures of the two societies also differed considerably. The political power of non-slaveholding whites was much greater in the U.S. South, while in Brazil a planter "squireocracy controlled the polity," which was itself highly centralized. Finally the general cultural ethos of the South was more infected by bourgeois attitudes toward "individualism, entrepeneurship, hard work, and social mobility"; nor was it unimportant, asserts Graham, that the mother countries, Britain and Portugal, were so different in social structure and cultural ethos. Thus Graham concludes, "what we at first separate–the economic from the cultural–end up being differing facets of the same reality".

With this in mind, what might be offered by way of comment or critique? First, despite its claim that economics and culture were "differing facets of the same reality," Graham's paper needs to polish the cultural facet a bit more assiduously. Except for the final comments concerning Portugal and Britain, to which he devotes relatively little space, the explanatory weight of his thesis is carried by economic and social factors. Put another way, I would have liked more discussion of explicit world-views, value systems, educational institutions and intellectual elites from a comparative perspective. For instance, were there Brazilian counterparts to the southern intellectuals that Drew Faust, Michael O'Brien and Eugene Genovese have called to our attention in their recent work?

Specifically, there are three areas in which Graham's paper could be more expansive, both to its and to our benefit. First, I was struck by the absence of attention to the differing racial demographics of the two societies and, more importantly, to the ideological functions of racial/racist modes of thinking, formal and articulate or embedded and tacit, in each place. It is surely important that "race" was the organizing concept in the South, while "color" was central to racial politics in Brazil. As long as it remains the case that all slaves were people of color, but not all people of color were slaves, that some people of color were slaves, but no whites were slaves, then the function of race and racial ideologies have to be related somehow to the economic and cultural dimensions of hemispheric slave societies, if only by their relative lack of importance. (I do not think that race is of negligible importance; but that is irrelevant to my point.)

Second, I miss much, if any, discussion of the religious life of the slave or free populations in either society. I am less concerned here about putting some new spin on the Weber thesis than I am with the need for some descriptive account of the religious cultures of the South and Brazil. Specifically, one might ask if slaves in Brazil made use of the Biblical culture of the European settlers in the way southern slaves did. For the latter the Old Testament was a fertile source of religious and quasipolitical models of organization, action and self-conception. They took, for instance, a religious narrative of deliverance (the Exodus story) and transformed it into a political story of liberation. Was there anything like this in Catholic Brazil?

To shift the focus to the white population, what is the validity of Allen Tate's assertion that the ante-bellum South possessed the wrong religion, i.e., if it had been Catholic rather than Protestant, its distinctive hiearchical, pre-bourgeois worldview might have found greater resonance during the sectional crisis and had greater sticking power, once the South had been defeated? How did the differences between Protestant and Catholic cultures influence styles of political and social thinking as well as tacit and explicit theories of political and social organization in the two societies?

This in turn points to Graham's discussion of the political culture and institutions of Brazil. It whetted my curiosity without quite satisfying it. Nineteenth-century America, including the South, had a political culture comprised of an unstable combination of fading republicanism, an emerging ideology of democracy and popular sovereignty, a residual political-legal rhetoric of natural rights and higher law, the disruptive politics of sectional interests and an overarching ideology of expansionist nationalism, i.e., manifest destiny. Each of these ingredients could have radical or conservative implications; some were hostile to modernity, while others were direct offshoots thereof; and some could be turned to sectional purposes, while others could not. Were there similar cross- and countercurrents at work in Brazilian political life? Was there an ideology of Tradition? of Emancipation? How was economic and social "development" opposed or encouraged in ideological terms?

In sum, if economics and culture really are "facets of the same reality," we cannot fully comprehend that reality until we have a clearer sense of the texture of the culture informing the societies in question. On the other hand, if economic and social forces actually are determining "in the last instance," then we might as well admit it. At present, Professor Graham's paper explicitly asserts the former, but its subtext, the drift of its emphasis, would suggest the latter.

Black-White Relations Since Emancipation: The Search for a Comparative Perspective

GEORGE M. FREDRICKSON

The advocacy and promotion of comparative history runs well ahead of its practice. In other words, historians are more likely to talk prescriptively about the value of sustained comparison than to demonstrate its fruitfulness by actually doing it. But there are a few historical topics that have been explored extensively from a cross-cultural perspective. Preeminent among them is the institution of slavery, especially the comparison of the Old South's "peculiar institution" with systems of unfree labor elsewhere in the world. For more than forty years, scholars have been probing the similarities and differences between African servitude in the southern United States and in other slave societies of the New World; more recently Africa itself has been brought into the comparison; and now we even have a major study of North American slavery and Russian serfdom.[1]

Some of these studies go beyond the discussion of slavery itself and argue that black-white relations in the postemancipation era were predetermined or at least strongly influenced by the character of the antecedent slave society.[2] Although it would be hard to deny that that the slave regime left an enduring legacy of attitudes and habits predisposing former masters and slaves to think and behave in certain ways, it is doubtful whether one can deal effectively with the subsequent history of race relations exclusively, or even principally, from this perspective. Circumstances and events of the postemancipation era, of a kind not clearly prefigured by slavery and the attitudes associated with it, may be of more importance in understanding postemancipation race relations than the

129

peculiarities of the slave past. This is especially true if we take the long view and consider not merely what happened to the freedmen immediately after the abolition of chattel servitude but attempt to trace the trajectory of black experience from the time of emancipation to the present. Such a longitudinal view reveals major changes as well as significant continuities, and it would seem unlikely that we could explain change and development in terms of the characteristics or effects of an institution that was abolished before these transformations took place.

The subject of race relations over the entire time span from the end of slavery to the present remains relatively undeveloped as an opportunity for comparative historical analysis. This paper is no more than prologue to such an undertaking, because it starts from the premise that fruitful comparison can only begin after we have a better idea as to what other case or cases of modern race or class relations would provide the most useful comparative perspectives on what has happened to African Americans since the Civil War. There is no substitute for in-depth bilateral or trilateral comparisons if we wish to get a purchase on particular historical experiences, but here I seek merely to point the way to appropriate comparisons without actually making them in more than a hypothetical or heuristic way.

My point of departure is a synthetic view of the course or trajectory of black-white relations in the South, and ultimately in the United States as a whole, since emancipation. From such a general understanding, it should be possible to look at some other cases or types of cases to determine what kinds of insights or perspectives a more systematic comparison might be expected to yield.

Black Americans were freed from bondage as the result of a Civil War that was fought primarily for the preservation of the federal union and not for their liberation. But as a result of the necessities and opportunities of war, as viewed from the Union side, emancipation was adopted as an expedient policy that also appealed to the ideals of democracy and free labor that many northerners espoused as the basis of their superiority to the "aristocratic" South with its reliance on an archaic form of unfree labor. It is often incorrectly asserted that the slaves made no significant contribution to their own liberation. In fact they voted against slavery with their feet and offered themselves *en masse* to the Union army as a source of manpower. Had they remained quietly at work on the plantations, the temptation to free them as "a war measure" would have been weaker and perhaps even resistable.[3]

By itself, emancipation did not determine the status of blacks in American society. Racial prejudice and white-supremacist ideology remained strong in the North as well as the South in the immediate postwar years, and a possible model for where the freedmen would fit in the new order was the status of the half-million free Negroes of the antebellum period, who had been, as much in the North as in the South, a segregated pariah class without citizenship or "rights white men were bound to respect," except the right to own their own bodies, possess such property as they might somehow be able to acquire, and choose their own employers when not apprenticed or under some form of labor contract. If one could have taken a poll of white Americans immediately after the Civil War, there seems little doubt that a majority would have favored such an arrangement. It was only because the ruling Republican party found that its own postwar agenda required black citizenship that the constitution was amended to provide for equality under the law and a nonracial suffrage. Republican motives have been much debated, and various efforts have been made to distinguish elements of principle and expediency in the formation of Radical race policy. What is important for our purposes is that some combination of practical circumstances and ideological pressures made the fundamental Law of the Land into a barrier to legalized or publicity-sanctioned racial discrimination, although the question of how far it went or what precisely it covered would long remain debatable.

Constitutional reform of this kind was not sufficient by itself to turn ex-slaves into citizens. Efficient enforcement and generous interpretation of the law was necessary, and these were not forth-coming except fitfully and for a relatively short period. By the late 1870s, the southern states were once again under the dominance of white supremacist majorities, and the rights accorded blacks dur-ing the Reconstruction era were largely nullified. In the period 1890–1910, the southern states, with the consent of the United States Supreme Court, segregated blacks by law in virtually all public facilities and amended their constitutions to bring about the de facto disfranchisement of most of the freedmen and their de-scendents. In the North, blacks retained many of their civil rights, including the right to vote and hold office, but they had no adequate defense against the private or extralegal discrimination that denied them equal access to jobs, housing, education, police protection, and public amenities. The organized and articulate black response to these developments took two forms. In the South, where opposition to black political rights was massive and unyielding, an accommodationist ideology condoning social segre-gation, stressing economic self-help, and deferring aspirations for full citizenship was clearly dominant. The accommodationist and gradualist approach of Booker T. Washington was also influential in the north, especially among a rising class of black entrepreneurs working within an increasingly segregated economy. But in the early 1900s, northern black professionals, seeking to turn back the tide of Jim Crow laws and practices, launched a protest movement, modelled on pre-Civil War abolitionism, that rejected Wash-ington's accommodationism and called for the end of enforced segregation, disfranchisement, and all publicly-sanctioned dis-crimination. In 1909 they joined with a group of white liberals and socialists to form the organization that soon became known as the National Association for the Advancement of Colored People (NAACP).

In the meantime, economic and demographic changes were occurring that would alter the contours of black-white relations. For the first half century of freedom, most blacks remained in the rural South as sharecroppers and farm laborers, or, in the case of a fortunate minority, as renters or owners of small farms. Except to the extent that they worked in such extractive industries as mining and lumbering, blacks were scarcely affected by industrialization; in the South most factory jobs were reserved for poor whites. Hamstrung by a credit system that kept many of them in perpetual debt, these rural blacks constituted part of a class that was not supposed to exist in America—an oppressed and impoverished peasantry, an agrarian lower stratum that had some limited access to the means of production but was denied upward mobility and full rights of citizenship.

This situation began to change in the era of the First World War when the combination of an economic boom and the restriction of European immigration provided new employment opportunities for blacks in the North, including the chance to gain a toehold in secondary industry. The great migration accelerated, except for a temporary hiatus during the Great Depression, until the 1970s.

This massive shift of black population from the South to the North and from the country to the city had profound effects on American race relations. Discrimination in the housing market, combined with the preference of American ethnic groups to cluster together in their own neighborhoods, produced the great urban ghettos. As has often been noted, the North was no promised land; blacks were often frustrated in their desire to find and keep decent jobs, sometimes encountered violence in their struggle for living space, and confronted, in addition to the special disabilities imposed by racial discrimination, the problems of social and cultural adjustment faced by any population of ex-peasants that finds itself thrust into an urban environment.

But there were also great advantages that followed from the migration. Despite the racial inequities, economic and educational opportunities were normally greater than they had been in the South. Furthermore, the less repressive northern environment accorded blacks the political space to air their grievances and mount protest movements. Blacks also regained the right to vote when they went north, and politicians began to appeal to black interests and feelings for the first time since Reconstruction. As early as the 1930s, it was clear that the black vote could be crucial in municipal, state, and even national elections. With the NAACP now functioning as a legislative lobby, blacks in the 1930s were able to block the confirmation of a racist judge to the Supreme Court and came close to getting a federal and antilynching law through Congress. In the same decade, blacks developed their first significant ties to organized labor when nondiscriminatory unions recruited them in such industries as autos and steel. The transformation of blacks from peasants to proletarians picked up further momentum during World War II. Wartime labor shortages, pressures from black organizations and movements, and federal policy encouraging nondiscriminatory hiring brought about a substantial increase in the proportion of blacks in steady, relatively skilled jobs, and the enormous gap between the average incomes of whites and blacks began to close for the first time.[4]

It was partly on the basis of progress already made and political clout already acquired that black activists and organizations were able to launch a successful assault on southern segregation and disfranchisement in the post-World War II period. But this victory was not simply a result of northern blacks being able to influence federal policy toward the South. The breakdown of the sharecropping economy and the accelerating urbanization of blacks within the South in the period before, during, and after World War II gave the growing proportion of southern African Americans living in cities greater freedom and capacity to organize for protest than those still living under flagrantly repressive rural or small town conditions. Urban black churches, unique in the extent to which they provided southern blacks with an experience of autonomy and self-government, became potential centers for community mobilization.[5] Encouraged by favorable Supreme Court rulings and a concept of national interest that made racism a liability in the international competition for "the hearts and minds of men" in Asia and Africa, the nonviolent direct action movement of the 1950s and 1960s was able to compel federal action to eliminate "Jim Crow" segregation and a variety of obstructions to black suffrage in the southern states. The Civil Rights Acts of 1964 and 1965 fulfilled the promise of the Reconstruction amendments to the Constitution and at long last put equality under the law and at the ballot box on a firm foundation.

Although it did not bring full equality or total liberation, the civil rights movement resulted in substantial and seemingly irreversible progress toward eliminating status inequality based on race in the United States. Its legislative and judicial successes appear to give the lie to the common assumption that patterns of race relations, once they become firmly established, are virtually immutable. It can now be argued on the basis of historical precedent that pariah groups or oppressed minorities, for however long they have been assigned an inferior status and to whatever extent a dominant group may have cherished a belief in their inferiority, *can* gain substantive legal and political equality with their former overlords.

One should not conclude, however, that the American black-white problem has been solved; it would be more accurate to say that it has changed character. The growing black middle class has been the main beneficiary of the civil rights movement and the affirmative action programs that came to be viewed as an essential means for achieving its goals. But the emergence of black judges, congressmen, presidential candidates, elite professionals, executives, and entrepreneurs should not obscure the fact that the impoverished black lower class—about a third of the black population—is in worse shape than ever before. Trapped in inner-city ghettoes from which the black middle class has now largely fled, these blacks remain poor, unemployed or underemployed, beset by problems of teenage pregnancy, crime, and drug abuse, and essentially cut off from the aspirations and opportunities that are available to most white Americans.[6] But this is not so much a problem involving civil rights in the traditional sense or even attitudinal racism as a challenge to the political economy of late twentieth-century American capitalism. Only reforms directed at changing the American economic system in a fundamental way are likely to emancipate the black poor from misery and desperation. Race-specific policies are still necessary, but solving the problem of accumulated economic and educational disadvantage—and rehabilitating the "underclass" it produces—depends on the growth of a broader and more inclusive movement for economic justice and equality.

What general conclusions can be drawn from this thumbnail sketch of the African-American experience since emancipation that might inform and guide our search for a comparative perspective? It should be clear enough, first of all, that black-white relations have not been static or fixed in their essential character, but have in fact changed substantially over time—first in the direction of greater separation and segmentation between the 1870s and the First World War and thereafter in the direction of greater openness and enhanced opportunities for the incorporation of at least some blacks into the mainstream of American life. Accounting for these changes requires not only an understanding of the effect of such large-scale and long-term processes as industrialization and urbanization but also a recognition of the creative historical impact of black leaders and movements.

It is also evident, however, that one essential aspect of American race relations has not changed fundamentally—the sense of race itself as socially and politically salient. The sharp color line that was drawn during the segregation era has ceased to be the basis of invidious laws, but it lives on in the form of black-white polarization on issues such as affirmative action and the responsibility of government for the relief of poverty and its consequences. Many social questions that in other countries would be debated on their merits for the entire society—or in terms of class—tend to be viewed in the United States through a prism of calculations on how they will affect this or that racial group. Even those whites who profess a lack of prejudice or ideological racism still tend to think that there are white "interests" that clash with black "interests."

Blacks also have a strong sense of racial cohesion and group interest. It was essential to the success of the civil rights struggle that blacks develop ethnic solidarity under their own leadership. Only through the group pride that came from independent action could the masses be aroused to confront white racism in the direct and courageous way necessary to accelerate reform. Liberal whites have of course supported civil rights movements, but since the earliest years of the NAACP they have not led them or constituted a major proportion of their membership. The great paradox of the struggle for desegregation was that blacks seemingly had to separate themselves from whites in order to gain the right to come together with them. But coming together has not meant assimilation to the point of surrendering black identity. As a result of their origin and peculiar historical experience, African Americans have developed a strong sense of ethnic distinctiveness. (Even in the days when "full integration" was proclaimed as the single goal of the Civil Rights Movement, no black leader seriously proposed eliminating separate black churches.) So long as one portion of the black population is excluded from the opportunities that American society offers to whites, and another, more successful, segment feels insecure about whether they can hold on to the gains they have recently made, race will continue to determine the political and social outlook of most African Americans. Black ethnic assertiveness risks bringing white prejudices to the surface and provoking white tribalism and violence against blacks. The color line in the mind persists long after the color line in the law has been eliminated.

The obvious way to begin a search for comparative perspectives on the experience just described is by asking to what extent the trajectory of black-white relations in the United States is the product of special American circumstances and to what extent it reflects some larger, international process. As in virtually all comparative studies involving the United States, the question comes down to the issue of American "exceptionalism." But it is not very helpful to frame this question as a simple either/or proposition. It is better to begin with the assumption that the American experi-

ence will share common elements with situations and transformations occurring elsewhere but will also show distinctive features
that may mean that comparable processes will have different consequences. This may sound like a truism, but if so it is one that is
often forgotten in the heat of debate over American exceptionalism.

The comparisons that most readily come to mind are with the
other former colonial societies of the New World that abolished
slavery during the nineteenth century and faced a similar problem
of incorporating freedpeople of African descent into a new social
order. For a sustained bilateral comparison, Brazil provides a case
study that presents many analogues to what happened in the
United States. As a large, independent continental nation with a
racial composition roughly similar to the North American, it might
be expected to yield valuable comparative insights. When slavery
was abolished in Brazil in 1889, the freedpeople instantly became,
on paper at least, citizens with equality under the law. After
attempting unsuccessfully to survive as agricultural workers or
subsistence farmers, substantial numbers of former plantation
slaves fled the countryside and migrated to the cities where they
found little demand for their labor and were often condemned to a
poverty-stricken existence on the margins of a slowly developing
economy. Furthermore, like North American blacks, they often
faced unequal competition from white immigrants also seeking
employment as wage workers in emerging industries. In some
ways, the predominantly black *favelas* on the periphery of Brazilian cities were analogous to the inner-city black ghettos in the
United States.

Faced with pervasive, if unofficial and extra-legal discrimination, black Brazilians began to organize along racial lines in the late
1920s and early 30s, forming the *Frente Negra Brasilera* in 1931.
But the Negro front was outlawed when Getulio Vargas took power
in 1937 and banned all political movements. It was not until the
1970s that the political atmosphere, as well as international examples of black insurgency, permitted a renewed expression of organ-

ized black protest. That decade saw the emergence of the *Movimento Negro Unificado.*[7]

One might conclude, therefore, that Brazilian blacks have been moving in the same direction as blacks in the United States but in a slower and less continuous fashion. Industrialization and the full protetarianization of the black peasantry has been inhibited by the general slowness of economic development, and black mobilization has been impeded by a lack of democratic political conditions in the country as a whole. Yet other differences between the two racial situations make it difficult to conclude that one is merely dealing with the same process occurring at different speeds. Brazil has never had a color line as clearly defined and rigid as the one characteristic of the United States. The well-known fluidity of racial definition and what Carl Degler called "the mulatto escape hatch" has meant that it was never entirely clear who was black and who was white and that upward mobility through a change in racial categorization was possible, as it has rarely been in the United States with its rigid "descent rule" for ascribing racial status.[8] Furthermore, the segregation of even those who were both dark-skinned and poor was never mandated by law or even enforced consistently and comprehensively by custom or private action. The presence of wealthy mulattoes among the "white" elite and poor whites living cheek to jowl with blacks in the *favelas* is indicative of an underlying pattern of race relations quite different from that of the United States.

The Brazilian comparison also suggests the extent to which an experience of segregation and overt racial discrimination may be a precondition for the development of successful black movements. Several of the black informants whom Florestan Fernandes interviewed for his classic study *The Negro in Brazilian Society* saw segregation as "the real cause of the Negro's progress in the United States" because it created a clear-cut set of grievances and led "Negroes to unite and fight for better things." One of them concluded that the Negro in Brazil was debilitated by a form of prejudice that was covert and "hypocritical," while the American Negro had "benefited" from "open" prejudice because it had "led him to look at himself and solve his own problems."[9] One does not have to wax lyrical over how fortunate it was that North American blacks had to face such intense and flagrant racism to acknowledge that black mobilization and militancy came more naturally in a situation of sharp racial definition and enforced segregation than in a more fluid and ambiguous context.

Hence Brazil makes for a good comparison if one is seeking to appreciate the role of race consciousness and black-white polarization in the United States. In Brazil, it seems, nonracial determinants of class and status have had a greater capability to bend or blur lines of demarkation based on color and ancestry. The Brazilian adage "money whitens" would be hard to apply to North American race relations, at least until very recently and in a somewhat different sense. If, however, one is seeking to learn how and why the political and social implications of a deep and polarizing sense of racial difference may change over time, Brazil is not such a useful analogue. For that purpose, it might be better to turn to another society in which official segregation and militant white supremacy emerged early in the modern industrial era and incited comparable forms of black mobilization and protest.

Comparing race relations in the United States and South Africa is a difficult enterprise full of traps for the unwary, particularly if one focuses on the period from the late nineteenth century to the present. In an earlier work on the development of white supremacist attitudes and policies in the two countries, I concluded that the differences in the circumstances surrounding the practice of "segregation," as well as in the actual functions performed by the legalized separation of racial groups, called into question the value of a detailed comparison of twentieth-century developments.[10] Clearly the demographic variable, the fact that blacks have been a minority in the United States (even in the South) and a substantial majority in South Africa, means that they have weighed differently in the social and economic calculus of whites

and that the consequences of racial equality for the politics and
power relations of these nations would vary enormously. Furthermore, it is difficult to make an equivalence between an ex-slave
population with its fragmented or problematic culture and indigenous peoples who, in many cases, retained vital links with traditional ethnic communities.[11] In fact, I found in my earlier study of
white supremacy that the South African population group most
analogous to Afro-Americans, both demographically and in terms
of its history, was the mixed race or Cape Colored minority rather
than the African majority.[12]

Nevertheless, one does get a strong whiff of similitude from *one*
kind of source—the documentary record of public discourse on
the race question from both sides of the color line. Both South
African segregationists and those Africans who were protesting
against segregation drew heavily on American racial ideologies or
from common sources of international thinking about black-white
relations. This was especially the case between the 1880s and the
1940s. Despite the demographic and structural differences between white hegemony and black resistance in the two societies,
many participants in these ethnic struggles defined the issues
similarly and engaged in debates on racial policy that echoed each
other, sometimes consciously. The similarities in these discourses
become evident if we compare either with the rather different
colloquy on race and class that is found in Brazil.

Ideological similarity must reflect some common features in the
two racial situations that would go at least part of the way toward
compensating for the demographic and cultural differences that
would seem to obviate comparison. In my book *White Supremacy*,
I probed the origins of attitudes that promoted racial hierarchy,
exclusiveness, and ultimately systematic segregation. It is a complex argument, but it involves a comparable legacy of ethno-
centrism, racial slavery, reactions to nineteenth-century humani-
tarianism on the part of the beneficiaries of racial domination, and
the adaptation of preexisting white-supremacist habits and attitudes to an emergent industrial capitalism. In short, I found a

comparable interaction between inherited, premodern attitudes toward race and the exigencies of industrial modernization.[13] Brazil, on the other hand, brought to the modern era a different conception of race relations, for reasons buried deep in its history as a slave society, and has not experienced until very recently the kind of massive and rapid shift to industrial capitalism that occurred in the United States after the Civil War and in South Africa after the Anglo-Boer War. Hence there were commonalities in both the ideological traditions of whites and in the economic and social transformations that they were facing in the late nineteenth and early twentieth centuries that would set off the general tenor of American and South African racial doctrines and policies from those predominating in Brazil during the same period.

The United States and South Africa shared a conjuncture of inherited cultural racism and industrial capitalist development that might account for the fact that racial issues were to be framed in a similar way and even seemed at times amenable to analagous solutions. Massive movement of black peasants into the city and into industrial work was a common new development of the early-to-mid twentieth century, although, admittedly, official responses to it differed significantly. Unlike the United States, where extra-legal or unofficial discrimination ghettoized the new arrivals, the South African state assumed a major role in trying to control the flow and its consequences through the kind of policies that were later centralized and extended under the name of apartheid. I refer here to the pass system, influx control, prohibition of black land ownership outside of designated reserves, and reliance on contract, migratory labor.

The proposition that there are fruitful comparisons to be made between black-white relations in the United States since emancipation and African-white relations in South Africa in the twentieth century appears even more compelling if we view matters from the other side of the color line and examine the development of black movements and ideologies. There is first of all a rich record of black South African awareness of African-American ideas and achievements and a willingness to be influenced by them. Allow me simply to enumerate some examples of the African-American connection: 1) the encouragement of religious separatism or, "Ethiopianism," by missionaries and bishops from the African Methodist Church of the United States between the 1890s and the First World War; 2) the reverence for Booker T. Washington and Tuskegee Institute among the first generation of African nationalist leaders; 3) the substantial impact in South Africa during the 1920s of Marcus Garvey and his robust version of black nationalism; 4) the great prestige of W. E. B. Du Bois and his journal *The Crisis* among educated Africans seeking to combine a Pan-African vision with a militant struggle for equal rights in a multiracial society; 5) the influence of African-American music, dance, and literature on urbanized Africans seeking to fashion a syncretic culture that would transcend ethnic differences and yet remain distinctively black; 6) the way that the South African Black Consciousness Movement of the 1970s appropriated the rhetoric of the American Black Power Movement of the late 1960s. One might find an even more recent example in the "Defiance Campaign" of 1989, in which black demonstrators adopted many of the techniques and even the songs of the American Civil Rights Movement. The role of African-American influences and examples in shaping the consciousness of black South Africans is being studied by a number of scholars, and the results to date suggest an important interchange of ideas and perspectives that only makes sense if the situation of blacks in the two societies were comparable in some significant respects.[14]

Perhaps the origins of this ideological affinity can be traced to the status situations that confronted black elites in the era of intensified white supremacy and segregationism in the period between the turn of the century and the First World War. During the late nineteenth century, a new class of educated blacks, the product of mission education or its equivalent, emerged in both countries and sought the opportunities for social mobility and incorporation in the larger society that seemed to be promised by the theoretically color-blind liberalism of the mid-Victorian era. Bitterly disappointed by the resurgence of ideological racism and discriminatory policies around the turn of the century—culminating by 1913 in such symbolically similar actions as the segregation of Federal employees in the United States and the denial to Africans of the right to purchase or rent land in the "white" areas of South Africa—the black intelligentsia moved from optimistic accommodation to moderate protest. The founding of the NAACP in 1909 and the South African Native National Congress (later the African National Congress) in 1912 were parallel expressions of black elite dissatisfaction with new color bars and diminishing opportunities for educated, Christianized, or "civilized" blacks. Although black elites organized increasingly along racial lines, they resisted an exclusionary nationalism and based their plea for equal treatment on a liberal and interracial vision of a just society. The Americans, who had been promised more, demanded more —the universal black suffrage and full public equality that had been affirmed during the Reconstruction era. The early South African nationalists claimed only the equal rights for a "civilized" minority that was the essence of the "Cape liberal tradition"; under its aegis blacks who could meet a general property and literacy qualification had been voting in the Cape Colony since 1852. The struggles of both movements for inclusion in a white-dominated political and economic system were based on an assumption that peaceful agitation, the petitioning of those in authority, legislative lobbying, and legal action based on constitutional guarantees or English common-law traditions would eventually induce the whites to live up to their own professed principles of equal opportunity and democratic citizenship.[15]

Because the NAACP had only a modest initial success and the ANC virtually none at all, and because both organizations failed to address the most pressing problems of black peasants and workers, they were challenged during the 1920s by popular movements drawing on a heightened racial or ethnic consciousness. These movements sanctioned overtly antiwhite sentiments and put forth utopian visions of a separate black nation. It is in this context that the appeal in both countries of Marcus Garvey and his Universal Negro Improvement Association can best be understood.

As the extravagant expectations of the ultranationalist and millennialist movements of the 1920s shattered against the obdurate reality of white power, a different and seemingly more efficaceous conception of revolutionary change gained a following among middle class black intellectuals, as well as among the politically conscious members of an emerging industrial working class. Marxian socialism did not gain a mass following among blacks in either the United States or South Africa during the period of the great Depression and the Second World War, but it had a significant impact on leaders and political activists. Serious efforts, emanating from the Comintern, to combine an orthodox Marxian class analysis with recognition of the primacy in some societies of a race or national question engendered similar debates among black and white leftists in both countries.

Enough has been said perhaps to give at least a crude sense of how it is possible to see a similar trajectory for black ideologies and movements up through the Second World War, and one could go on to suggest parallels between the coming of nonviolent mass protest to South Africa in the early 1950s and to the southern United States in the late fifties and early sixties. But now the outcomes of comparable protest initiatives diverged widely and the American example became increasingly less relevant to the calculations of the South African resistance. The massive American nonviolent campaigns of the 1960s did not come until after the African National Congress had already tried such tactics and had been forced to abandon them by a repressive regime.

The turning point for both societies was possibly the election of 1948. In that year the Nationalist party came to power in South Africa and began to implement an even more rigid and systematic policy of racial separation and discrimination. The same year saw the surprising victory of Harry S. Truman and the Democratic party in the United States, despite the fact that the Democrats had a civil rights plank in their platform and faced a third party challenge from southern white-supremacists. In effect the black vote in the North more than counterbalanced the white defections in the South. Up to 1948 it might have been possible to argue that there were prospects for racial reform in South Africa that were comparable to those in the United States. Hopes for a peaceful evolution toward equal rights became patently unrealistic in one context at the same time that they were becoming quite credible in the other.

There are many ways that the shift from parallelism to divergence might be explained. Some were suggested by our earlier discussion of the factors involved in the victories of the American civil rights movement, none of which were present, or present to the same degree, in the South African case. Demography, legal-constitutional traditions, and geopolitical circumstances were clearly more conducive to reform in one case than the other. An international development with significant implications for the status of blacks in white-dominated societies—decolonization and the emergence of independent nations in black Africa—had quite contrary effects on short-term black prospects. In the United States, it gave added weight to the cause of reform, while in South Africa it provoked a beleaguered white minority to greater repression. But the elections of 1948 brought one crucial factor into sharp relief. In one election the black vote was a decisive factor; in the other it did not figure at all, for the electorate was all white except for a small number of Coloreds who would soon be disfranchised by the Nationalist government.

If any general truth emerges from this admittedly very tentative exploration of comparative possibilities, it is that politics and power are crucial to understanding evolving patterns of race relations. In Brazil blacks have not been able to challenge a system that makes them de facto, if not de jure, inferiors because a confused and ambiguous ideological situation, a lack of group resources, and an unstable, often undemocratic, political system have made it impossible for them to exert political power as a distinctive element in the population. In South Africa, blacks have gained a clear understanding of their situation and what would be required to change it, but ruthless repression has up to now denied them the capability to influence the government by peaceful means or through a non-revolutionary, reformist politics. In the United States blacks have been able to acquire some power and leverage within a functioning democratic political system—not enough to address the problems of an impoverished lower class but enough to keep hopes of progressive reform alive. In the end the solution to South Africa's problems will also come through politics, but it may well be the politics of revolution rather than reform. (I should add, however, that very recent developments provide a glimmer of hope for nonviolent change.) In short, the history of race relations should be viewed, not as illustrating some iron law of social and cultural determinism, but rather as the record of a dynamic process that can be made to change course as a result of political action and initiative. Black people, like people in general, make their own history even if they cannot make it exactly as they choose.

Commentary / Michael Craton

As a practitioner of microhistory—the nature of which enjoins one constantly to ask questions concerning typicality and atypicality, and to place a particular microscopic case in its larger contexts before making any claims that it sheds new general light—one might tend to be dismissive of, or at least not quickly attuned to, that form of macrohistory that takes whole nations and cultures and places them in comparative counterpoint. Certainly, to compare one culture with another, as Tannenbaum and Degler most notably have done with the systems of American and Brazilian slavery, or Fredrickson did in *White Supremacy* with American and South African systems of racial supremacy, is to serve as an invaluable corrective to the fallacy of exceptionalism which infected many previous American historians, while at the same time to guard

against the equal tendency to regard a single case as normative.[1]
Even so, *White Supremacy* itself, as Fredrickson more or less
admits, bears out the fact that when two systems are compared in
more than superficial ways—and especially in the dimension of
time as well as space—the contrasts tend greatly to outnumber the
similarities, so that the historian is tempted to cast the net ever
wider in order to arrive at nonspecious generalizations.[2] This
seems to be why in the present paper Fredrickson extends his
comparison to a third system or culture, including the Brazilian as
well as the South African cases. But if three is better than two, why
not more? Where do we draw the line? And when does comparative history become simply a comparative *survey* of systems?
Where for that matter do we draw the internal comparative lines?
The South in comparative perspective might imply for many a
comparison with one or more other areas within the United States,
particularly between South and North. Others might point out
that there are substantial, even limitless, variations within the
South itself—as with any comparable large cultural entity. In
these respects, to take it to the perhaps absurd extreme, all history
is basically microhistory, all history properly is comparative history.[3]

Before I go too far let me hasten to say that I believe that
Professor Fredrickson's addition of Brazil to his comparative analysis strengthens his arguments, and modestly to suggest that I
might be able to add a few comparative and contrasting points
toward the final resolution of the question of black-white relations
since emancipation from a fourth base, that of my own special area
of interest. This is the British West Indies, which plays no part in
Fredrickson's present analysis—though he did write comparatively of Jamaica in a 1978 article, recently republished. Some of
my points may qualify Fredrickson's admittedly tentative findings,
though others undoubtedly corroborate them.[4]

The first obvious point of comparison is what one might call the
numbers variable. Perhaps Fredrickson does not make quite
enough of the great differences in ratios between blacks and whites

in each of the areas compared, both in the region overall, and in its separate subregions, from those with the greatest to those with the least disparity. The fact that the United States has about 10 per cent blacks in its total population has a certain overall significance, which is subtly qualified when one looks at greater regional concentrations of blacks in former plantation areas, northern industrial towns, individual ghettos, or freakish areas like the District of Columbia. But how fundamentally different a country—or large region of similar territories like the West Indies—must be when the overall proportions of whites and blacks are reversed! In the South African case the ratio is something like five to one, but in the British West Indies as a whole more like twenty to one, with some small countries like Antigua being almost exclusively black. Incidentally, I think Fredrickson's statement that Brazil and the United States are broadly comparable on the basis of similar ratios of blacks and whites is misleading. There is a far higher proportion of blacks in Brazil than in the United States, especially if one uses the American rather than the Brazilian definition of what constitutes a black—quite apart from the fact that a very large number of the Brazilian whites who help to reshape the ratios there as a result of migrations since Brazilian slavery ended and the United States began to restrict immigration at much the same time, at the end of the nineteenth century. The numbers variable (as well as disproportions in sexual ratios), of course, also had an important effect on the patterns of miscegenation, the effects of which one could discuss at far greater length than is possible here.[5]

A second factor which I believe is underplayed in Professor Fredrickson's comparative analysis is what I would term the original status variable in respect of the labor requirements of colonial and later economies, and this touches on what are fundamental differences in legal systems—between Brazil and other areas with a Roman Law tradition and those, like the United States and the British West Indies which have the British traditions of Statute and Common Law, not to mention those areas like South Africa where the two systems coexist and conflict. We are supposed to be concentrating on postemancipation race relations, but it is surely significant that almost all whites come out of a Western European tradition in which the hereditary chattel enslavement of their own kind had faded in favour of other forms of agricultural, commercial and industrial labour relations. This system, it was assumed, transferred along with the folk themselves to the colonies, English, Dutch and Portuguese alike, at least until large numbers of black slaves became available, and was actually reinforced by the notions that evolving systems of white democracy were speeded by the "freer air"—the wide-open spaces and cheaper land—of North and South America and southern Africa. When they looked for alternative and more suitably bonded laborers, white European colonizers naturally looked first to the indigenous peoples, but very soon found there were legalistic as well as practical reasons for preferring imported rather than indigenous people as slaves.[6] Fredrickson points out the anomaly, but perhaps does not sufficiently stress its importance, that for South Africa it was Africans who were the indigenous people, never quite enslaved as they were once shipped to the New World (mainly from other parts of Africa), while the majority of early slaves were transhipped Indonesians. In the Americas, Amerindians were enslaved by Europeans, but not in large numbers or for long, Africans being soon preferred for a type of chattel and hereditary reification and debasement regarded as unsuitable, impractical and illegal for Amerindians as well as for whites. Since the story of black-white relations in South Africa is essentially that of relations between the indigenous people and the descendants of white settlers, rather than those between the descendants of two phenotypically different settler ethnicities, one is somewhat surprised to find that Fredrickson takes absolutely no account in his comparative analysis of relations in the Americas between whites, and for that matter blacks, on the one hand, and the Amerindian natives on the other.

The numbers involved and questions of ethnicity and legal status clearly affect, though not fully explain, the third area of comparison and contrast that needs further exploration: that is the

very different degrees of race/class polarisation. Fredrickson succinctly explains how, in different phases and for subtly different
reasons both the North American and the South African whites
constructed a cultural-legal system absolutely distinguishing if not
quite absolutely separating whites and nonwhites. He also goes far
to explain how and why demographic and economic realities determined a far more fluid and mobile system in Brazil. But including
the case of the West Indies into the analysis would surely shed light
on developments in all three other areas. For in the West Indies we
have the clearest example of what is sometimes termed the three-
tier model of socio-political-racio-economic development; that is,
the evolution of an intermediate formerly free colored (or black),
later increasingly dominant, largely brown middle class. At the
very least this should help to illuminate such phenomena, men-
tioned by Fredrickson, that it has been a black or brown elite
(albeit steadily expanding) that has been the chief beneficiary so
far of changes in the United States, leaving a black underclass
more disadvantaged and even oppressed than ever before.[7]

We must, however, mention an additional complicating factor in
the West Indies that has its parallels and corollaries elsewhere.
The period after slave emancipation saw a very large influx of a new
type of laborer from a new area. These were the East Indians
indentured under what Hugh Tinker has called "A New System of
Slavery," whose descendants, replacing blacks who spurned plantation labor and became peasant farmers or migrated to the towns,
now constitute, for example, at least half the populations of
Guyana and Trinidad. These "East Indian West Indians" are only
now emerging from a status both socioeconimically and politically
subordinate, and the condition of being regarded as sociocultur-
ally inferior, by the descendants of black slaves. In contrast, later
migrants to both the United States and Brazil have been mainly
whites, able to keep the descendants of American slaves in a
position of inferiority in almost every respect. Only in recent
years, with the influx of large numbers of new immigrants—many
of them nonwhites of nontraditional ethnicities, and many of

them "illegals"—have United States blacks had the questionable advantage (some might say "questionably the advantage") of a new immigrant underclass over which they could establish some kind of marginal superiority. The South African case is more complex and not analagous in every respect, but the importation of Asiatic "coolies" and of mainly English-speaking whites in the postslave period had both positive and negative (I should say some initially positive but mostly ultimately negative) repercussions on black-white relations in South Africa.[8]

In comparing the development of black-white relations in different areas since slave emancipation, one is more struck than Professor Fredrickson seems to be by the different dates at which emancipation occurred—occurring, that is, at widely spaced intervals in the general development of the world at large, as well as providing widely different lengths of time for postemancipation development in different areas. The United States slaves were freed in 1865, but this was merely midway in a process that began in the British West Indies (and South Africa) in 1834, just over 150 years ago, and was not completed in Brazil until 1888, 100 years ago last year. To what extent could the different cases be expected to follow identical or even similar trajectories at different periods of world history? To what extent was each related to the period of world history in which they were set? And to what extent was each regional development affected by antecedent developments elsewhere?[9]

Certainly, other factors than the dating of slave emancipation and the length of time since have determined the nature of black-white relations, but what are the crucial determinants? Fredrickson in his paper suggests a plausible case for the importance of the shift from the slave mode of production through a peasantry phase to the creation of an industrial proletariat, or (to use that non-Marxian analysis which many American commentators prefer), of the process of modernization, in all its ramifications. Thus the nature and speed of modernization (alias capitalistic intensification) and the consequent migration, urbanization and proletarianization of blacks, affected the change in black-white relations in both the United States and South Africa in the twentieth century, whereas in Brazil the situation changed more slowly, and less, because of the slower and less complete shift towards industrialization and the development of an urban proletariat. But how well does this attune to what one notices in the British West Indies, and what additional factors do we discern there that modify or qualify Fredrickson's arguments?[10]

The Caribbean shares modernization characteristics with the rest of the Third World, especially the unfortunate features of hugely expanding populations pressing on limited resources and the factors commonly lumped together as underdevelopment. Among these are a gross urbanization without concomitant industrialization and thus the absence of an urbanized proletariat akin to the American, South African, or even Brazilian cases. The West Indies have seen the prolonged evolution and partial survival of a special type of peasantry, including elements that Richard Frucht labelled "part-peasant, part-proletarian." This process has even been antedated, by Sidney Mintz and others, to the slavery period itself, when there was a kind of "protopeasantry" based on the existence and vitality of slave provision grounds and slave-dominated internal marketing. Brazilian Marxist historians, specifically Ciro Flamarion Cardoso, have christened the phenomenon "the peasant breach in the slave mode of production"—a preliminary to a postemancipation phase that is characterized in Marxist terms as an intermediate era of small commodity production. Whatever we call it, the condition of most West Indian ex-slaves, and their relations with their former owners, was clearly different from those applying to United States blacks, whose peasanty phase was so short-lived, or South African Blacks who were proletarianized out of an ancient peasant tradition without necessarily going through a stage of formal slavery.[11]

Another distinguishing and divisive feature was what one could term the imperial factor. Surely it is relevant on many counts that the British West Indies remained colonial dependencies until well after World War II, whereas the United States has been an independent republic for two hundred years, Brazil ceased to be a colony in 1822 and a monarchy the year after slavery ended, and even South Africa has been virtually autonomous since 1910. I know that white southerners, like the West Indian planters, saw slave emancipation and the subsequent impositions of the post-emancipation or Reconstruction era as a kind of imperialist dictation. And there is certainly a concurrence in the way that political forces in Britain and the United States North alike (as well as the liberal and progressive elements in Brazil) combined humanitarian egalitarianism with economic arguments concerning the superiority of free wage labor over chattel slavery. But how different was a process bound to be that emerged respectively (and sequentially) from imperial persuasion and legislation in the 1830s, a bloody civil war and its subsequent turmoil in the 1860s, and a kind of operational inertia in Brazil in the 1880s?[12]

Even so, there was a sense in which the prevailing British liberal ideology of free trade and *laissez faire* was conducive to the pragmatic continuation of patterns of white socioeconomic domination in the British West Indies for a century after 1834. This was little different in effect from the practical reversal of black gains in the United States between 1880 and 1910, the steady imposition and intensification of Afrikaner Nationalist notions of black-white relations in South Africa after the Anglo-Boer War, or even the way that the predominantly white Brazilian ruling class (epitomized by the fascistic regime of Getulio Vargas) was able to superimpose itself and pragmatically create an almost exclusively black underclass. Such concurrences surely indicate the kind of ideological and strategic crosscurrents and generalizations that bear out a Gramscian view of late imperialism. Parenthetically, I might add here that perhaps the best places to examine the crosscutting of North American socioeconomic and European colonial factors in the shaping of black-white relations might be those former Spanish slave colonies which became actual or virtual United States dependencies at the turn of the twentieth century; that is, Cuba, Puerto Rico and, perhaps, the Philippines.[13]

Another factor with lasting and wide-ranging effects that should not be forgotten is the way that in the West Indies, and arguably in Brazil, the blacks were agents in their own emancipation through the many ways that they resisted both slavery and later forms of oppression. Fredrickson notes that United States slaves too voted with their feet by running to the Union side in the Civil War. He might have added the ways that slave noncooperation convinced many who were not necessarily humanitarians that slavery was impractical on economic grounds, and also might have stressed the effects of the constant threat of overt black resistance even in a culture where slaves and ex-slaves were outnumbered, unorganised and overpowered. But how (despite what Herbert Aptheker argues) can anything in the history of United States black-white relations fully compare with the scale and the effects of the Jamaican maroon wars, the great rebellion of 1760, the late slave rebellions throughout the British West Indies between 1816 and 1832, or of the Morant Bay Rebellion in Jamaica in 1865, let alone the creation of the independent Maroon state of Palmares in Brazil, the Haitian slave revolution of 1791–1804, or the virtual achievement by the Danish slaves of the Virgin Islands of their own emancipation in 1848?[14]

Two further general points before I try to make a conclusion of sorts. Professor Fredrickson mentions the importance of factors influencing black-white relations in the twentieth century, especially since mid-century—and I have left myself too little space to focus adequately on all his elegantly expressed arguments. But could I perhaps suggest that he says too little about the effects of World War II on a global scale, and of the way that black-white relations everywhere have been affected by the communications revolutions that have made the whole world a smaller place, if not yet quite a global village? Remember that World War II was officially fought and won on the principles expressed in the Atlantic Charter—including opposition to racialist oppression as well as imperialism—and was successfully concluded by the United Nations itself. (It was also, incidentally, the last occasion when the United States, Britain, South Africa, the British West Indies and Brazil fought ostensibly for a common cause.) World War II was followed by the first of several waves of decolonization, though the degree to which these represented the victory of abstract principles, anticolonialist forces, or the decline of power and will on the part of the imperialists remains open to debate. During this phase, the British West Indies, for example, built on the widespread unrest, agitation and labor, and political organization of the later 1930s to become a galaxy of independent, predominantly black nations dedicated to the highest principles, including those of multiculturalism. This was expressed in national mottoes like those of Jamaica and Trinidad, which echoed, in English, the United States' motto, which had always been "cloaked in the decent obscurity of a foreign tongue," E pluribus unum. World War II had also given black people everywhere the chance to travel and share experiences, aspirations, strategies and tactics with others from all over the world—leading to a heightening of consciousness and increase in organization and action even greater than had happened, in somewhat similar ways, as a result of World War I.[15]

Professor Fredrickson points out the ways that the movement of black consciousness in the 1950s, 1960s and 1970s was a global phenomenon, but perhaps overly stresses the ways in which the rest of the world followed the lead of United States blacks. It was, of course, an universal movement, in which, I would argue, the contribution of United States blacks, though vital, was not predominant. Surely we should remember that Marcus Garvey was not American but Jamaican born, and that many West Indians, paradoxically coming from territories that were still colonies, helped to spark and shape the forms of black activism in the United States, as well as in the colonial dependencies in Africa and the Caribbean. Similarly we must not underestimate the contribution of Africans—both native to Africa and products of the great diaspora—in the Pan African Movement and the cultural renaissance of *Negritude*. For that matter, we should also not forget that the concept of black power, the very definition of who is black, was in the 1960s and 1970s disseminated to include all oppressed and subject people of (almost) whatever race. My own wife, who is a Trinidadian Chinese (her parents escapees from mainland China in 1949) has just been invited to join an organization called the Waterloo Council of Black Women. She says, incidentally, that if black here means West Indian, and if the Women do not plan to exclude men from consideration, she will be proud to join![16]

In the last analysis we are discussing here a much narrower concept—perhaps too narrow a concept—the nature of black-white relations since emancipation. Yet even if the task is to a dangerous degree self-defining and artificially exclusionist, it is surely clear from all the comparative evidence that there has always been something special about the black-white relationship that distinguishes it from all other relationships of power, class, caste and race throughout history. Perhaps we ought to get back to some of the questions that Winthrop Jordan poses and descants on in his monumental *White Over Black*. What is it that makes the African and the Afro-American a special case, or, more appositely, what has there always been special and distinct in the relationship between white Europeans, or whites of European stock, and persons native to Africa or of African descent?[17]

Certainly it is one of the longest interracial relationships as well as that most obviously polarised by phenotypical difference. By the same token it is also one of the closest of historical bonds, if too often a sybiotic, paradox-ridden and tension-loaded kind. From a detached height we might characterize it as a form of ever-so-gradual syncresis or creolization. Optimists might look to Brazil and see the process most advanced, while pessimists agree with Professor Fredrickson that at the other extreme, in South Africa, the only resolution lies in revolution. Where does this place the United States on the spectrum? Somewhere in the middle? Or is the United States, after all, an exceptional case? I do not think so, and will conclude by noting—if not take unequivocal hope from— the ways in which American whites and blacks in their relationships with each other participate in the lexicon of common humanity. Is there not significance—a special type of bonding not necessarily involving formal bondage—in the way that while an American white slaveholder, and his employing descendant, might refer to his male slave or servant as "My Man", the black slaves and their descendants—male and female—use just the same term for a black soul brother or an "affective other," and at the same time American slaves and modern blacks alike have referred to their male owner, employer or member of the continuing ruling class—or all of these in the abstract—simply as "The Man"? Why does someone's "other man" (or, for that matter, other woman) necessarily have to be of another race?

Such an ending may suggest that, unlike Fredrickson, I ascribe more importance to class than to racial distinctions. In a sense this is true; but I do not intend to defend class distinctions. What I would rather we do is to more clearly recognize and distinguish the class component in black-white relations. That way we would be able to face up more squarely to the alternative proposed by W. E. B. Du Bois in *Dusk of Dawn* (in a quotation already used by Fredrickson in *The Arrogance of Race*)—seeing the black-white split as depending merely, or mainly, on the surely more superficial, and perhaps reversible, matter of "a racial folklore grounded on centuries of instinct, habit, and thought and implemented by the conditioned reflex of visible color."[18]

Notes

Notes to INTRODUCTION

1. This is not the case for Eugene Genovese's essay, which is based on his opening address to the symposium.

Notes to HONOR AND MARTIALISM IN THE U.S. SOUTH AND PRUSSIAN EAST ELBIA DURING THE MID-NINETEENTH CENTURY
by Shearer Davis Bowman

1. Michael Stephen Hindus, *Prison and Plantation: Crime, Justice, and Authority in Massachusetts and South Carolina, 1767–1878* (Chapel Hill: University of North Carolina Press, 1980); and William H. and Jane H. Pease, *The Web of Progress: Private Values and Public Styles in Boston and Charleston, 1828–1843* (New York: Oxford University Press, 1985).
2. John Hope Franklin, *The Militant South, 1800–1861* (Boston: Beacon Press, 1956), viii, 10.
3. Marcus Cunliffe, *Soldiers & Civilians: The Martial Spirit in America, 1775–1865*, 2nd ed. (New York: Free Press, 1973), x.
4. Bertram Wyatt-Brown, *Honor and Violence in the Old South* (New York: Oxford University Press, 1986), 20. This book is Wyatt-Brown's abridgment of his *Southern Honor: Ethics and Behavior in the Old South* (New York: Oxford University Press, 1982).
5. Gerald F. Linderman, *Embattled Courage: The Experience of Combat in the American Civil War* (New York: Free Press, 1987), 15–16.
6. Jeannette Hussey, *The Code Duello in America: An Exhibition at the National Portrait Gallery, December 18, 1980 to April 19, 1981* (Washington, D.C.: Smithsonian Institution Press for the National Portrait Gallery, 1980), 26.
7. Harnett T. Kane, *Gentlemen, Swords and Pistols* (New York: William Morrow, 1951), ix.
8. V. G. Kiernan, *The Duel in European History: Honour and the Reign of Aristocracy* (Oxford: Oxford University Press, 1988), 218.
9. See James T. Moore, "The Death of the Duel: The Code Duello in Readjuster Virginia, 1879–1883," *Virginia Magazine of History and Biography*, 83 (1975): 259–76; and Jerry L. Butcher, "Cash-Shannon Duel" [in South Carolina], in *Encyclopedia of Southern History*, ed. David C. Roller and Robert W. Twyman (Baton Rouge: Louisiana State University Press, 1979), 187.
10. Kiernan, *The Duel in European History*, 215–9.
11. Jack K. Williams, *Dueling in the Old South: Vignettes of Social History* (College Station, Texas: Texas A & M University Press, 1980), 37.
12. [Anonymous], "Duelling," *Southern Literary Messenger* (March, 1861), quotations from pp. 222–39.

13. Edward L. Ayers, *Vengeance and Justice: Crime and Punishment in the 19th-Century American South* (New York: Oxford University Press, 1984), 28.

14. On the ambiguities of gentleman, see Stow Persons, *The Decline of American Gentility* (New York: Columbia University Press, 1973); and David Castronovo, *The English Gentleman: Images and Ideals in Literature and Society* (New York: Ungar, 1987). On the ambiguities of honor, see Karl Demeter, *The German Officer-Corps in Society and State, 1650–1945*, trans. Angus Malcolm (New York: Frederick A. Praeger, 1965), Chapter 14, "The Dual Nature of Honor"; and Friedrich Zunkel, "Ehre," in *Geschichtliche Grundbegriffe: Historisches Lexikon zur politisch-sozialen Sprache in Deutschland*, ed. Otto Bruner, Werner Conze, and Reinhart Koselleck, (Stuggart: Ernst Klett, 1975), vol. 2, 1–63.

15. Ayers, *Vengeance and Justice*, 31.

16. Kiernan, *The Duel in European History*, 217.

17. *Richmond Enquirer*, 27 May 1856 and 30 May 1856.

18. Daniel J. Boorstin, *The Americans: The National Experience* (New York: Vintage Books, 1965), 212.

19. Demeter, *The German Officer-Corps*, 116. For an etymological discussion see Kiernan, *The Duel in European History*, 6.

20. Konrad H. Jarausch, *Students, Society, and Politics in Imperial Germany: The Rise of Academic Illiberalism* (Princeton: Princeton University Press, 1982), 238.

21. Williams, *Dueling in the Old South*, 43, notes that "fencing was pretty much out of style in America, even Louisiana, by the midpoint of the antebellum era."

22. Albrecht von Boguslawski, *Die Ehre und das Duell*, 2nd ed. (Berlin: Schall und Grund, 1897), 90–1.

23. Demeter, *The German Officer-Corps*, 143–4.

24. Boguslawski, *Die Ehre und das Duell*, 78.

25. These two duels are discussed at length in Dickson D. Bruce, Jr., *Violence and Culture in the Antebellum South* (Austin: University of Texas Press, 1979), Chapter 1, "The Southern Duel."

26. See Steven M. Stowe, *Intimacy and Power in the Old South: Ritual in the Lives of the Planters* (Baltimore: Johns Hopkins University Press, 1987), 38–49 (a section entitled "Cilley-Graves: Serving Honor"). It is ironic that Stowe, who posits distinctly different cultural values among the Northern and Southern elites, should discuss this particular affair at such length.

27. Erich Eyck, *Bismarck* 3 vols. (Erlenbach-Zürich: Eugen Rentsch Verlag, 1941–4), vol. 1, 369.

28. Quoted in Ibid., vol. 2, 58–9.

29. See esp. Fritz Stern, *Gold and Iron: Bismarck, Bleichröder, and the Building of the German Empire* (New York: Vintage Books, 1977), 55–6. Edwin H. Ackerknecht, *Rudolpf Virchow: Doctor, Statesman, Anthropologist* (Madison: University of Wisconsin Press, 1953), 26, says that "Virchow declined the honor."

30. For the older nation, see William E. Dodd, *The Cotton Kingdom: A Chronicle of the Old South* (New Haven: Yale University Press, 1919), 49; and Carl L. Becker, *The Declaration of Independence: A Study in the History of Political Ideas* (New York: Knopf/Vintage Books, 1922), 247, 255; and Lowell Harrison, "Thomas Roderick Dew, Philosopher of the Old South," *Virginia Magazine of History and Biography* 57 (1949): 390–1. For the lack of evidence, see Stephen Mansfield, "Thomas Roderick Dew at William and Mary: 'A Main Prop of That Venerable

Institution,'" *Virginia Magazine of History and Biography* 75 (1965): 429–30. Mansfield also authored "Thomas Roderick Dew: Defender of the Southern Faith" (Ph.D. dissertation, University of Virginia, 1968).

31. The quotation is taken from Stanley K. Schultz, "Lieber, Francis," in *Encyclopedia of American Biography*, ed. John A. Garraty and Jerome L. Sternstein (New York: Harper & Row, 1974), 662–4.

32. John McAuley Palmer, *General von Steuben* (New Haven: Yale University Press, 1937), 38. His grandfather was "a protestant parson of plebeian descent" who late in life simply assumed the noble prefix "von." His mother, however, was of authentic noble descent; and his father was a captain in the Prussian army. "When Steuben received the title of Baron is unknown." Ibid. 14, 64.

33. Ibid., 50.

34. See James Kirby Martin and Mark Edward Lender, *A Respectable Army: The Military Origins of the Republic, 1763–1789* (Arlington Heights, Illinois: Harlan Davidson, 1982), 123.

35. Palmer, *General von Steuben*, 200–1.

36. Borcke makes numerous appearances in *Mary Chestnut's Civil War*, ed. C. Vann Woodward (New Haven: Yale University Press, 1981).

37. His decision to resign may have come after a quarrel with his father over how much financial support the son should receive. See James R. Belcher, Jr. and Ronald L. Heinemann, "Heros von Borcke: Knight Errant of the Confederacy," *Virginia Cavalcade* 35 (1985): 86–95.

38. Heros von Brocke, *Memoirs of the Confederate War for Independence* (Philadelphia: J. R. Lippincott & Co., 1867; repr. Gaithersburg, Maryland: Butternut Press, Inc., 1985), 4. Like many racist southern Confederates, Borcke always believed, as he told a reunion of some 300 former Confederate cavalrymen in Richmond in 1884, that he fought "in the defense of right and liberty." Quoted in Major Edgar Erskine Hume, US Army, "Colonel Heros von Borcke: A Famous Prussian Volunteer in the Confederate States Army," in *Southern Sketches*, First Series, No. 2, ed. J.D. Eggleston (Charlottesville, Virginia: Historical Publishing Co., 1935), 20.

39. His father, a Prussian infantry officer, became a member of the Prussian House of Lords in the 1850s, and at his death in 1878 bequeathed a knight's estate in Brandenburg to his son. The estate, Giesenbrügge, was located in the Soldin district of Brandenburg. See Heros von Borcke, *Mit Prinz Friedrich Karl: Kriegs- und Jagdfahrten und am häuslichen Herd*, 2nd ed. (Berlin: Paul Kittel, 1893), 304; and Karl Friedrich Rauer, ed., *Alphabetischer Nachweis (Adressbuch) des in den Preussischen Staaten mit Rittergütern angesessenen Adels* (Berlin: Durch die Herausgeber, 1857), 29.

40. Heros von Borcke, *Mit Prinz Friedrich Karl: Kriegs- und Jagdfahrten und am häuslichen Herd*, 30–1.

41. Fanny Lewald, *Meine Lebensgeschichte* quoted in *Deutsche Sozialgeschichte: Dokumente und Skizzen, Band I: 1815–1870*, ed. Werner Pols (Munich: C. H. Beck, 1973), 101–2.

42. Marc Bloch, "Toward a Comparative History of European Societies," trans. Jelle C. Riemersma, in *Enterprise and Secular Change: Readings in Economic History*, ed. Frederick C. Lane and Riemersma (Homewood, Illinois: R. D. Irwin, 1953), 496. Bloch was a French medievalist advocating comparative studies of different European societies; but his observations are germane to all comparativists.

43. Robert Brentano, *Two Churches: England and Italy in the Thirteenth Century* (Princeton: Princeton University Press, 1968), v.

44. Hans-Jürgen Puhle, "Aspekte der Agrarpolitik im 'Organisierten Kapitalismus,'" in *Sozialgeschichte Heute: Festschrift für Hans Rosenberg zum 70. Geburtstag*, ed. Hans-Ulrich Wehler (Göttingen: Vandenhoeck & Ruprecht, 1974), 547.

45. Thomas R. Dew, "On the Influence of the Federative Republican System of Government upon Literature and the Development of Character," *Southern Literary Messenger* (December, 1836): 279. This essay has recently been reprinted in *All Clever Men Who Make Their Way: Critical Discourse in the Old South*, ed. Michael O'Brien (Fayetteville, Arkansas: University of Arkansas Press, 1982), 125–76.

46. Otto Ernst Schuddekopf, *Die deutschen Innenpolitik im letzten Jahrhundert und der konservative Gedanke: Die Zusammenhänge zwischen Aussenpolitik, innerer Staatsführung und Parteigeschichte, dargestellt an der Geschichte der Konservativen Partei von 1807 bis 1918* (Braunschweig: Albert Limbach, 1951), 23.

47. Edward M. Coffman, *The Old Army: A Portrait of the American Army in Peacetime, 1784–1898* (New York: Oxford University Press, 1986), 92.

48. Ibid., 70.

49. See the helpful discussion in V. R. Berghahn, *Militarism: The History of an International Debate, 1861–1979* (Cambridge: Cambridge University Press, 1981), esp. 123.

50. There is a wealth of information on Southern violence in Ayers, *Vengeance and Justice*.

51. Ulrich Bonnell Phillips, *The Slave Economy of the Old South: Selected Essays in Economic and Social History* [1903–1928], ed. Eugene D. Genovese (Baton Rouge: Louisiana State University Press, 1968), Chapter 1, "Plantation and Frontier."

52. Graf Arnim-Boitzenburg, *Ueber die Vereidigung des Heeres auf die Verfassung* (Berlin: Verlag der Deckerschen Geheimen Ober-Hofbuchdruckerei, 1849), 11–2.

53. See William J. Cooper, Jr., *Liberty and Slavery: Southern Politics to 1860* (New York: Knopf, 1983), esp. 180, 257, 268; and Kenneth S. Greenberg, *Masters and Statesmen: The Political Culture of American Slavery* (Baltimore: Johns Hopkins University Press, 1985), esp. 16, 20–2; and Lacy K. Ford, Jr., *Origins of Southern Radicalism: the South Carolina Upcountry, 1800–1860* (New York: Oxford University Press, 1988), esp. 132–9, 350, 362.

54. I rely heavily here on Manfred Messerschmidt, "Einführung. Werden and Prägung des Preußischen Offizierkorps—Ein Überblick," in *Offiziere im Bild von Dokumenten aus Drei Jahrhunderten*, ed. Hans Meier-Welcker, Manfred Messerschmidt, and Ursula von Gersdorff (Stuttgart: Deutsche Verlags-Anstalt, 1964), 66–81, which persuasively modifies Karl Demeter's argument that fom 1800 to 1914 in the officer corps "the elements of extroverted class-honor (*Standesehre*) were very gradually displaced—not without sharp setbacks—by the elements of introverted personal honor." Demeter, *German Officer-Corps*, 116.

55. The quotation is from Saxon *Rittergutsbesitzer* von Wedell's comments before the United Diet on 2 May 1847, in *Der Erste Vereinigte Landtag in Berlin, 1847, Zweiter Teil*, ed. Eduard Bleich (Vaduz/Liechtenstein: Topos Verlag, 1977), 253.

56. Although an honorable man could hold antidueling convictions, Boyen told the United Diet on 8 May 1847, such convictions "are perhaps not appropriate for the military," and such a man should resign from the army. Ibid., 500. See the discussion of Boyen in Demeter, *German Officer-Corps*, 131–3.

57. A detailed discussion of the regulations is available in Boguslawski, *Die Ehre und das Duell*, 58–63.

58. Martineau cited in Williams, *Dueling in the Old South*, 64–5. Clement Eaton, "The Role of Honor in Southern Society," in *Southern Humanities Review* (1976 Bicentennial Issue) 52, tells of a Court of Honor instituted by the Mississippi Anti-Dueling Society in 1844 to prevent duels.

59. See Boguslawski, *Die Ehre und das Duell*, 61–2; and Demeter, *German Officer-Corps*, 134.

60. See Demeter, *German Officer-Corps*, 136–8; and Messerschmidt, "Einführung: Werden and Prägung des Preußischen Offizierkorps," 79–80.

61. Georg Friedrich Knapp, "Die Erbuntertänigkeit und die kapitalistische Wirtschaft," in his *Die Landarbeiter in Knechtschaft und Freiheit*, 2nd ed. (Leipzig: Duncker & Humblot, 1909), 57.

62. See my "U.S. Plantations and the Development of Capitalism," in *One World, One Institution: the Plantation. Proceedings of the Second World Plantation Conference, Shreveport, Louisiana, October 6–10, 1986*, ed. Sue Eakin and John Tarver (Baton Rouge: Louisiana State University Agricultural Center and The Everett Companies, 1989), 7–19.

63. Hans Rosenberg, "Die Ausprägung der Junkerherrschaft in Brandenburg-Preussen 1410–1618," in his *Machteliten und Wirtschaftskonjunkturen: Studien zur neureren deutschen Sozial- und Wirtschaftsgeschichte* (Göttingen: Vandenhoeck & Ruprecht, 1978), 78. He writes of the Junkers' "transformation into progressive, expansive economic entrepreneurs with very pronounced interest in commercial profit." Ibid., 66–7.

64. Eighteenth-century Chesapeake planters continued "to devote themselves to the active and energetic pursuit of profit through the production of tobacco for an international commercial market." Jack P. Greene, *Pursuits of Happiness: The Social Development of Early Modern British Colonies and the Formation of American Culture* (Chapel Hill: University of North Carolina Press, 1988), 96–8.

65. James Westphall Thompson, "East German Colonization in the Middle Ages," *Annual Report of the American Historical Association for the Year 1915* (Washington, D.C.: Government Printing Office, 1917), 149–50.

66. Quoted in Hermann von Petersdorff, *Kleist-Retzow: Ein Lebensbild* (Stuttgart & Berlin: J. G. Cotta'sche Buchhandlung Nachfolger, 1907), 3–4. See also Wolfgang Schröder, "Hans Hugo von Kleist-Retzow: Ein Junker von Schrot und Korn," in *Gestalten von Bismarckzeit*, ed. Gustav Seeber (East Berlin: Akademie-Verlag, 1978), 218–9.

67. David O. Whitten, "Slave Buying in 1835 in Virginia as Revealed by Letters of a Louisiana Negro Sugar Planter," *Louisiana History* 11 (1970): 231–4.

68. Michael P. Johnson and James L. Roark, *Black Masters: A Free Family of Color in the Old South* (New York: W. W. Norton, 1984).

69. See Eduard Bleich, ed., *Der Erste Vereinigte Landtag in Berlin, 1847, Erster Teil* (Vaduz/Liechtenstein: Topos Verlag, 1977), 733 ff.

70. Demeter, *German Officer-Corps*, 250.

71. *Somerville Reporter*, Saturday, 9 April 1842 (Microfilm in the Memphis State University library). The announcement was taken from the *Memphis Appeal*.

72. *Richmond Whig*, 1 May 1849.

73. See Max Weber, "National Character and the Junkers," in *From Max Weber: Essays in Sociology*, ed. H. H. Gerth and C. Wright Mills (New York: Oxford University Press, 1946), 392.

74. Winston's address as reprined in the *Richmond Enquirer*, 4 January 1856, with an editorial note commending the governor's "just views" to the newspaper's readers. In "Antebellum Planters and Vormärz Junkers in Comparative Perspec-

tive," *American Historical Review* 85 (1980): 796, note 56, I mistakenly identified this newspaper as the *Richmond Whig* for 4 January 1856.

75. Kiernan, *The Duel in European History,* 31–2.

Notes to COMMENTARY
by Edward L. Ayers

1. F. L. Carsten, *A History of the Prussian Junkers* (Brookfield, VT: Gower Pub. Co. 1989), 97.

2. Richard Evans, *Rethinking German History: Nineteenth-Century Germany and the Origins of the Third Reich* (Boston: Allen & Unwin, 1987), 111.

3. David Blackbourn, *Populists and Patricians: Essays in Modern German History* (Boston: Allen & Unwin, 1987), 12–13.

Notes to SOCIAL ORDER AND THE FEMALE SELF: THE CONSERVATISM OF SOUTHERN WOMEN IN COMPARATIVE PERSPECTIVE
by Elizabeth Fox-Genovese

1. Russell Kirk, *The Conservative Mind from Burke to Eliot.* (Chicago: Regnery Books, 1986).

2. Elizabeth Fox-Genovese and Eugene D. Genovese, "The Argument for Slavery in the Abstract," unpublished paper delivered at annual meeting of the Southern Historical Association, New Orleans, 1987.

3. Richard Weaver, *The Southern Tradition at Bay* (New Rochelle, NY: Arlington House, 1968); Louis P. Simpson, *The Dispossessed Garden* (Athens: University of Georgia Press, 1975) and *The Man of Letters in New England and the South* (Baton Rouge: Louisiana State University Press, 1973).

4. David Brion Davis, *The Problem of Slavery in the Age of Revolution;* (Ithaca: Cornell University Press, 1966); Eugene D. Genovese, *From Rebellion to Revolution* (Baton Rouge: Louisiana State University Press, 1979); Elizabeth Fox-Genovese, *The Female Self in the Age of Bourgeois Individualism,* Joanne Goodman Lectures, delivered at the University of Western Ontario, September 1987.

5. Eugene D. Genovese and Elizabeth Fox-Genovese, "Slavery, Economic Development, and the Law," *Washington and Lee Law Review* 41 (Winter 1984): 1–29; Elizabeth Fox-Genovese and Eugene D. Genovese, "The Divine Sanction of Social Order: The Religious Foundations of the Southern Slaveholders' World View," *Journal of the American Academy of Religion* 55, 2 (Summer 1987): 211–33. On the law, see Mark Tushnet, *The American Law of Slavery: Considerations of Humanity and Interest* (Princeton: Princeton University Press, 1981).

6. Elizabeth Fox-Genovese, *Within the Plantation Household: Black and White Women of the Old South* (Chapel Hill: University of North Carolina Press, 1988).

7. Elizabeth Fox-Genovese, "The Religion of Slaveholding Women," in *That Gentle Strength: Aspects of Female Spirituality,* ed. Lydia L. Coon (Charlottesville; 1989).

8. Campbell Family Papers, Perkins Library, Duke University

9. The references to Washington are ubiquitous. See, e.g., Mary Moragne, *The Neglected Thread*, ed. Del Mullen Craven, 66 (22 February 1838).

10. John Boles, *The Great Revival, 1787–1805: The Origins of the Southern Evangelical Mind* (Lexington: University of Kentucky Press, 1972); Jan Lewis, *The Pursuit of Happiness: Family and Values in Jefferson's Virginia* (New York: Cambridge University Press, 1983).

11. Moragne, *Neglected Thread*, 233 (26 February 1842).

12. Fox-Genovese, *Within the Plantation Household*, ch. 5.

13. Eugene D. Genovese, "Toward a Kinder and Gentler America: The Southern Lady in the Greening of the Politics of the Old South," in *Marriage and the Family in the Victorian South*, ed. Carol Bleser (New York: Oxford University Press, 1990).

14. Julia Gardiner Tyler, "To the Duchess of Sutherland and the Ladies of England," *Southern Literary Messenger* 19, no. 20 (Feb. 1853): 121.

15. Ibid., 120, 121.

16. Ibid.

17. Ibid.

18. Ibid., 125.

19. Caroline Lee Hentz, *The Planter's Northern Bride* (Chapel Hill: University of North Carolina Press, 1970).

20. Mrs. Henry Schoolcraft, *The Black Gauntlet* (Philadelphia: Lippincott, 1860), 93.

21. Ibid., 227.

22. Ibid., 306–7.

23. Ibid., iv.

24. Ibid., v.

25. Augusta Jane Evans, *Beulah* (Atlanta: Hoyt and Martin, 1898; orig. ed., 1859).

26. Augusta Jane Evans, *Inez: A Tale of the Alamo* (New York: Grossett and Dunlap 1887).

27. Louisa S. McCord [L.S.M.], "Woman and Her Needs," *DeBow's Review* 13 (September 1852): 168, and her "Enfranchisement of Women," *Southern Quarterly Review* 21 (April 1852): 322–41.

28. Thomas Roderick Dew, *Digest of the Laws* (New York: Appleton and Co., 1852).

29. Elizabeth Fox-Genovese and Eugene D. Genovese, *Fruits of Merchant Capital* (New York: Oxford University Press, 1983), ch. 11.

30. Elizabeth Fox-Genovese, "Women, Affirmative Action, and the Myth of Individualism," *George Washington Law Review* 54, 2 & 3 (January and March 1986): 338–74.

31. Marilyn Butler, *Jane Austen and the War of Ideas* (Oxford: Oxford University Press, 1975), 293.

32. Butler, *Jane Austen*, 299.

33. Elizabeth Fox-Genovese, "The Female Self in the Age of Bourgeois Individualism," Joanne Goodman Lectures, 1987.

34. Hannah More, *Coelebs in Search of a Wife and Strictures on the Modern System of Female Education*, in *The Works of Hannah More*, 2 vols. (New York: Harper and Brothers, 1841); Catherine Hall, "The Early Formation of Victorian Domestic Ideology," in *Fit Work for Women*, ed. Sandra Burman (New York: St. Martin's Press, 1979); M. G. Jones, *Hannah More* (New York: Greenwood Press, 1968; orig. ed., 1952).

Notes to COMMENTARY
by Barbara Jeanne Fields

1. *Within the Plantation Household: Black and White Women of the Old South* (Chapel Hill: University of North Carolina Press, 1988).
2. Fox-Genovese, *Within the Plantation Household,* 98.
3. I have developed this argument at greater length in "Slavery, Race, and Ideology," *New Left Review* (forthcoming). See also David Brion Davis, *The Problem of Slavery in the Age of Revolution, 1770–1823* (Ithaca: Cornell University Press, 1975), esp. chs. 4, 6, and 7; and Barbara J. Fields, "Ideology and Race in American History," in *Region, Race, and Reconstruction: Essays in Honor of C. Vann Woodward,* ed. J. Morgan Kousser and James M. McPherson (New York: Oxford University Press, 1982), 143–77.
4. Virginia Foster Durr, *Outside the Magic Circle: The Autobiography of Virginia Foster Durr* (New York: Simon and Schuster, 1985), 96–7.
5. Suzanne Lebsock, *The Free Women of Petersburg: Status and Culture in a Southern Town, 1784–1860* (New York: Norton, 1984), 138.
6. Fox-Genovese, *Within the Plantation Household,* 366.

Notes to EMANCIPATION AND THE DEVELOPMENT OF CAPITALIST AGRICULTURE: THE SOUTH IN COMPARATIVE PERSPECTIVE
by Steven Hahn

1. Historians differ, at times vociferously, in explaining the course by which servile relations and peasant claims were abolished. Some emphasize demographic cycles, some the growth of towns and trade, and some the social struggles between exploiters and direct producers in the countryside. Most would, however, agree that the "agricultural revolution" required the loosening of servile constraints and the reorganization of property rights. The literature touching this subject is vast, but for very useful introductions to the points of contention see Rodney Hilton, ed., *The Transition From Feudalism to Capitalism* (London: NLB, 1976); T. H. Aston and C. H. E. Philpin, eds., *The Brenner Debate: Agrarian Class Structure and Economic Development in Pre-Industrial Europe* (Cambridge: Cambridge University Press, 1985); J. D. Chambers and G. E. Mingay, *The Agricultural Revolution, 1750–1880* (London: Batsford, 1966).
2. See, for example, the contributions by Robert Brenner, Patricia Croot and David Parker, and Guy Bois in Ashton and Philpin, eds., *Brenner Debate,* 10–63, 79–90, 107–18, 213–327; Peter Kolchin, *Unfree Labor: American Slavery and Russian Serfdom* (Cambridge: The Belknap Press of Harvard University Press, 1987), 1–46.
3. E.J. Hobsbawm, *The Age of Revolution, 1789–1848* (London: Weidenfeld & Nicolson, 1962), 149–67; E.J. Hobsbawm, *The Age of Capital, 1848–1875* (New York: Scribner, 1975), 189–211; Robin Blackburn, *The Overthrow of Colonial Slavery, 1776–1848* (London: Verso, 1988), 519–49; Gareth Stedman Jones, "Society and Politics at the Beginning of the World Economy," *Cambridge Journal of Economics* 1 (March, 1977): 82–3.
4. Barbara Jeanne Fields, *Slavery and Freedom on the Middle Ground: Maryland During the Nineteenth Century* (New Haven: Yale University Press, 1985), 1–22; Steven Hahn, *The Roots of Southern Populism: Yeoman Farmers and the Transformation of the Georgia Upcountry, 1850–1890* (New York: Oxford Univer-

sity Press, 1983), 15–85; Ira Berlin and Herbert G. Gutman, "Natives and Immigrants, Free Men and Slaves: Urban Workingmen in the Antebellum South," *American Historical Review* 88 (December, 1983): 1175–1200. The existence of social relations and formations based on some type of free labor in slave and servile societies, just as the existence of social relations and formations based on coerced and dependent labor in capitalist societies, poses for historians the analytic problem of articulation: of the linkage between different sets of social relations and formations. For some important discussions see, Aidan Foster-Carter, "The Modes of Production Controversy," *New Left Review* 107 (January-February, 1978): 50–62; Steve J. Stern, "Feudalism, Capitalism, and the World-System in the Perspective of Latin America and the Caribbean," *American Historical Review* 93 (October, 1988): 829–71; Barbara Jeanne Fields, "The Nineteenth Century American South: History and Theory," *Plantation Society* 2 (April, 1983): 9–14; Florencia E. Mallon, *The Defense of Community in Peru's Central Highlands: Peasant Struggle and Capitalist Transition, 1860–1940* (Princeton: Princeton University Press 1983), 5–7.

5. In Brazil, Cuba, and the American South, the free population surpassed the slave at all points in the nineteenth century, and in Cuba whites claimed either a near or real majority. On these and related matters concerning demographic patterns see, Emilia Viotti da Costa, *The Brazilian Empire: Myths and Histories* (Chicago: University of Chicago Press, 1985), 125–71; Stanley J. Stein, *Vassouras: A Brazilian Coffee County, 1850–1890* (Cambridge: Harvard University Press, 1957), 295–96; Franklin W. Knight, *Slave Society in Cuba During the Nineteenth Century* (Madison: University of Wisconsin Press, 1970), 3–46; Rebecca J. Scott, *Slave Emancipation in Cuba: The Transition to Free Labor, 1860–1899* (Princeton: Princeton University Press, 1985), 3–41.

6. William W. Hagen, "The Junkers' Faithless Servants: Peasant Insubordination and the Breakdown of Serfdom in Brandenburg-Prussia, 1763–1811," in *The German Peasantry: Conflict and Community in Rural Society From the Eighteenth to the Twentieth Centuries*, eds. Richard J. Evans and W. R. Lee (London: Croom Helm, 1986), 71–101; Scott, *Slave Emancipation in Cuba*, xiii, 29; Fe Iglesias Garcia, "The Development of Capitalism in Cuban Sugar Production, 1860–1900," in *Between Slavery and Free Labor: The Spanish-Speaking Caribbean in the Nineteenth Century*, ed. Manuel Moreno Fraginals, Frank Moya Pons, and Stanley L. Engerman (Baltimore: Johns Hopkins University Press, 1985), 64–66; Thomas H. Holloway, "The Coffee *Colono* of São Paulo, Brazil: Migration and Mobility, 1880–1930," in *Land and Labour in Latin America: Essays in the Development of Agrarian Capitalism in the Nineteenth and Twentieth Centuries*, ed. Ian Rutledge and Kenneth Duncan (Cambridge: Cambridge University Press, 1977), 305–10; Emilia Viotti da Costa, *Da senzala à colônia* (São Paulo: Difusão Europbeia do Livro, 1966), 188–202.

7. Eugene D. Genovese, *The Political Economy of Slavery: Studies in the Economy and Society of the Slave South* (New York: Pantheon, 1965), 155–274; Ira Berlin, *Slaves Without Masters: The Free Negro in the Antebellum South* (New York: Pantheon, 1974), 343–80; Frederick F. Siegel, *The Roots of Southern Distinctiveness: Tobacco and Society in Danville, Virginia, 1780–1865* (Chapel Hill, University of North Carolina Press, 1987).

8. I have attempted to develop this argument in *The Roots of Southern Populism*, 15–85, and in "The 'Unmaking' of the Southern Yeomanry: The Transformation of the Georgia Upcountry, 1860–1890," in *The Countryside in the Age of Capitalist Transformation: Essays in the Social History of Rural America*, ed. Steven Hahn

and Jonathan Prude (Chapel Hill: University of North Carolina Press, 1985), 179–203. See also, Elizabeth Fox-Genovese, "Antebellum Southern Households: A New Perspective on a Familiar Question," *Review* 7 (Fall, 1983): 215–53. Recent research on the northern and western countryside has suggested that the transition to capitalist relations may have been far more extended than previously assumed, and the Old South may well have anchored a broad-based anti-bourgeois coalition that at least slowed the pace of capitalist development throughout the nation. The destruction of slavery in the South, together with the destruction of servile relations and the commercialization of the rural economies in southern and eastern Europe, as I will argue shortly, sped the advance of capitalist agriculture all over the United States.

9. Eugene D. Genovese, *The World the Slaveholders Made: Two Essays in Interpretation* (New York: Pantheon, 1969), 21–113; Jerome Blum, *The End of the Old Order in Rural Europe* (Princeton: Princeton University Press, 1978), 357–417.

10. On the protracted route to capitalist social relations, see especially, Jonathan M. Wiener, "Class Structure and Economic Development in the American South: 1865–1955," *American Historical Review* 84 (October, 1979): 970–92; Jay R. Mandle, *The Roots of Black Poverty: The Southern Economy After the Civil War* (Durham: Duke University Press, 1978); Roger Ransom and Richard Sutch, *One Kind of Freedom: The Economic Consequences of Emancipation* (Cambridge: Cambridge University Press, 1977); Dwight Billings, *Planters and the Making of a 'New South': Class, Politics, and Development in North Carolina, 1865–1900* (Chapel Hill: University of North Carolina Press, 1979). On comparisons emphasizing the implementation of coercive mechanisms, see Wilhelmina Kloosterboer, *Involuntary Servitude Since the Abolition of Slavery: A Survey of Compulsory Labour Throughout the World* (Leiden: E.J. Brill, 1960); C. Vann Woodward, "The Price of Freedom," in *What Was Freedom's Price?* ed. David J. Sansing (Jackson: University Press of Mississippi, 1978), 101–5.

11. William A. Green, *British Slave Emancipation: The Sugar Colonies and the Great Experiment, 1830–1865* (Oxford: Clarendon Press, 1965), 131–218; Eric Foner, *Nothing But Freedom: Emancipation and Its Legacy* (Baton Rouge: Louisiana State University Press, 1983), 14–20, 24–29; Stanley L. Engerman, "Economic Adjustments to Emancipation in the United States and the British West Indies," *Journal of Interdisciplinary History*, 13 (Autumn, 1982): 194–203. Much is made of the so-called "land/labor ratio" in explaining the outcomes of emancipation. Where the ratio was high, it is often argued, planters had difficulty in controlling freed-labor and plantation production suffered; where it was low, the freedpeople had few alternatives to the estates and the plantations rode the transition far more easily. In other words, a high land/labor ratio was related to greater freedom for the ex-slaves. Compelling as it seems, the very same logic is used to explain the rise of slavery. Which is merely to emphasize the importance of politics and power, the land/labor ration being only an aspect. For a critique in light of a distinctive example, see, O. Nigel Bolland, "Systems of Domination After Slavery: The Control of Land and Labor in the British West Indies After 1838," *Comparative Studies in Society and History* 23 (October, 1981): 591–619.

12. Walter Rodney, *A History of the Guyanese Working People, 1881–1905* (Baltimore: Johns Hopkins University Press, 1981), 31–59; Alan H. Adamson, "The Reconstruction of Plantation Labor After Emancipation: The Case of British Guiana," in *Race and Slavery in the Western Hemisphere: Quantitative Studies*, ed. Eugene D. Genovese and Stanley L. Engerman (Princeton: Princeton Univer-

sity Press, 1975), 457–73; Stanley L. Engerman, "Servants to Slaves to Servants: Contract Labour and European Expansion," in *Colonialism and Migration: Indentured Labour Before and After Slavery*, ed. P. C. Emmer (Dordrecht: Nijhoff, 1986), 270–76; Green, *British Slave Emancipation*, 192–218; George L. Beckford, *Persistent Poverty: Underdevelopment in Plantation Economies of the Third World* (New York: Oxford University Press, 1972), 84–113; L. S. Stavrianos, *Global Rift: The Third World Comes of Age* (New York: Morrow, 1981), 230–52.

13. Viotti da Costa, *Brazilian Empire*, 128–70; Joseph L. Love, *São Paulo in the Brazilian Federation, 1889–1937* (Stanford: Stanford University Press, 1980), 8–10.

14. Thomas H. Holloway, *Immigrants on the Land: Coffee and Society in São Paulo, 1886–1934* (Chapel Hill: University of North Carolina Press, 1980); Steven Topik, *The Political Economy of the Brazilian State, 1889–1930* (Austin: University of Texas Press, 1987), 59–92; Barbara Weinstein, "Brazilian Regionalism," *Latin American Research Review* 17 (1982): 262–76; Stein, *Vassouras*, 250–76; George Reid Andrews, "Black and White Workers: São Paulo, 1888–1928," in Rebecca Scott et al., *The Abolition of Slavery and the Aftermath of Emancipation in Brazil* (Durham: Duke University Press, 1988), 96–109.

15. Peter L. Eisenberg, *The Sugar Industry in Pernambuco, 1840–1910: Modernization Without Change* (Berkeley: University of California Press, 1974), 180–214; Peter L. Eisenberg, "The Consequences of Modernization for Brazil's Sugar Plantations in the Nineteenth Century," in *Land and Labour in Latin America*, ed. Rutledge and Duncan, 345–67.

16. Scott, *Slave Emancipation in Cuba*, 3–41, 63–226; Eisenberg, "Consequences of Modernization," 348–49.

17. Manuel Moreno Fraginals, "Plantations in the Caribbean: Cuba, Puerto Rico, and the Dominican Republic in the Nineteenth Century," in *Between Slavery and Free Labor*, eds., Fraginals, Pons, and Engerman, 4–8, 14–21; Scott, *Slave Emancipation in Cuba*, 227–78.

18. Hartmut Harnisch, "Peasants and Markets; The Background to the Agrarian Reforms in Feudal Prussia East of the Elbe, 1760–1807," in *German Peasantry*, eds., Evans and Lee, 38–66; Hagan, "Junkers' Faithless Servants," 71–101; Jerome Blum, "The Rise of Serfdom in Eastern Europe," *American Historical Review* 62 (July, 1957): 807–36.

19. Blum, *End of the Old Order*, 377–400; Theodore S. Hamerow, *Revolution, Restoration, and Reaction: Economics and Politics in Germany, 1815–1871* (Princeton: Princeton University Press, 1958), 38–55; J. A. Perkins, "The Agricultural Revolution in Germany, 1850–1914," *Journal of European Economic History* 10 (Spring, 1981): 101–08; Alan Richards, "The Political Economy of *Gutswirtschaft*: A Comparative Analysis of East Elbian Germany, Egypt, and Chile," *Comparative Studies in Society and History* 21 (October, 1979): 487–88, 510–12.

20. Gordon A. Craig, *Germany, 1866–1945* (New York: Oxford University Press, 1980), 85–99; Hans-Jürgen Puhle, "Lords and Peasants in the Kaisserreich," in *Peasants and Lords in Modern Germany*, ed. Robert G. Moeller (Boston: Allen & Unwin, 1986), 81–109; Kenneth Barkin, *The Controversy Over German Industrialization, 1890–1902* (Chicago: University of Chicago Press, 1970), 37–40; Alexander Gerschenkron, *Bread and Democracy in Germany* (New York: H. Fertig, 1966), 42–4; Robert G. Moeller, "Peasants and Tariffs in the Kaisserreich: How Backward Were the 'Bauern'?" *Agricultural History* 55 (October, 1981): 370–84.

21. The case of St. Domingue is well known, but as P. M. Jones argues in his recent study of rural France during the Revolutionary era, the bourgeois assault on peasant common rights did not have the success of the more general attack on

seigneurialism. Indeed, the outcome was something of a draw, giving breathing room to small property and the larger agricultural sector. See, P. M. Jones, *The Peasantry in the French Revolution* (Cambridge: Cambridge University Press, 1988); C. L. R. James, *The Black Jacobins: Toussaint L'Ouverture and the San Domingo Revolution* (New York: Vintage Books, 1963); Eugene D. Genovese, *From Rebellion to Revolution: Afro-American Slave Revolts in the Making of the Modern World* (Baton Rouge: Louisiana State University Press, 1979), 82–125.

22. On this point, see, Richards, "Political Economy of *Gutswirtschaft*," 496.

23. John Alfred Heitmann, *The Modernization of the Louisiana Sugar Industry, 1830–1910* (Baton Rouge: Louisiana University Press, 1987), 68–97; Joseph P. Reidy, "The Development of Central Factories and the Rise of Tenancy in Louisiana's Sugar Economy, 1880–1910" (Paper Presented to the Annual Meeting of the Social Science History Association, 1982); Joseph P. Reidy, "Sugar and Freedom: Emancipation in Louisiana's Sugar Parishes" (Paper Presented to the Annual Meeting of the American Historical Association, 1980).

24. Foner, *Nothing But Freedom*, 74–110; Julie Saville, "A Measure of Freedom: From Slave to Wage Labor in South Carolina, 1860–1868" (Ph.D. diss., Yale University, 1986); C. Vann Woodward, *Origins of the New South, 1877–1913* (Baton Rouge: Louisiana State University Press, 1951), 107–41; Pete Daniel, *Breaking the Land: The Transformation of Cotton, Tobacco, and Rice Cultures Since 1880* (Urbana, Il: University of Illinois Press, 1985), 39–61, 215–36; Barbara Jeanne Fields, "The Advent of Capitalist Agriculture: The South in a Bourgeois World," in *Essays on the Postbellum Southern Economy*, eds., Thavolia Glymph and John J. Kushma (College Station: Texas A & M University Press, 1985), 80–81.

25. Crandall A. Shifflett, *Patronage and Poverty in the Tobacco South: Louisa County, Virginia, 1860–1900* (Knoxville: University of Tennessee Press, 1982), 22–23, 52–54; Fields, *Slavery and Freedom*, 167–93; V. I. Lenin, *The Development of Capitalism in Russia* (Moscow: Progress Pubs., 1974), 181.

26. *A Compendium of the Ninth Census of the United States, 1870* (Washington: U.S. Government Printing Office, 1872), 672; Lawanda F. Cox, "The American Agricultural Wage Earner: The Emergence of a Modern Labor Problem," *Agricultural History*, 22 (April, 1948): 96. For the most recent and sophisticated treatment of the development of sharecropping which emphasizes the importance of capital scarcity and of squads in the transition from gang labor, see, Gerald D. Jaynes, *Roots Without Branches: Genesis of the Black Working Class in the American South, 1862–1882* (New York: Oxford University Press, 1986), 163–90 and passim.

27. Richards, "Political Economy of *Gutswirtschaft*," 497; Harold D. Woodman, "Post-Civil War Southern Agriculture and the Law," *Agricultural History* 53 (January, 1979): 324–27; Steven Hahn, "Hunting, Fishing, and Foraging: Common Rights and Class Relations in the Postbellum South," *Radical History Review* 26 (1982): 37–67; Foner, *Nothing But Freedom*, 39–73.

28. Robert L. Brandfon, *Cotton Kingdom of the New South: A History of the Yazoo Mississippi Delta From Reconstruction to the Twentieth Century* (Cambridge: Harvard University Press, 1967); Harold D. Woodman, "The Reconstruction of the Cotton Plantation in the New South," in *Essays on Postbellum Southern Economy*, eds. Glymph and Kushma, 113–15; Fields, "Advent of Capitalist Agriculture," 84–89; Jeannie Whayne, "Reshaping the Rural South: Land, Labor, and Federal Policy in Poinsett County, Arkansas, 1900–1940" (Ph.D. diss., University of California, San Diego, 1989). I have tried to develop this argument in "Class and State in Postemancipation Societies: Southern Planters in Comparative Perspective," *American Historical Review* 95, 1 (February, 1990): 75–98.

29. Hahn, *Roots of Southern Populism*, 137–203; Jacquelyn Hall et al., *Like a Family: The Making of a Southern Cotton Mill World* (Chapel Hill: University of North Carolina Press, 1987), 31–113; Gavin Wright, *Old South, New South: Revolutions in the Southern Economy Since the Civil War* (New York: Basic Books, Inc., Publishers, 1986), 51–156. Many of the features associated with the capitalist transformation of nonplantation districts—the centrality of merchant capital, the persistence of the household with a shrinking subsistence base as the unit of production, and the nature of the crop—suggest useful comparisons with the unfortunately named but historically significant phenomenon of "proto-industrialization" in Europe.

30. Ronald D. Eller, *Miners, Millhands, and Mountaineers: Industrialization of the Appalachian South, 1880–1930* (Knoxville: University of Tennessee Press, 1982), 39–85; Woodward, *Origins of the New South*, 175–263.

31. Howard Lamar, "From Bondage to Contract: Ethnic Labor in the American West, 1600–1900," in *The Countryside in the Age of Capitalist Transformation*, ed. Hahn and Prude, 310–17; Cox, "American Agricultural Wage Earner," 98–114; David Montgomery, *The Fall of the House of Labor: The Workplace, the State, and American Labor Activism, 1865–1925* (Cambridge: Cambridge University Press, 1987), 70–73; June Mei, "Socioeconomic Origins of Emigration: Guandong to California, 1850–1882," in *Labor Immigration Under Capitalism: Asian Workers in the United States Before World War II* eds. Licie Cheng and Edna Bonacich, (Berkeley: University of California Press, 1984), 219–45; Yuji Ichioka, *The Issei: The World of the First Generation of Japanese Immigrants, 1885–1924* (New York: The Free Press, 1988), 80–82.

32. Cox, "American Agricultural Wage Earner," 105–06; Paul Wallace Gates, "Land Policy and Tenancy in the Prairie States," *Journal of Economic History* 1 (May, 1941): 77–82; Gilbert C. Fite, *The Farmers' Frontier, 1865–1900* (New York: Holt, Rinehart and Winston, 1966), 34–155.

33. On the South-West axis in the postbellum period see, Carl V. Harris, "Right Fork or Left Fork?: The Section-Party Alignments of Southern Democrats in Congress, 1873–1897" *Journal of Southern History* 42 (November, 1976): 471–506.

Notes to COMMENTARY
by Peter Kolchin

1. Eugene D. Genovese, *The Political Economy of Slavery: Studies in the Economy and Society of the Slave South* (New York: Vintage Books, 1965), *The World the Slaveholders Made: Two Essays in Interpretation* (New York: Pantheon, 1969), *Roll, Jordan, Roll: The World the Slaves Made* (New York: Vintage Books, 1974); Elizabeth Fox-Genovese and Eugene D. Genovese, "The Janus Face of Merchant Capital," *Fruits of Merchant Capital: Slavery and Bourgeois Property in the Rise and Expansion of Capitalism* (New York: Oxford University Press, 1983), 3–25.

2. Kenneth M. Stampp, *The Peculiar Institution: Slavery in the Ante-Bellum South* (New York: A. A. Knopf, 1956); Robert William Fogel and Stanley L. Engerman, *Time on the Cross: The Economics of American Negro Slavery* (Boston: Little, Brown, 1974).

3. James Oakes, *The Ruling Race: A History of American Slaveholders* (New York: A. A. Knopf, 1982), xiii.

4. See Peter Kolchin, "American Historians and Antebellum Southern Slavery,"

in *A Master's Due: Essays in Honor of David Herbert Donald*, ed. William J. Cooper *et al.* (Baton Rouge: Louisiana State University Press, 1985), 95–102.

5. Crandall A. Shifflett, *Patronage and Poverty in the Tobacco South: Louisa County, Virginia, 1860–1900* (Knoxville: University of Tennessee Press, 1982), 64–5, 103; Jonathan M. Wiener, *Social Origins of The New South: Alabama, 1860–1885* (Baton Rouge: Louisiana State University Press, 1978); Jay R. Mandle, *The Roots of Black Poverty: The Southern Plantation Economy After the Civil War* (Durham: Duke University Press, 1978).

6. Robert Higgs, *Competition and Coercion: Blacks in the American Economy, 1865–1914* (Cambridge: Cambridge University Press, 1977); Stephen J. DeCanio, *Agriculture in the Postbellum South: The Economics of Production and Supply* (Cambridge, Mass.: MIT Press, 1974).

7. For two major works that also reject these positions—although from perspectives different from Hahn's (and from each other's)—see Roger L. Ransom and Richard Sutch, *One Kind of Freedom: The Economic Consequences of Emancipation* (Cambridge: Cambridge University Press, 1977); and Gavin Wright, *Old South, New South: Revolutions in the Southern Economy Since the Civil War* (New York: Basic Books, Inc., Pubs., 1986).

8. Eric Foner, *Reconstruction: America's Unfinished Revolution, 1863–1877* (New York: Harper & Row, 1988), 11; C. Vann Woodward, *Origins of the New South, 1877–1913* (Baton Rouge: Louisiana State University Press, 1951); Barbara Jeanne Fields, "The Advent of Capitalist Agriculture: The New South in a Bourgeois World," in *Essays on the Postbellum Southern Economy*, ed. Thavolia Glymph and John J. Kushma (College Station: Texas A&M University Pess, 1985), 73–94.

9. Donald Mackenzie Wallace, *Russia on the Eve of War and Revolution*, ed., Cyril E. Black (New York: Vintage Books, 1961; first pub.,1877), 338–9.

Notes to ECONOMICS OR CULTURE: THE DEVELOPMENT OF THE U.S. SOUTH AND BRAZIL IN THE DAYS OF SLAVERY
by Richard Graham

1. The slave population of the United States totalled 3,953,696 in 1860: United States, Bureau of the Census, *Population of the United States in 1860 Compiled from the Original Returns of the Eighth Census* (Washington, D.C.: U.S. Government Printing Office, 1864). It is estimated that in 1850 the slave population of Brazil totaled 2,500,000: Joaquim Norberto de Souza Silva, *Investigações sobre os recenseamentos da população geral do Imperio e de cada provincia de per si tentados desde os tempos coloniaes até hoje* (Rio de Janeiro: Perseverança, 1870), 9. A census taken in Brazil in 1872 showed 1,510,806 slaves: Brazil, Directoria Geral de Estatistica, *Recenseamento da população do Imperio do Brazil a que se procedeu no dia 1° de agosto de 1872* (Rio de Janeiro: Leuzinger, 1873–6). I published some portions of this chapter in altered form in *Comparative Studies in Society and History*, 23: 4 (Oct. 1981): 620–55, and included them here by kind permission of Cambridge University Press.

2. Elizabeth Fox-Genovese and Eugene D. Genovese, *Fruits of Merchant Capital: Slavery and Bourgeois Property in the Rise and Expansion of Capitalism* (New York: Oxford University Press, 1983), 43.

3. Certainly comparing seventeenth-century sugar planters in Brazil with nineteenth-century cotton planters in the U.S.—as is often done—seems to be inviting

even greater difficulties. Celso Furtado argues that the difference in timing in export strength during the 19th century is the major factor to be considered in the differing records of development in the two countries: *The Economic Growth of Brazil: A Survey from Colonial to Modern Times*, trans. Ricardo W. de Aguiar and Eric Charles Drysdale (Berkeley: University of California Press, 1963), 164–5. The geographical spread of coffee within the province of São Paulo is graphically presented in Sérgio Milliet, *Roteiro do café: análise histórico-demográfica da expansão cafeeira no estado de São Paulo*, Estudos Paulistas, no. 1 (São Paulo: n.p., 1938), 23–8; similar maps have not been prepared for the province of Rio de Janeiro but, for the distribution of slaves in 1883, see Orlando Valverde, *La fazenda de café esclavista en el Brasil*, Cuadernos Geograficos, no. 3 (Merida, Venezuela: Universidad de los Andes, 1965), 41. Maps showing similar movement of slaves and cotton can be found in Robert William Fogel and Stanley L. Engerman, *Time on the Cross: The Economics of American Negro Slavery* (Boston: Little, Brown, 1974), 45; and Lewis Cecil Gray, *History of Agriculture in the Southern United States to 1860* (New York: Peter Smith, 1941), 684, 890–1. Cotton was planted in new areas of the South after slavery, but not with the same impact as in the case of coffee in Brazil.

4. On shipments on the Paraíba River, see Louis Agassiz and Elizabeth Cabot Gary Agassiz, *A Journey to Brazil*, 2nd ed. (Boston: Ticknor and Fields, 1868), 121. On the difficulty of using the São Paulo rivers for transportation, see Sérgio Buarque de Holanda, *Monções*, 2nd ed., Biblioteca Alfa-Omega, História, no. 8 (São Paulo: Alfa-Omega, 1976), 40–6, 77–107. For lack of financial resources governments did little then or later to construct locks and canals to make these rivers navigable; cf. Carter Goodrich, ed., *Canals and American Economic Development* (New York: Columbia University Press, 1961).

5. Frederick Law Olmstead, *The Cotton Kingdom: A Traveller's Observations on Cotton and Slavery in the American Slave States*, Arthur M. Schlessinger, ed. (New York: Knopf, 1953), 128–9, 343–4; George Rogers Taylor, *The Transportation Revolution, 1815–1860*, Economic History of the United States, no. 4 (New York: Harper and Row, 1951), 15–16; U. B. Phillips, *A History of Transportation in the Eastern Cotton Belt to 1860* (New York: Columbia University Press, 1908), 12, 59–61, 69, 127, 129; William Eleijus Martin, *Internal Improvements in Alabama*, Johns Hopkins University Studies in Historical and Political Science, ser. 20, no. 4 (Baltimore: Johns Hopkins Press, 1902), 27–32; Alfred Glaze Smith, *Economic Readjustment of an Old Cotton State: South Carolina, 1820–1860* (Columbia: University of South Carolina Press, 1958), 137–8, 143, 153–4; Milton S. Heath, *Constructive Liberalism: The Role of the State in Economic Development in Georgia to 1860* (Cambridge: Harvard University Press, 1954), 233–4, 239, 249–52.

6. José Alípio Goulart, *Tropas e tropeiros na formação do Brasil*, Coleção Temas Brasileiros (Rio de Janeiro: n.p., 1961); Luis C. Almedia, *Vida e morte do tropeiro* (São Paulo: Martins, 1971); Carlos Borges Schmidt, *Tropas e tropeiros* (São Paulo; n.p., 1932); Jean Baptiste Debret, *Voyage pittoresque et historique au Brésil: ou séjour d'un artiste français au Brésil, depuis 1816 jusqu'en 1831 inclusivement*, facsim. ed., 3 vols. (Rio de Janeiro: Record: New York: Continental News, 1965), II, 117, and plate 37; Richard M. Morse, "Some Themes of Brazilian History," *South Atlantic Quarterly* 51 (Spring 1962): 169; Richard P. Momsen, Jr., *Routes Over the Serra do Mar: The Evolution of Transportation in the Highlands of Rio de Janeiro and São Paulo* (Rio de Janeiro: [privately printed?], 1964); Alberto Ribeiro Lamego, *O homem e a serra*, 2nd ed. (Rio de Janeiro: Instituto Brasileiro de Geografia e Estatística, 1963); Caio Prado Júnior, *The Colonial Background of Modern Brazil*,

trans. Suzette Macedo (Berkeley: University of California Press, 1967), 298–307, 481 n. 42; Emília Viotti da Costa, *Da senzala à colônia*, Corpo e Alma do Brasil, no. 19 (São Paulo: Difusão Européia do Livro, 1966), 154–73; Maria Thereza Schorer Petrone, *A lavoura canavieira em São Paulo: Expansão e declínio (1765–1851)*, Corpo e Alma do Brasil, no. 21 (São Paulo: Difusão Européia do Livro, 1968), 186–222; Stanley J. Stein, *Vassouras, a Brazilian Coffee County, 1850–1900*, Harvard Historical Studies, no. 69 (Cambridge: Harvard University Press, 1957), 91–101; Vânia Fróes Bragança, "Contribuição para o estudo da crise e extinção do Município de Estrela," in *Ensaios sobre a política e economia da provincia fluminense no seculo xix*, ed. Richard Graham (Rio de Janeiro: Arquivo Nacional for the Universidade Federal Fluminense, 1974), 104–28; Robert H. Mattoon, Jr., "Railroads, Coffee, and the Growth of Big Business in São Paulo, Brazil," *Hispanic American Historical Review* 57 (May 1977): 276–77; A. R. Neto, *A Estrada da Graciosa* (Rio de Janeiro: Revista Rodovia, 1945); Fulvio C. Rodrigues, *A União e Industria, pioneira das estradas de rodagem brasileiras (ensaio)* (Rio de Janeiro: Grafica do "Jornal do Brasil," 1934). The oxcart had long been used in Brazil but, having a fixed axle, was not suitable for the steep inclines of the coffee region: José B. Sousa, *O ciclo do carro de boi no Brasil* (São Paulo: Editôra Nacional, 1958). Some wagon roads traversed the flat sugar regions of northern Rio de Janeiro province.

7. E.g., Harold D. Woodman, *King Cotton and His Retainers: Financing and Marketing the Cotton Crop of the South, 1800–1925* (Lexington: University of Kentucky Press, 1968), 152, 188. On Southern railroads, see Phillips, *History of Transportation*, 132–396; Robert C. Black, III, *The Railroads of the Confederacy* (Chapel Hill: University of North Carolina Press, 1952); Robert S. Cotterill, "Southern Railroads, 1850–1860," *Mississippi Valley Historical Review* 10 (March 1924): 396–405; Smith, *Economic Readjustment*, 148, 156–60, 170–6, 191–2; Heath, *Constructive Liberalism*, 254–92.

8. On Brazilian railroads, see Richard Graham, *Britain and the Onset of Modernization in Brazil, 1850–1914*, Cambridge Latin American Studies, no. 4 (Cambridge: Cambridge University Press, 1968), 51–72 and the sources cited therein; Mattoon, "Railroads"; Odilon Nogueira de Matos, *Café e ferrovias: a evolução ferroviária de São Paulo e o desenvolvimento da cultura cafeeira*, 2nd ed., Biblioteca Alfa-Omega, História, no. 2 (São Paulo: Alfa-Omega, 1974).

9. John F. Stover, *The Railroads of the South, 1865–1900: A Study of Finance and Control* (Chapel Hill: University of North Carolina Press, 1955), 5, 193; J. P. Wileman, comp., *The Brazilian Year Book, Second Issue—1909* (London: McCorquodale, 1909), 612.

10. E.g., Fogel and Engerman, *Time on the Cross*, 191–209; Fox-Genovese and Genovese, *Fruits of Merchant Capital*, 34–60.

11. Paul W. Gates, *The Farmer's Age: Agriculture, 1815–1860*, The Economic History of the United States, no. 3 (New York: Harper and Row, 1960), 142–4.

12. Franklee Gilbert Whartenby, *Land and Labor Productivity in United States Cotton Production, 1800–1840* (New York: Arno, 1977), 109–12; Gates, *Farmer's Age*, 135–6, 144; John Hebron Moore, *Agriculture in Ante-Bellum Mississippi* (New York: Bookman Associates, 1958), 114, 121, 165, 167, 169–73, 182–3, 187–9; Gray, *History of Agriculture*, 792–800; T. Lynn Smith, *Brazil: People and Institutions*, 3rd ed. (Baton Rouge: Louisiana State University Press, 1963), 372–90; Carlos Borges Schmidt, *Técnicas agrícolas primitivas e tradicionais* (Rio de Janeiro: Conselho Federal de Cultura, 1976), 91–117.

13. The quotations are, respectively, from Wilson Cano, *Raízes da concentração indus-*

trial em São Paulo (São Paulo: Difel, 1977), 28, and João Manuel Cardoso de Mello, "O capitalismo tardio (contribuição a revisão crítica da formação e desenvolvimento da economia brasileira)" (Ph. D. diss., Universidade Estadual de Campinas, 1975), 54. It is well known that slaves worked cotton gins and compresses as well as coffee hulling and drying equipment much of which, in both cases, meant working with complicated steam-driven equipment: Robert S. Starobin, *Industrial Slavery in the Old South* (New York: Oxford University Press, 1970), 22; Stuart Bruchey, *The Roots of American Economic Growth, 1607–1861; An Essay in Social Causation* (New York: Harper and Row, 1968), 173; Graham, *Britain*, 45–6; C. F. van Delden Laerne, *Brazil and Java: Report on Coffee-Culture in America, Asia, and Africa to H. E. the Minister of the Colonies* (London: W. H. Allen, 1885), 310–21; Herbert H. Smith, *Brazil—the Amazons and the Coast* (New York: Scribner's, 1879), 512–27; and Affonso de Escragnolle Taunay, *História do café no Brasil*, 15 vols. (Rio de Janeiro: Departmento Nacional do Café, 1939–1943), VII, 225–82. Brazilian authors have argued that the use of slaves slowed the introduction of such machinery or that the use of the machinery undermined the slave system. Costa, *Da senzala à colônia*, 177–88; Jacob Gorender, *O escravismo colonial*, Ensaios, no. 29 (São Paulo: Ática, 1978), 563. A comparative study of processing machinery has yet to be made. It is probably true that technical improvements were not as essential to the growth of a slave system as they were to a capitalist one based on salaried labor.

14. Gray, *History of Agriculture*, 197; T. L. Smith, *Brazil: People and Institutions*, 364–72.

15. Avery O. Craven, *Soil Exhaustion as a Factor in the Agricultural History of Virginia and Maryland, 1606–1860*, University of Illinois Studies in Social Sciences, vol. 13, no. 1 (Urbana: University of Illinois, 1926), 11–12, 19, 163; A. G. Smith, *Economic Readjustment*, 58, 68, 84, 90, 95, 97, 106; Fogel and Engerman, *Time on the Cross*, 196–9; Maxine Margolis, "Historical Perspectives on Frontier Agriculture as an Adaptive Strategy," *American Ethnologist* 4 (February 1977): 42–64.

16. Stein, *Vassouras*, 214; Mello, "O capitalismo tardio," 80.

17. Gray, *History of Agriculture*, 199, 700–01, 801–07; Gates, *Farmer's Age*, 134, 135–7, 140, 144; Moore, *Agriculture in Mississippi*, 112–21, 145, 164–205, 239 n. 35; Rosser H. Taylor, "The Sale and Application of Commercial Fertilizers in the South Atlantic States to 1900," *Agricultural History* 21 (January 1947): 46–8; *idem*, "Commercial Fertilizers in South Carolina," *South Atlantic Quarterly*, 29 (April 1930): 179–89; Weymouth T. Jordan, "The Peruvian Guano Gospel in the Old South," *Agricultural History* 24 (October 1950): 211–21; William K. Scarborough, *The Overseer: Plantation Management in the Old South* (Baton Rouge: Louisiana State University Press, 1966), 175; Stein, *Vassouras*, 33–4, 50; Schmidt, *Técnicas*, 159–63. The precise extent to which scientific practices were used in the South is the subject of some debate among North American historians, partly because they have not firmly decided what the comparative standard will be, that is, how much is a lot? Eugene Genovese, *The Political Economy of Slavery: Studies in the Economy and Society of the Slave South* (New York: Pantheon, 1965), 85–99, has convincingly denied that there was widespread use of fertilizer in the South, but my point here relates to a comparison with Brazil. See also A. G. Smith, *Economic Readjustment*, 88–100. Gorender, *Escravismo colonial*, 222, relying too heavily on Genovese, also fails to consider the difference in degree between Brazil and the American South. Julius Rubin, "The Limits of Agricultural Progress in the Nineteenth-Century South," *Agricultural History* 49 (April 1975): 362–72, has argued that not slavery but climate inhibited the spread of many of these practices in the South.

18. Gates, *Farmer's Age*, 138, 143–4; Fogel and Engerman, *Time on the Cross*,

198; Scarborough, *Overseer*, 136; *O Auxiliador da Industria Nacional* (Rio de Janeiro, 1835–88); Rio de Janeiro, Instituto Fluminense de Agricultura, *Revista Agricola* (1869–91); Francisco Peixoto de Lacerda Werneck, *Memoria sobre a fundação e costeio de uma fazenda na provincia do Rio de Janeiro* (Rio de Janeiro: Laemmert, 1847); Stein, *Vassouras*, 121–4; John D. Wirth, *Minas Gerais in the Brazilian Federation, 1889–1937* (Stanford: Stanford University Press, 1977), 192–201.

19. On the hesitations see Genovese, *Political Economy of Slavery*, 221–39. My own view of "development" would focus more on human needs and a just social order; but that was not the general nineteenth-century attitude either in Brazil or in the South.

20. Starobin, *Industrial Slavery*, 13–25; Victor Clark, "Manufactures During the Antebellum and War Periods," in *The South in the Building of the Nation*, Vol. 5 of *Economic History*, ed. James C. Ballagh, (Richmond: Southern Historical Publications Society, 1909), 313–35, esp. 331; Robert Royal Russel, *Economic Aspects of Southern Sectionalism, 1840–1861*, University of Illinois Studies in the Social Sciences, vol. 9, nos. 1–2 (Urbana: University of Illinois, 1924), 225–30; Fred Bateman and Thomas Weiss, "Manufacturing in the Antebellum South," in *Research in Economic History: An Annual Compilation of Research*, ed. Paul Uselding (Greenwich, CT: JAI Press, 1976), I: 3; idem, *A Deplorable Scarcity: The Failure of Industrialization in the Slave Economy* (Chapel Hill: University of North Carolina Press, 1981); Charles B. Dew, *Ironmaker to the Confederacy* (New Haven: Yale University Press, 1966); J. F. Normano, *Brazil, a Study of Economic Types* (Chapel Hill: University of North Carolina Press, 1935), 97–103; Stanley J. Stein, *The Brazilian Cotton Manufacture: Textile Enterprise in an Underdeveloped Area, 1850–1950* (Cambridge: Harvard University Press, 1957), 1–77; Warren Dean, *The Industrialization of São Paulo, 1880–1945*, Latin American Monographs, no. 17 (Austin: University of Texas Press for the Institute of Latin American Studies, 1969), 3–80; Graham, *Britain*, 125–59. William N. Parker, in his article "Slavery and Southern Economic Development: An Hypothesis and Some Evidence," *Agricultural History* 44 (January 1970): 115–26, makes the point that it is important to distinguish among small, medium, and large-scale industries and that medium-size factories may be most conducive to economic development. He then presents an exhaustive list of manufacturing enterprises in the South. Were the sources available in Brazil, I am sure no list equivalent in size could be compiled.

21. Ernest M. Lander, *The Textile Industry in Antebellum South Carolina* (Baton Rouge: Louisiana State University Press, 1969), 79; U.S. Census Office, *Manufactures of the United States in 1860* (Washington, D.C.: U.S. Government Printing Office, 1865), 14, 82, 203, 299, 437, 559, 578, 638; Stein, *Brazilian Cotton Manufacture*, 21, 191.

22. Cf. Kathleen Bruce, *Virginia Iron Manufacture in the Slave Era* (1940; rpt. New York: Augustus M. Kelley, 1968), esp. p. 452, map showing location of iron furnaces, with William S. Callaghan, "Obstacles to Industrialization: The Iron and Steel Industry in Brazil during the Old Republic" (Ph.D. diss., University of Texas at Austin, 1981), 44–8.

23. Costa, *De senzala à colônia*, 154–220; Fernando Henrique Cardoso, *Capitalismo e escravidão no Brasil meridional. O negro na sociedade escravocrata do Rio Grande do Sul*, Corpo e Alma do Brasil, no. 8 (São Paulo: Difusão Européia do Livro, 1962), 133–62, 186–204; Florestan Fernandes, *A Revolução burguesa no Brasil: ensaio de interpretação sociológica* (Rio de Janeiro: Zahar, 1975), 86–146;

Cano, *Raízes da concentração*, 31–42. See references to these same themes among United States historians cited by Stanley L. Engerman, "Marxist Economic Studies of the Slave South," *Marxist Perspectives* 1: 1 (Spring, 1970): 150, 154–6, 163 n. 266.
24. Starobin, *Industrial Slavery*, esp. 11, 15, 126, 168–73, 182–6. Unfortunately, Starobin did not make the essential distinction on size of factories, but see p. 50 on their rural locations and cf. p. 59; on the profitability of using slaves in industry, see pp. 146ff., although some of his calculations and argument may be subject to question, as on pp. 156 and 186. Other sources on the use of slaves in industries include A.G. Smith, *Economic Readjustment*, 126–7; Bruce, *Virginia Iron Manufacture*, 231–58; Charles B. Dew, "Disciplining Slave Ironworkers in the Antebellum South: Coercion, Conciliation, and Accommodation," *American Historical Review* 79 (April 1974): 393–418; Ernest M. Lander, *The Textile Industry in Antebellum South Carolina* (Baton Rouge: Louisiana State University Press, 1969), 43–4, 49, 88–93; Tom E. Terrill, "Eager Hands: Labor for Southern Textiles, 1850–1860," *Journal of Economic History* 36 (March 1976): 84–99, esp. 86; and Gavin Wright, "Cheap Labor and Southern Textiles before 1880," *Journal of Economic History* 39 (September 1979): 655–80. On one point evidence from the South supports the views advanced for Brazil that sabotage and other forms of resistance were a distinct possibility: See Starobin, *Industrial Slavery*, 42, 77–91, and Lander, *Textile Industry*, 35.
25. Starobin, *Industrial Slavery*, 12, 128ff.; Dew, "Disciplining Slave Ironworkers." The comparative costs of renting as against buying a slave are calculated for the United States by Robert Evans, Jr., "The Economics of American Negro Slavery, 1830–1860," in Universities-National Bureau Committee for Economic Research, *Aspects of Labor Economics* (Princeton: Princeton University Press, 1962), 185–243, and for Brazil by Pedro Carvalho de Mello, "The Economics of Labor in Brazilian Coffee Plantations, 1850–1888," University of Chicago, Department of Economics, Report no. 7475-8 (Chicago: 1974); but see Robert Wayne Slenes, "The Demography and Economics of Brazilian Slavery, 1850–1888" (Ph.D. diss., Stanford University, 1975), 249–54. On the use of slaves in industry in Brazil, see Stein, *Brazilian Cotton Manufacture*, 51; and on hiring out slaves in Brazil for domestic duties, see Sandra Lauderdale Graham, *House and Street: The Domestic World of Servants and Masters in Nineteenth-Century Rio de Janeiro*, Cambridge Latin American Studies no. 68 (Cambridge: Cambridge University Press, 1988), 19–21.
26. Gilberto Freyre, *Sobrados e mucambos* 3rd ed., 2 vols. (Rio de Janeiro: José Olympio, 1961), 500; Frank Tannenbaum, *Slave and Citizen, the Negro in the Americas* (New York: Knopf, 1947), 58–61; Mary C. Karasch, *Slave Life in Rio de Janeiro, 1808–1850* (Princeton: Princeton University Press, 1987), 128, 185–214, *passim*; Richard C. Wade, *Slavery in the Cities: The South, 1820–1860* (New York: Oxford University Press, 1964), 38–54; Starobin, *Industrial Slavery*, 135–7; Peter H. Wood, *Black Majority: Negroes in Colonial South Carolina from 1670 through the Stono Rebellion* (New York: Norton, 1975), 207–11, 214–5, 229. I have found no evidence that skilled whites in Brazil objected to the self-hire system, as they did in the United States South: Clement Eaton, *The Growth of Southern Civilization, 1790–1860* (New York: Harper, 1961), 167; Starobin, *Industrial Slavery*, 128, and 128n.
27. Some historians have even seen in provision grounds elements of a peasant economy: Ciro Flamarion S. Cardoso, "The Peasant Breach in the Slave System: New Developments in Brazil," *Luso-Brazilian Review* 25: 1 (Summer, 1988): 49–57.

28. Laerne, *Brazil and Java*, 301–302.

29. North, *Economic Growth*, 101–21; but cf. criticisms of his model in Morton Rothstein, "The Cotton Frontier of the Antebellum United States: a Methodological Battleground," *Agricultural History* 44: 1 (January 1970): 153–4.

30. Wade, *Slavery in the Cities*, 243–81; Claudia Goldin, *Urban Slavery in the American South, 1820–1860; A Quantitative History* (Chicago: University of Chicago Press, 1976), challenges Wade, but Barbara Fields, *Slavery and Freedom on the Middle Ground: Maryland During the Nineteenth Century* (New Haven: Yale University Press, 1985), 49–54 comes to his defense. Also see Fogel and Engerman, *Time on the Cross*, 102. Fields conflates urban society with industrial economy; the city of Salvador was for centuries a thriving urban center with a very large slave population that worked alongside a free one.

31. Genovese, *Political Economy of Slavery*, 221–35; Richard Graham, "Causes for the Abolition of Negro Slavery in Brazil: An Interpretive Essay," *Hispanic American Historical Review* 46 (May 1966): 123–7. Whether immigrants in Brazil joined abolitionist ranks in large numbers and whether they did so for fear of competition from slave labor is not yet known, but seems doubtful: Rebecca Baird Bergstresser, "The Movement for the Abolition of Slavery in Rio de Janeiro, Brazil, 1880–1889" (Ph.D. diss., Stanford University, 1973). Black Brazilian freedmen complained about immigrants competing with them for jobs rather than vice-versa: Karasch, *Slave Life* 321.

32. See censuses cited in note 1. It is true that in the coffee counties of Rio de Janeiro the proportion of slaves among agricultural workers reached 46% in 1872. The reasons for the larger number of slaves in the U.S. South, despite much smaller importation of Africans, has been addressed by many authors. See especially Carl Degler, *Neither Black nor White: Slavery and Race Relations in Brazil and the United States* (New York: Macmillan, 1971).

33. Barrington Moore, Jr., *Social Origins of Dictatorship and Democracy: Lord and Peasant in the Making of the Modern World* (Boston: Beacon, 1966), 111–55.

34. Nelson Werneck Sodré, *História da burguesia brasileira*, Retratos do Brasil, no. 22 (Rio de Janeiro: Civilização Brasileira, 1965), 77–88, 142–57; Fernandes, *Revolução burguesa*, 179–97. Ciro F. S. Cardoso makes the point that international dependence and slavery together explain underdevelopment, and criticizes those, especially North American historians, who stress only one half of the formula: "Sobre os modos de produção coloniais da America," in *America colonial*, ed. Théo Santiago, (Rio de Janeiro: Pallas, 1975), 110–1.

35. Taylor, *Transportation Revolution*, 451; Brazil, Conselho Nacional de Estatística, Instituto Brasileiro de Geografia e Estatística, *Anuario estatístico do Brasil*, Ano V: *1939/1940* (Rio de Janeiro: Imp. Nacional, 1941), 1379.

36. Stuart W. Bruchey, *Cotton and the Growth of the American Economy, 1700–1860: Sources and Readings* (New York: Harcourt, Brace, 1967), Table 3-A. The country as a whole did not focus as much on the production of exports as did Brazil, but the South did.

37. Rothstein, "Cotton Frontier," 153, 163–4; Woodman, *King Cotton*, 150n.; Ralph W. Hidy, *The House of Baring in American Trade and Finance: English Merchant Bankers at Work, 1763–1861*, Harvard Studies in Business History, no. 14 (Cambridge: Harvard University Press, 1949), 74–5, 105–7, 173–6, 184–9, 254–9, 298–301, 359–64; A. G. Smith, *Economic Readjustment*, 162.

38. Ephraim Douglas Adams, *Great Britain and the American Civil War*, 2 vols. (London: Longmans, Green, 1925); Brian Jenkins, *Britain and the War for the Union* (Montreal: McGill-Queen's University Press, 1974), I, esp. 281–305: "Bibliographical Essay."

39. Stein, *Vassouras*, 101–2; Graham, *Britain*, 51–72, 99–105; Julian S. Duncan, *Public and Private Operation of Railways in Brazil*, Studies in History, Economics, and Public Law, no. 367 (New York: Columbia University Press, 1932); Black, *Railroads*, 40, 42, 44–5; Stover, *Railroads of the South*, 7–8; A. G. Smith, *Economic Readjustment*, 167–70, 176–90; Merl E. Reed, "Government Investment and Economic Growth: Louisiana's Ante-Bellum Railroads," *Journal of Southern History* 28 (May 1962): 183–201; Milton S. Heath, "Public Railroad Construction and the Development of Private Enterprise in the South before 1861," *Journal of Economic History* 10 (supplement 1950): 40–53; Heath, *Constructive Liberalism*, 254–92, esp. 287–8; Carter Goodrich, *Government Promotion of American Canals and Railroads, 1800–1890* (New York: Columbia University Press, 1959), 87–120, 152–62, 270; Cotterill, "Southern Railroads," 404–5.

40. Bruchey, *Cotton*, Table 3–K; Brazil, *Anuário estatístico*, pp. 1374–75. Nathaniel H. Leff, in his article "Economic Development and Regional Inequality: Origins of the Brazilian Case," *Quarterly Journal of Economics* 86 (May 1972): 258–9, in effect argues that Brazil's lagging northeast could have brought the result of its export earnings closer home had the area not been part of the Brazilian polity; could the same argument not be made for the American South? Perhaps the secessionists were right, cf. Thomas F. Huertas, "Damnifying Growth in the Antebellum South," *Journal of Economic History* 39 (March 1979): 98–100.

41. The flow of capital between nations is extremely difficult to calculate and it is even harder (perhaps impossible) to specify the exact region that received the funds. Certainly a much larger amount of British investment went to the United States as a whole than to Brazil, but we cannot readily determine how much of that share went to the South. The difficulties of investigating both the balance of payments and transfers of capital for the nineteenth century are suggested by Albert H. Imlah, "British Balance of Payments and Export of Capital, 1816–1913," *Economic History Review* 2nd ser., 5: 2 (1952): 208–39; also see S.E. Saul, *Studies in British Overseas Trade, 1870–1914* (Liverpool: Liverpool University Press, 1960), esp. 67; Leland H. Jenks, *The Migration of British Capital to 1875* (1927; rpt. New York: Barnes & Noble, 1973); Bruchey, *Roots of American Economic Growth*, 133; J. Fred Rippy, *British Investments in Latin America, 1822–1949: A Case Study in the Operations of Private Enterprise in Retarded Regions* (Minneapolis: University of Minnesota Press, 1959), 150–8.

42. Woodman, *King Cotton*, 162 and passim; Joseph E. Sweigart, *Coffee Factorage and the Emergence of a Brazilian Capital Market, 1850–1888* (New York: Garland, 1987); David Joslin, *A Century of Banking in Latin America; To Commemorate the Centenary in 1962 of the Bank of London and South America, Limited* (London: Oxford University Press, 1963), 163; Charles Jones, "Commercial Banks and Mortgage Companies," in *Business Imperialism, 1840–1930: An Inquiry Based on British Experience in Latin American*, ed. D.C.M. Platt, (Oxford: Clarendon, 1977), 17–52.

43. Pinto de Aguiar, *Bancos no Brasil colonial: tentativas de organização bancária em Portugal e no Brasil até 1808*, Coleção de Estudos Brasileiros Série Marajoara, no. 31 (Salvador: Progresso, 1960); Barbara Levy, *História dos bancos commerciais no Brasil* (Rio de Janeiro: IBMEC, 1972); Anyda Marchant, "A New Portrait of Mauá, the Banker: A Man of Business in Nineteenth-Century Brazil," *Hispanic American Historical Review* 30 (November 1950): 411–31; idem, "A sorte não o permitiu," *Revista do Instituto Histórico e Geográfico Brasileiro* 192 (1946): 46–59; Jones, "Commercial Banks," 31–32; Sweigart, *Coffee Factorage*; A. G. Smith, *Economic Readjustment*, 193–217; George D. Green, *Finance and Economic Development in the Old South: Louisiana Banking, 1804–1861* (Stanford:

Stanford University Press, 1972), 202; J. van Fenstermaker, *The Development of American Commercial Banking, 1782–1837*, Printed Series, no. 5 (Kent, Ohio: Kent State University Bureau of Economic and Business Research, 1965), 77–95; Earl Sylvester Sparks, *History and Theory of Agricultural Credit in the United States* (New York: Crowell, 1932), 83–111; Bruchey, *Roots of American Economic Growth*, 148; Heath, *Constructive Liberalism*, 159–230.

44. The prevailing interest rates provide another test for the relative availability of capital. Unfortunately, no one has compiled regular series on interest rates for the South or for Brazil. But rates in the South appear, on the whole, to have been substantially lower, and loans there more easily raised, than in Brazil. Alfred Smith reports rates in the South beween 4 and 7 percent, but Harold Woodman speaks of a range from 5 to 18 percent, settling finally on 8 percent as the most prevalent. Historians similarly disagree about Brazil, but tend toward higher figures. A contemporary observer reported 10 to 12 percent "at least" as the cost of borrowing in the coffee districts of São Paulo in the early 1880s. Whereas Robert Greenhill refers to rates in the coffee zones as being "up to 24 percent," Pedro Carvalho de Mello estimates that the rate ranged from 8 to 12 percent: A. G. Smith, *Economic Readjustment*, 76, 105, 107, 108; Woodman, *King Cotton*, 52–3; Laerne, *Brazil and Java*, 225; Robert Greenhill, "Brazilian Coffee Trade," in *Business Imperialism, 1840–1930: An Inquiry Based on British Experience in Latin America*, ed. D. C. M. Platt (Oxford: Clarendon, 1977), 205; Pedro Carvalho de Mello, "The Economics of Labor in Brazilian Coffee Plantations, 1850–1888" (Ph.D. diss., University of Chicago, 1977), 147. Hélio Oliveira Portocarrero de Castro, however, in his article on "Viabilidade econômica da escravidão no Brasil: 1880–1888," *Revista Brasileira de Economia* 27 (January-March 1973): 49, puts the range at 7 to 10 percent, going on to acknowledge that it was "common" to find coffee planters borrowing at 12 percent in the 1880s. Finally, Nathaniel H. Leff, "Long-term Viability of Slavery in a Backward, Closed Economy," *Journal of Interdisciplinary History* 5 (Summer 1974): 106, compares rates of 6 to 8 percent for American cotton planters with 12 to 18 percent for Brazilian coffee growers. See also Sidney Homer, *A History of Interest Rates*, 2nd ed. (New Brunswick, N.J.: Rutgers University Press, 1977).

45. William Otto Henderson, *The Lancanshire Cotton Famine, 1861–1865*, Economic History Series, no. 9 (Manchester, England: Manchester University Press, 1934).

46. E.g., Estate inventory, Deceased: Baronesa de Vassouras, 31 Jan. 1881 Primeiro Officio de Vassouras, Inventories, 1880 [sic], ff. 32–34v.

47. The relationship between income distribution, market size, and industrial growth is admittedly still subject to much dispute; see, for instance, Stanley L. Engerman, "Discussion," in "Slavery as an Obstacle to Economic Growth in the United States: A Panel Discussion," eds. Alfred H. Conrad et al., *Journal of Economic History* 27 (December 1967): 543; Bateman and Weiss, "Manufacturing in the Antebellum South," I, 1–44.

48. Frank L. Owsley, *Plain Folk of the Old South* (Baton Rouge: Louisiana State University Press, 1949), 7, 16, 200–1; also see Herbert Weaver (one of Owsley's many students), *Mississippi Farmers, 1850–1860* (Nashville: Vanderbilt University Press, 1945).

49. Owsley, *Plain Folk*, 17; according to data on pp. 174 and 200, 0.88 percent of slaveholders in Lowndes County, Mississippi, and 0.24 percent of those in the Georgia black belt owned more than 5,000 acres each in 1850.

50. Fabian Linden, "Economic Democracy in the Slave South: An Appraisal of

Some Recent Views," *Journal of Negro History* 31 (1946): 163; he showed (p. 159) that, in the Delta region of Mississippi, estates larger than 2,000 acres held by 8.8 percent of the landholders accounted for 34.2 percent of the land. Linden agreed however, that the two-class stereotype is invalid, p. 187.

51. A. G. Smith, *Economic Readjustment*, 80; Randolph B. Campbell, "Planters and Plain Folk: Harrison County, Texas, as a Test Case, 1850–1860," *Journal of Southern History* 40 (August 1974): 369–98; Gavin Wright, *The Political Economy of the Cotton South: Household, Markets, and Wealth in the Nineteenth Century* (New York: Norton, 1978), 24–42; idem, "'Economic Democracy' and the Concentration of Agricultural Wealth in the Cotton South, 1850–1860," *Agricultural History* 44 (January 1970): 63–93. Lee Soltow, *Men and Wealth in the United States, 1850–1870* (New Haven: Yale University Press, 1975), 136, has concluded that 80 percent of free men in the South in 1860 owned no slaves; but Otto H. Olsen, "Historians and the Extent of Slave Ownership in the Southern United States," *Civil War History* 18 (June 1972): 111, focusing on white families in the cotton South, shows that this number declines to 52 percent in South Carolina and Mississippi.

52. Franco has argued that Brazilian planters tended to engross the better land as it increased in value during the spread of coffee cultivation, but Warren Dean has shown that owners of small tracts on marginal soils were useful to the planters as suppliers of foodstuffs and that they encouraged small owners to stay: Maria Sylvia de Carvalho Franco, *Homens livres na ordem escravocrata* (São Paulo: Instituto de Estudos Brasileiros, 1969), 94–5; Warren Dean, *Rio Claro: A Brazilian Plantation System, 1820–1929* (Stanford: Stanford University Press, 1976), 19. Also see Stein, *Vassouras*, 47–8; Alcir Lenharo, *As Tropas da moderação (o abastecimento da Corte na formação política do Brasil, 1808–1842)*, Coleção Ensaio e Memoria, no. 21 (São Paulo: Símbolo, 1979). In contrast, Robert E. Gallman, "Self-Sufficiency in the Cotton Economy of the Antebellum South," *Agricultural History* 44 (January 1970): 5–23, shows that in the United States large planters sold foodstuffs to small farmers rather than vice versa; see also Moore, *Agriculture in Mississippi*, 179, 182. If for coffee as for cotton, harvesting took more workers than any other operation on the plantation, then there would have been labor available to grow food during the remainder of the year in Brazil as was true in the South: Harold D. Woodman, "New Perspectives on Southern Economic Development: A Comment," *Agricultural History* 49, 2 (April 1975): 379; Gorender, *Escravismo colonial*, 241.

53. Some studies on the history of land tenure in Brazil include José da Costa Porto, *Estudos sobre o sistema sesmarial* (Recife: Imp. Universitária, 1965); Rui Cirne Lima, *Pequena história territorial do Brasil: Sesmarias e terras devolutas*, 2nd ed. (Pôrto Alegre: Livraria Sulina, 1954); idem, *Terras devolutas* (Porto Alegre: Globo, 1936); Alberto Passos Guimarães, *Quatro séculos de latifundio* (Rio de Janeiro: Paz e Terra, 1968); Felisbello Freire, *Historia territorial do Brasil* (Rio de Janeiro: Typ. "Jornal do Commercio," 1906); Louis Couty, *Pequena propriedade e immigração européia* (Rio de Janeiro: Imprensa Nacional, 1887). A comparison between the North American homestead law and the Brazilian land law of 1850 is made by Emília Viotti da Costa, *The Brazilian Empire: Myths and Realities* (Chicago: University of Chicago Press, 1985), 78–93.

54. Alice P. Cannabrava, "A repartição da terra na Capitania de São Paulo, 1818," *Estudos Econômicos*, 2 (December 1972), 113; Wright, *Political Economy*, 23; Wright also uses (p. 26) the value of real estate and ends up with a Gini Index number of 0.73. There is much debate on this issue among United States historians: Soltow, *Men and Wealth*, 130, calculated a Gini Index among all landowners in the

182 Notes to Pages 113–115

entire United States in 1860 at 0.62 and showed that if all farmers were included—not just landowners—the figure would rise to 0.78. For the South, he presented data only for landowners (p. 183) and—working with value, not acreage—pushed the figure up to Brazilian levels at 0.88. Meanwhile, rural townships in the United States North yield Gini Index figures hovering around 0.50: Gloria L. Main, "Inequality in Early America: The Evidence from Probate Records of Massachusetts and Maryland," *Journal of Interdisciplinary History*, 7 (Spring 1977): 560.

55. On landownership in two parishes of the county of Vassouras see Stein, *Vassouras*, p. 225; on population see Brazil, Directoria Geral de Estatística, *Synopse do recenseamento de 31 de dezembro de 1890* (Rio de Janeiro: Officina da Estatística, 1898), 115 and idem, *Idades da população recenseada em 31 de dezembro de 1890* (Rio de Janeiro: Officina da Estatística, 1901), 353–7. I computed the Gini index by using the method indicated in Charles M. Dollar and Richard J. Jensen, *Historian's Guide to Statistics: Quantitative Analysis and Historical Research* (New York: Holt, Rinehart, 1971), 122–4.

56. On Brazil see Guimarães, *Quatro séculos*, 39–55. Subsequently, these *sesmarias* were broken up by sale and inheritance to a degree not usually considered by Brazilian historians: Cf. Fernandes, *Revolução burguesa*, 16–26, with Rae J. D. Flory, "Bahian Society in the Mid-Colonial Period: The Sugar Planters, Tobacco Growers, Merchants, and Artisans of Salvador, 1680–1725" (Ph.D. diss., University of Texas, 1978), 24. Still they remained very large. For the situation in the U.S., see Gray, *History of Agriculture*, 325, 381–403; Samuel G. McLendon, *History of the Public Domain of Georgia* (Atlanta: Foote and Davies, 1924); Robert S. Cotterhill, "The National Land System in the South," *Mississippi Valley Historical Review* 16 (March 1930): 495–506; Richard R. Beeman, "Labor Forces and Race Relations: A Comparative View of Colonization of Brazil and Virginia," *Political Science Quarterly* 86 (December 1971): 633. All this is not to deny that in Brazil as in the South there were many more social strata than the very rich and the very poor.

57. Warren Dean, "Latifundia and Land Policy in Nineteenth-Century Brazil," *Hispanic American Historical Review* 51 (November 1971): 606–25.

58. Soltow, *Men and Wealth*, 136, concluded that the Gini Index figure for the distribution of slaves among slaveowners in the South in 1860 was 0.62; but if all free men were considered the figure would be 0.93. Furthermore, if slaves were included as potential property holders, the number would rise still further. See Lee Soltow, "Comment," in *Six Papers on the Size Distribution of Wealth and Income*, ed. Lee Soltow (New York: Columbia University Press for the National Bureau of Economic Research, 1969), 26. Also see Wright, *Political Economy*, 27 where the Gini Index for slaveholding among slaveowners is calculated at 0.79, rising in some places to 0.85. For the placer mining region of Brazil, long after its decline, Gorender shows a rather even distribution of slaves: *Escravismo colonial*, 435. Stuart Schwartz suggests this was the trend in all of Brazil: *Sugar Plantations in the Formation of Brazilian Society* (Cambridge: Cambridge University Press, 1985), 439–67. Also see, for eighteenth- and early nineteenth-century Brazil, Iraci del Nero da Costa, "Nota sobre a posse de escravos nos engenhos e engenhocas fluminenses (1778)," *Revista do Instituto de Estudos Brasileiros* 28 (1988), 111–3, and Francisco Vidal Luna, "Estrutura de posse de escravos e atividades produtivas em Jacareí (1777 a 1829)," *Revista do Instituto de Estudos Brasileiros* 28 (1988), 23–35.

59. In the United States land taxes antedate even independence. Gray, *History of Agriculture*, 618.

60. On the failure of this group to provide an adequate market for industrial goods, see Genovese, "The Significance of the Slave Plantation," 422–37; but see the qualifying remarks on this matter made by Parker, "Slavery and Southern Economic Development," 177. Also see Bruchey, *Roots of American Economic Growth*, 162–72, esp. 171.

61. Cf. Eaton, *Growth of Southern Civilization*, 169–70, with Monteiro Lobato, *Urupês*, 2nd ed. (São Paulo: Brasiliense, 1947), 235–6. Historians of Brazil need to differentiate among the *caipiras* more carefully, as Eaton does, and as Emílio Willems begins to do in "Social Differentiation in Colonial Brazil," *Comparative Studies in Society and History* 12, 1 (January 1970): 31–49.

62. Eni de Mesquita, "O papel do agregado na região de Itú—1780 a 1830," *Coleção Museu Paulista* 6 (1977): 13–121; Laerne, *Brazil and Java*, 309n.; James W. Wells, *Exploring and Travelling Three Thousand Miles Through Brazil from Rio de Janeiro to Maranhão* (London: S. Low, Marston, Searle & Rivington 1886), 168; Stein, *Vassouras*, 32n, 57n, 58; Franco, *Homens livres*, 94–107.

63. Thomas H. Holloway, *Immigrants on the Land: Coffee and Society in São Paulo, 1886–1934* (Chapel Hill: University of North Carolina Press, 1980); idem, "The Coffee Colono of São Paulo: Migration and Mobility, 1880–1930," *Land and Labour in Latin America*, eds. Kenneth Duncan and Ian Rutledge (Cambridge: Cambridge University Press, 1977), 301–32; idem, "Creating the Reserve Army? The Immigration Program of São Paulo, 1886–1930," *International Migration Review* 12 (Summer 1978): 187–209; Michael M. Hall, "The Origins of Mass Immigration in Brazil, 1871–1914" (Ph.D. diss., Columbia University, 1969); Alfredo Ellis Júnior, *Populações paulistas*, Biblioteca Pedagógica Brasileira, ser. 5, no. 27 (São Paulo: Editôra Nacional, 1934), 57–79; Nathaniel H. Leff, "Tropical Trade and Development in the Nineteenth Century: the Brazilian Experience," *Journal of Political Economy* (May-June 1973): 688, 690–1.

64. Brazil, Directoria Geral de Estatistica, *Recenseamento . . . 1872*; Elizabeth Fox-Genovese, *Within the Plantation Household: Black and White Women of the Old South* (Chapel Hill: University of North Carolina Press, 1988), 78.

65. Cf., e.g., Olmstead, *Cotton Kingdom*, 212–21, with Richard F. Burton, *Explorations of the Highlands of the Brazil, with a Full Account of the Gold and Diamond Mines; Also, Canoeing down 1500 miles of the Great River São Francisco from Sabará to the Sea*, 2 vols. (London: Tinsley, 1869), I, 34–115. Also see Woodman, *King Cotton*, 189–91; Goldin, *Urban Slavery*, 11–27; Thomas W. Merrick and Douglas H. Graham, *Population and Economic Development in Brazil, 1800 to the Present* (Baltimore: The Johns Hopkins University Press, 1979), 186–89. The fact that the Brazilian census did not distinguish town and country derives, of course, not just from the nature of political units, but from the very concept of the urbs, another subject for comparative study; see Richard W. Morse, "Prolegomenon to Latin American Urban History," *Hispanic American Historical Review* 52 (August 1972): 359–94.

66. Joaquim Nabuco, *Abolitionism: The Brazilian Antislavery Struggle*, trans. and ed. Robert Conrad (Urbana: University of Illinois Press, 1977), 125. A similar description appears in Olmstead, *Cotton Kingdom*, 528–9.

67. Fletcher M. Green, "Democracy in the Old South," *Journal of Southern History* 12 (February 1946): 14–5; Genovese, *Political Economy of Slavery*, 28–31; the property held by southern legislators has been studied by Ralph A. Wooster, *The People in Power: Courthouse and Statehouse in the Lower South, 1850–1860* (Knoxville: University of Tennessee Press, 1969); but Eugene D. Genovese has retorted that studies of the social place of politicians reveal "what every fool always

184   Notes to Pages 118–119

knew," namely, that politicians were usually lawyers, "Yeoman Farmers in the
Slaveholders' Democracy," *Agricultural History* 49 (April 1975): 339. Also see
Douglas F. Dowd, "Discussion," in "Slavery as an Obstacle," ed. Conrad et al., 537;
and Roger W. Shugg, *Origins of Class Struggle in Louisiana: A Social History of
White Farmers and Laborers during Slavery and After, 1840–1875* (1939; rpt.,
Baton Rouge: Louisiana State University Press, 1972), 121–56. James Oakes, *The
Ruling Race: a History of American Slaveholders* (New York: Vintage, 1982) has
challenged the view that large planters exercised a cultural hegemony over the rest
of society.
    68. Michael P. Johnson, *Toward a Patriarchal Republic: The Secession of Georgia*
(Baton Rouge: Louisiana State University Press, 1977). Also see Eaton, *Growth of
Southern Civilization*, 173, 175–6.
    69. José Honório Rodrigues, *Conciliação e reforma no Brasil, Um desafio histó-
rico-político*, Retratos do Brasil, no. 32 (Rio de Janeiro: Civilização Brasileira,
1965), 135–62. On measuring the political power of landowners, see Richard
Graham, "Political Power and Landownership in Nineteenth-Century Latin America," in *New Approaches to Latin American History*, eds. Richard Graham and
Peter H. Smith (Austin: University of Texas Press, 1974), 112–36. Note, however,
that Raymundo Faoro, *Os donos do poder; formação do patronato político
brasileiro*, 2nd ed. (Porto Alegre and São Paulo: Globo and Editôra da Universidade de São Paulo, 1975), has argued that the Brazilian state was totally independent of the influence of landowners and was even antagonistic to them. Roderick J.
Barman maintains that even poor whites had considerable power: "The Brazilian
Peasantry Reexamined: The Implications of the Quebra-Quilos Revolt,
1874–1875," *Hispanic American Historical Review* 57 (August 1977): 401–24; but
Linda Lewin presents strong evidence to the contrary in "Some Historical Implications of Kinship Organization for Family-based Politics in the Brazilian Northeast,"
Comparative Studies in Society and History 21, 2 (April 1979): 266–7, 277–8,
289–90, and also in her "The Oligarchical Limitations of Social Banditry in Brazil:
The Case of the 'Good' Thief Antonio Silvino," *Past and Present* 82 (February 1979):
46.
    70. Congresso Agricola, *Congresso Agricola: Coleção de Documentos* (Rio de
Janeiro, 1878), 17.
    71. Stein, *Vassouras*, 16–20, 120, 159; Sweigart, *Coffee Factorage*, 86.
    72. Acta da Eleição de Eleitores, Freguezia de N.S. da Conceição do Paty do
Alferes, 9 Sept. 1842, AN, SAP, Cód. 112, Vol. 4, Doc. 110. Lacerda Werneck
became state assemblyman the next year: Actas da Camara de Nictheroy para a
apuração de 36 deputados á Assembleia Provincial, 22 Dec. 1843, ibid.
    73. *Almanak [Laemmert] administrativo, mercantil e industrial do Rio de Janeiro
e indicador. . . . Obra estatistica e de consulta* (Rio de Janeiro: E. H. Laemmert,
1855), Supplemento, 135–41. For an earlier example of these families' monopoly of
official positions, see Thomas Flory, *Judge and Jury in Imperial Brazil, 1808–1871:
Social Control and Political Stability in the New State*, Latin American Monographs no. 53 (Austin: University of Texas Press, 1981), 95.
    74. E.g., in the sugar-rich county of Escada in Pernambuco, the planter and
seigneur Henrique Marques Lins had a son-in-law as police commissioner and a
brother-in-law as deputy police commissioner. As commandant of a militia bat-
talion, Lins himself issued orders through fifteen company commanders, eight of
whom possessed, among them, sixteen sugarmills. The county council there
included three members who together owned thirteen plantations. Out of seven-
teen justices of the peace in the various parishes, twelve owned nineteen sugar-

mills: Peter L. Eisenberg, *The Sugar Industry in Pernambuco: Modernization without Change, 1840–1910* (Berkeley: University of California Press, 1974), 131–4. For similar control by sugar families in Bahia, see Flory, *Judge*, 78–80.

75. José Murilo de Carvalho, *A construção da ordem: A elite política imperial* (Rio de Janeiro: Campus, 1980), 87.

76. Robert Conrad, *The Destruction of Brazilian Slavery, 1850–1888* (Berkeley: University of California Press, 1972); Costa, *Da senzala à colônia*, 428–55; Costa, *Brazilian Empire*, 202–03; Dean, *Rio Claro*, 124–155; Richard Graham, "Landowners and the Overthrow of the Empire," *Luso-Brazilian Review* 7:2 (Dec. 1970): 44–56.

77. Here again one thinks of Barrington Moore, *Social Origins of Dictatorship and Democracy.* To enforce slavery slaveowners must have some control of the state and I do not wish to ignore their power in Washington; but their power in Rio de Janeiro was uncontested.

78. The Brazilian figures are derived from the 1872 census and refer to the percentage of total literates among the total free over six years of age, Brazil, Directoria Geral de Estatistica, *Recenseamento . . . 1872* (Rio de Janeiro: Leuzinger, 1873–76); the data on the United States are from Eaton, *Growth of Southern Civilization*, 160. Also see Engerman, "Reconsideration," 353 n., who reports the literacy rate among whites in the South at 84 percent.

79. U.S. Census Office, *Population of the United States in 1860* (Washington, D.C.: U.S. Government Printing Office, 1864); Brazil, *Recenseamento . . . 1872.* Fox-Genovese and Genovese use roughly the same data to contrast southern backwardness with Northern progress, *Fruits of Merchant Capital*, 49.

80. Fernandes, *Revolução burguesa;* Genovese, *Political Economy of Slavery.*

81. Luiz Peixoto de Lacerda Werneck, *Idéias sobre colonização, precedidads de uma sucinta exposição dos princípios que regem a população* (Rio de Janeiro, 1855), 28.

82. The two positions on the South are most clearly expressed in Genovese, *Political Economy of Slavery*, 13–36, and Fogel and Engerman, *Time on the Cross.* Also see Oakes, *Ruling Race;* Carl N. Degler, "Plantation Society: Old and New Perspectives on Hemispheric History," *Plantation Society in the Americas* 1 (February 1979): 13–4. For critiques of Fogel and Engerman's positions on this matter, see Paul A. David and Peter Temin, "Capitalist Masters, Bourgeois Slaves," *Journal of Interdisciplinary History* 5 (Winter 1975): 445–57; idem, "Slavery: The Progressive Institution," *Journal of Economic History* 34 (September 1974): 739–83; and Elizabeth Fox-Genovese, "Poor Richard at Work in the Cotton Fields: A Critique of the Psychological and Ideological Presuppositions of *Time of the Cross*," *Review of Radical Political Economics* 7 (Fall 1975): 67–83. The hegemony of the Northern bourgeoisie in this one nation-state may have forced southern planters, in self-defense, to articulate a more seigneurial position than their behavior belied. On mortgage law and clarity of land titles, see Sweigart, *Coffee Factorage*, 109–217. On the relationship of culture to economic growth, see William H. Nicholls, *Southern Tradition and Regional Progress* (Chapel Hill, University of North Carolina Press, 1960).

83. Oakes, *Ruling Race.*

84. The highlights of the debate are noted succinctly in Thomas C. Barrow, "The American Revolution as a Colonial War for Independence," *William and Mary Quarterly* 25 (July 1968): 452n.-453n.

85. José Honório Rodrigues, *Independência: revolução e contra-revolução*, 5 vols. (Rio de Janeiro: Francisco Alves, 1975); Carlos Guilherme Mota, ed., *1822:*

Dimensões (São Paulo: Perspectiva, 1972); F. W. O. Morton, "The Conservative Revolution of Independence: Economy, Society, and Politics in Bahia, 1790–1840" (Ph.D. diss., University of Oxford, 1974); and Fernandes, *Revolução burguesa*, 31–85. But cf. Faoro, *Os donos do poder*, I, 241–312.

86. Fernandes, *Revolução burguesa*, 15–30; R. J. D. Flory, "Bahian Society," 96–157; Gary B. Nash, *Class and Society in Early America* (Englewood Cliffs, N.J.: Prentice-Hall, 1970), and especially the readings he suggests.

87. Lawrence Stone, *The Causes of the English Revolution, 1529–1642* (New York: Harper and Row, 1972); Eduardo d'Oliveira França, "Portugal na época da Restauração" (Ph.D. diss., Universidade de São Paulo, 1951). The debate on the situation in England can be followed in Lawrence Stone, "Social Mobility in England, 1500–1700," *Past and Present* 33 (April 1966): 16–55; Alan Everitt, "Social Mobility in Early Modern England," *Past and Present* 33 (April 1966): 56–73; W. A. Speck, "Social Status in Late Stuart England," *Past and Present* 34 (July 1966): 127–9; and Lawrence Stone, "Social Mobility," *Past and Present* 35 (December 1966): 156–7.

Notes to BLACK-WHITE RELATIONS SINCE EMANCIPATION: THE SEARCH FOR A COMPARATIVE PERSPECTIVE
by George M. Fredrickson

1. Among the major studies comparing slavery in the United States and Latin America are Frank Tannenbaum, *Slave and Citizen: the Negro in the Americas* (New York: A. A. Knopf, 1946); Marvin Harris, *Patterns of Race in the Americas* (New York: Walker, 1964); Herbert S. Klein, *Slavery in the Americas: A Comparative Study of Cuba and Virginia* (Chicago: University of Chicago Press, 1967); David Brion Davis, *The Problem of Slavery in Western Culture* (Ithaca: Cornell University Press, 1966), 223–288; Carl N. Degler, *Neither Black Nor White: Slavery and Race Relations in Brazil and the United States* (New York: Macmillan, 1971); and *Comparative Perspectives on Slavery in New World Plantation Societies*, ed. Vera Rubin and Arthur Tuden (New York: The Free Press, 1977). For comparisons with slavery in South Africa, see George M. Fredrickson *White Supremacy: A Comparative Study in American and South African History* (New York: Oxford University Press, 1981), 54–135. Comparative perspectives on slavery elsewhere in Africa can be found in *Slavery in Africa: Historical and Antropological Perspectives* ed. Suzanne Miers and Igor Kopytoff (Madison: University of Wisconsin Press, 1977); Frederick Cooper, *Plantation Slavery on the East Coast of Africa* (New Haven: Yale University Press, 1977); and *The End of Slavery in Africa* ed. Suzanne Miers and Richard Roberts (Madison: University of Wisconsin Press, 1988). The latest extension of the scope of comparative slavery studies is Peter Kolchin, *Unfree Labor: American Slavery and Russian Serfdom* (Cambridge, Mass.: The Belknap Press of Harvard University Press, 1987).

2. Although they disagree sharply on whether or not how slaves were treated had a determining effect on post-emancipation race relations, or indeed on the question of what, if any differences there were in the harshness or leniency of servitude in the areas being compared, the books cited in note 1 by Tannenbaum,

Harris, Klein, and Degler all attribute the creation of enduring racial patterns to the kinds of distinctions and modes of stratification that developed in the context of a slave society.

3. See *The Destruction of Slavery*, series 1, vol. 1 of *Freedom: A Documentary History of Emancipation* ed. Ira Berlin, et al. (Cambridge: Cambridge University Press, 1985).

4. William Julius Wilson's work drew my attention to how an increase of black resources during World War II made effective protest more likely in the post-war period. See *Power, Racism, and Privilege: Race Relations in Theoretical and Socio-Historical Perspective* (New York: Macmillan, 1973), 122–7.

5. See Aldon D. Morris, *The Origins of the Civil Rights Movement: Black Communities Organizing for Change* (New York: The Free Press, 1984).

6. My view of current black-white relations has been influenced by two books by William Julius Wilson, *The Declining Significance of Race: Blacks and Changing American Institutions* (Chicago: University of Chicago Press, 1978) and *The Truly Disadvantaged: The Inner City Underclass and Public Policy* (Chicago: University of Chicago Press, 1987). I agree with Wilson that economic class has become relatively more important in recent years as a determinant of black disadvantage but would not go quite so far as he does in deemphasizing the current role of racial attitudes. Racial prejudice continues to exist and may never entirely disappear, but it can be made less harmful and even neutralized to a considerable extent by successful efforts to empower blacks economically and politically.

7. Florestan Fernandes, *The Negro in Brazilian Society* (New York: Columbia University Press, 1971), 210–20; and D.K. Sundiatta, "Late Twentieth Century Patterns of Race Relations in Brazil and the United States," *Phylon* 48 (1987): 71.

8. See Degler, *Neither Black Nor White*.

9. Fernandes, *Negro in Brazilian Society*, 300–01, 416–17, 430.

10. Fredrickson, *White Supremacy*, 239–54.

11. This point is made by Shula Marks in *The Ambiguities of Dependence: Class, Nationalism, and the State in Twentieth-Century Natal* (Baltimore: Johns Hopkins University Press, 1986), 5.

12. Fredrickson, *White Supremacy*, 255–81.

13. Ibid., passim.

14. Recent works on the connection of black America and black South Africa includes the following: J. Mutero Chirenje, *Ethiopianism and Afro-Americans in Southern Africa, 1883–1916* (Baton Rouge: Louisiana State University Press, 1987); James Campbell, "Our Fathers, Our Children: A History of the African Methodist Episcopal Church in the United States and South Africa," unpublished Ph.d. dissertation, Stanford University, 1989; William Manning Marable, "African Nationalist: the Life of John Langalibele Dube," unpublished Ph. D. dissertation, the University of Maryland, 1976; Robert A. Hill and Gregory A. Pirio, "Africa for the Africans: the Garvey Movement in South Africa, 1930–1940," in *The Politics of Race, Class, and Nationalism in Twentieth-Century South Africa*, ed. Shula Marks and Stanley Trapido (New York: Longman, 1987); Tim Couzens, Johannesburg, 1918–1936 in *Industrialisation and Social Change in South Africa: African Class Formation, Culture, and Consciousness, 1870–1930* ed. Shula Marks and Richard Rathbone (London: Longman, 1982); and David B. Coplan, *In Township Tonight! South Africa's Black City Music and Theatre* (New York: Longman, 1985).

15. These generalizations and those that follow are based on my work in progress

for a book-length study comparing black movements and ideologies in the United States and South Africa from the 1880s to the 1980s.

Notes to COMMENTARY
by Michael Craton

1. Frank Tannenbaum, *Slave and Citizen: The Negro in the Americas* (New York: A. A. Knopf, 1946); Carl N. Degler, *Neither Black nor White: Slavery and Race Relations in Brazil and the United States* (New York: Macmillan, 1971); George M. Fredrickson, *White Supremacy: A Comparative Study in American and South African History* (Oxford: Oxford University Press, 1981).

2. "It follows from this persistent concern for what is special or unique in each situation that the comparative historian will be drawn at least as much to differences as to similarities. Similitude must first be established to make comparison meaningful—it is essential to show that one is dealing with the same type or category of phenomena in each case, and that the larger historical contexts are sufficiently alike to make comparison more than forced analogy or obvious contrast. But after a firm common ground is established, it is differences that will compel most of the historian's attention because of the way that they can suggest new problems of interpretation and point to discrete patterns of causation." Fredrickson, *White Supremacy*, xv.

3. There is, of course, a considerable literature on microhistory vs. macrohistory, as on comparative history, but I am not aware of an historiographical essay adequately integrating the two topics, let alone relating them to the interdisciplinary and cliometric concerns of the New Social History. The only relevant comparative microhistory with which I am familiar is the ongoing work by Richard S. Dunn on specific slave plantations in Virginia and Jamaica, from which a book is anticipated in due course; "A Tale of Two Plantations: Slave Life at Mesopotamia in Jamaica and Mount Airy in Virginia, 1799–1828," *William and Mary Quarterly* 34 (1977): 32ff.

4. The daunting diversity of the Caribbean region has ensured both a dearth of bilateral comparative studies of slavery and its aftermath—internal as well as external—and a tendency to loose generalization. One brave recent exception is Rebecca Scott, "Comparing Emancipations: A Review Essay," *Journal of Social History*, Spring 1987, 565–83. To the few direct external comparisons such as Herbert S. Klein, *Slavery in the Americas: A Comparative Study of Cuba and Virginia* (Chicago: University of Chicago Press, 1967). Richard S. Dunn, "Masters, Servants and Slaves in the Colonial Chesapeake and the Caribbean," in *Early Maryland in a Wider World*, ed. David B. Quinn (Detroit: Wayne State University Press, 1982), 242–66; Thomas Holt, "An Empire over the Mind: Emancipation, Race and Ideology in the British West Indies and the American South," in *Region, Race, and Reconstruction: Essays in Honor of C. Vann Woodward*, ed. J. Morgan Kousser and James M. McPherson (New York: Oxford University Press, 1982), and a forthcoming book comparing slavery and race relations in Georgia by Stephen Small of the University of Massachusetts (which conclusively lays to rest Tannenbaum's dichotomy), must be added George Fredrickson's own 1978 essay "White Responses to Emancipation: The American South, Jamaica, and the Cape of Good Hope," in *The Arrogance of Race: Historical Perspectives on Slavery, Racism, and Social Inequality* (Middletown: Wesleyan, 1983), 236–53. More general com-

parative studies include David Brion Davis, *The Problem of Slavery in Western Culture* (Ithaca: Cornell University Press, 1966); David Barry Gaspar, *Bondmen and Rebels: A Study of Master-Slave Relations in Antigua, with Implications for Colonial British America* (Baltimore: Johns Hopkins University Press, 1985); and Jack P. Greene, *Pursuits of Happiness: The Social Development of Early Modern British Colonies and the Formation of American Culture* (Chapel Hill: University of North Carolina Press, 1988). There are at least three excellent comparative readers: Laura Foner and Eugene D. Genovese, *Slavery in the New World: A Reader in Comparative History* (Englewood Cliffs: Prentice-Hall, 1969); David W. Cohen and Jack P. Greene eds., *Neither Slave Nor Free: The Freedmen of African Descent in the Slave Societies of the New World* (Baltimore: Johns Hopkins University Press, 1971); and Richard Price, *Maroon Societies: Rebel Slave Communities in the Americas*, 2nd. ed. (Baltimore: Johns Hopkins University Press, 1979). The very few direct internal comparisons include Sidney W. Mintz, "Labor and Sugar in Puerto Rico and Jamaica," *Comparative Studies in Society and History* 7, 3 (March 1959): 273–83; Harry Hoetink, "Diferencias en Relaciones Raciales entre Curazao y Surinam," *Revista de Ciencias Sociales* 5, 4 (December 1961): 499–514; Gwendolyn Midlo Hall, *Social Control in Slave Plantation Societies: A Comparison of St. Domingue and Cuba* (Baltimore: Johns Hopkins University Press, 1971); Arnold A. Sio, "Race and Colour in the Status of the Free Coloured in the West Indies: Jamaica and Barbados," *Journal of Belizean Affairs* 4 (December 1976); and Bridget Brereton, "Society and Culture in the Caribbean: The British and French West Indies, 1870–1980," in *The Modern Caribbean*, Franklin W. Knight and Colin A. Palmer (Chapel Hill: University of North Carolina Press, 1989), 85–110. Particularly useful among comparative surveys of the Caribbean region are David Lowenthal, *West Indian Societies* (Oxford: Oxford University Press, 1972), and Barry Higman, *Slave Populations of the British Caribbean, 1807–1834* (Baltimore: Johns Hopkins University Press, 1984). Much more, though, is expected from the projected six volume UNESCO general History of the Caribbean, in gestation since the early 1980s.

5. For cliometric concerns relating to Caribbean slavery and race relations, see, for example, Higman, *Slave Populations*, David Watts, *The West Indies: Patterns of Development, Culture and Environmental Change since 1492* (Cambridge: Cambridge University Press, 1987), and David Eltis, *Economic Growth and the Ending of the Transatlantic Slave Trade* (New York: Oxford University Press, 1987).

6. These are, of course, aspects of the "problem" discussed in David Brion Davis's *Problem of Slavery in Western Culture*. See also the same author's *Slavery and Human Progress* (Oxford: Oxford University Press, 1984), especially Chapter 5, 51–82; and Elsa V. Goveia, *The West Indian Slave Laws of the 18th Century* (Barbados: Caribbean University Press, 1970).

7. For the intersection of race and class relations during and after slavery in the Caribbean region and plantation America at large, see, for example, Marvin Harris, *Patterns of Race in the Americas* (New York: Walker, 1964); Arnold A. Sio, "Interpretations of Slavery: The Slave Status in the Americas", *Comparatve Studies in Society and History* 7 (1965): 289–308; Magnus Morner, *Race Mixture in the History of Latin America* (Boston: Little Brown, 1967); Talcott Parsons, "The Problem of Polarization on the Axis of Color," in *Color and Race*, ed. John Hope Franklin (Boston: Houghton Mifflin, 1968); Sidney W. Mintz, "Groups, Group Boundaries and the Perception of Race," *Comparative Studies in Society and History* 13 (1971): 444; Robert Brent Toplin, "Reinterpreting Comparative Race Relations," *Journal of Black Studies* 2 (1971–2): 135–55; Harry Hoetink, *Slavery*

190 Notes to Pages 151–155

and Race Relations in the Americas (New York: Harper, 1973); Verena Martinez-
Allier, *Marriage, Class and Colour in Nineteenth-Century Cuba: A Study of Racial
Attitudes and Sexual Values in a Slave Society* (Cambridge: Cambridge University
Press, 1974); Michael Banton, *Rational Choice: A Theory of Racial and Ethnic
Relations* (SSRC, University of Bristol, 1977); Harry Hoetink, "Slavery and Race,"
in *Roots and Branches: Current Directions in Slave Studies*, ed. Michael Craton
(Toronto: Pergamon, 1979), 255–74: O. Nigel Bolland, "Systems of Domination
after Slavery: The Control of Land and Labor in the British West Indies after 1838,"
and the subsequent exchange with William A. Green, *Comparative Studies in
Society and History* 23 (1981): 591–619: ibid. 26 (1984): 112–25.

   8. Keith O. Laurence, *Immigration into the West Indies in the 19th Century*
(Jamaica: University of the West Indies, 1971); Hugh Tinker, *A New System of
Slavery: The Expatriation of Indian Labour Overseas, 1830–1920* (Oxford: Oxford
University Press, 1974); Selwyn D. Ryan, *Race and Nationalism in Trinidad and
Tobago: A Study of Decolonization in a Multiracial Society* (Toronto: University of
Toronto Press, 1972).

   9. Manuel Moreno Fraginals, Frank Moya Pons and Stanley L. Engerman,
*Between Slavery and Free Wage Labor: The Spanish-Speaking Caribbean in the
Nienteenth Century* (Baltimore: Johns Hopkins University Press, 1985); Robin
Blackburn, *The Overthrow of Colonial Slavery, 1776–1848* (London: Verso, 1988).

   10. Immanuel M. Wallerstein, *The Modern World System: Capitalist Agriculture
and the Origins of the Modern World System* (New York: Academic Press, 1976).
We also look forward eagerly to Robin Blackburn's announced second volume,
tracing the ending of slavery in the Americas, 1848–1888.

   11. Richard Frucht, "A Caribbean Social Type: Neither 'Peasant' nor 'Pro-
letarian'," in *Peoples and Cultures of the Caribbean: An Anthropological Reader*,
ed. Michael M. Horowitz (Garden City: Natural History Press, 1971), 190–97;
Sidney W. Mintz, *Caribbean Transformation* (Chicago: Aldine Press, 1974). Ciro
Flamarion S. Cardoso, "A brecha camponesa no sistema escravista," *Agricultura,
escravidao e capitalismo* (Petropolis; 1979).

   12. For the debate on the ending of British slavery, particularly in relation to the
"Williams Thesis," see Barbara L. Solow and Stanley L. Engerman, *British Capitalism and Caribbean Slavery: The Legacy of Eric Williams* (Cambridge: Cam-
bridge University Press, 1987). For Brazil and the United States respectively,
Robert Conrad, *The Destruction of Brazilian Slavery, 1850–1888* (Berkeley: Uni-
versity of California Press, 1972): Robert Brent Toplin, *The Abolition of Slavery in
Brazil* (New York: Atheneum, 1972); Edwin C. Rozwenc, *Slavery as a Cause of the
Civil War* (Boston: Heath, 1949). As yet, the most suggestive multicausal analysis of
the ending of slavery in at least one Caribbean territory is by Rebecca Scott, *Slave
Emancipation in Cuba: The Transition to Free Labor, 1860–1899* (Princeton:
Princeton University Press, 1985).

   13. Ken Post, *Arise Ye Starvelings: The Jamaica Labour Rebellion of 1938 and its
Aftermath* (The Hague: Nijhoff, 1978); Eric Foner, *Reconstruction: America's
Unfinished Revolution, 1863–1877* (New York: Harper, 1988); Robert M. Levine,
The Vargas Regime: The Critical Years, 1934–1938 (New York: Columbia University
Press, 1970). Louis A. Perez Jr., *Cuba Between Empires, 1878–1902* (Pittsburgh:
University of Pittsburgh Press, 1983); *Cuba Under the Platt Amendment,
1902–1934* (Pittsburgh: University of Pittsburgh Press, 1986): History Task Force,
Centro de Estudios Puertorriquenos, *Labor Migration Under Capitalism: The
Puerto Rico Experience* (New York: Monthly Review Press, 1979); Stephen R.
Shalom, *The United States and the Philippines: A Study in Neocolonialism* (Phila-
delphia: ISHI, 1981).

14. Michael Craton, *Testing the Chains: Resistance to Slavery in the British West Indies* (Ithaca: Cornell University Press, 1982); "Forms of Resistance to Slavery," Chapter 7 of vol. 6, UNESCO general History of the Caribbean, forthcoming; Bernard Semmel, *Jamaican Blood and Victorian Conscience* (Boston: Houghton Mifflin, 1963); Richard Price, *Maroon Societies;* C. L. R. James, *Black Jacobins: Toussaint L'Ouverture and the Domingo Revolution,* rev. ed. (London: Alison & Busby, 1980); Blackburn, *Overthrow of Colonial Slavery,* 507–8.

15. Gordon K. Lewis, *The Growth of the Modern West Indies* (New York: Monthly Review Press, 1969); Knight and Palmer *The Modern Caribbean.*

16. John H. Clarke, *Marcus Garvey and the Vision of Africa* (New York: Random House, 1974); Robert A. Hill, *The Marcus Garvey and Universal Negro Improvement Association Papers,* 6 vols. (Berkeley: University of California Press, 1983–1989: Imanuel Geiss, *The Pan African Movement: A History of Pan-Africanism in America* (New York: Africana, 1974); Colette Verger Michael, *Negritude: An Annotated Bibliography* (West Cornwall, Conn.: Locust Hill, 1988); August Meier, ed., *Black Protest in the Sixties* (Chicago: Quadrangle, 1970); Walter Rodney, *The Groundings with my Brothers* (London: Bogle-L'Ouverture, 1971); Herman L. Bennett, "The Challenge to the Post-Colonial State: A Case study of the February Revolution in Trinidad," in *The Modern Caribbean,* ed., Knight and Palmer, 129–46.

17. Winthrop D. Jordan, *White Over Black: American Attitudes Toward the Negro, 1550–1812* (Chapel Hill: University of North Carolina Press, 1968); George M. Fredrickson, *The Black Image in the White Mind: The Debate on Afro-American Character and Destiny, 1817–1914* (New York: Harper & Row, 1972); Kenneth Kiple, *The Caribbean Slave: A Biological History* (Cambridge: Cambridge University Press, 1984).

18. W.E.B. Du Bois, *Dusk of Dawn: An Essay Toward the Autobiography of a Race Concept* (New York: Harcourt, Brace & Co., 1940), 205, quoted in Fredrickson, *Arrogance of Race,* 4.

Contributors

Edward Ayers is associate professor of history at the University of Virginia. He is the author of *Vengeance and Justice: Crime and Punishment in the Nineteenth-Century American South* (Oxford University Press, 1984) and a number of essays and reviews in southern history.

Shearer Davis Bowman is assistant professor of history at the University of Texas at Austin. He is the author of several articles and reviews in southern and comparative history and of *Lords and Masters: Mid-Nineteenth-Century Planters and Junkers* (forthcoming, Oxford University Press).

Michael Craton is professor of history at the University of Waterloo. He is the author of numerous books and essays about slavery in the West Indies, including *Searching for the Invisible Man: Slaves and Plantation Life in Jamaica* (Harvard University Press, 1978) and *Testing the Chains: Resistance to Slavery in the British West Indies* (Cornell University Press, 1982).

Barbara Jeanne Fields is professor of history at Columbia University. She is the author of *Slavery and Freedom on the Middle Ground: Maryland During the Nineteenth Century* (Yale University Press, 1985) and many articles on southern history.

Elizabeth Fox-Genovese is director of Women's Studies and professor of history at Emory University. She is the author of *The Origins of Physiocracy: Economic Revolution and Social Order in Eighteenth-Century France* (Cornell University Press, 1976), *Within the Plantation Household: Black and White Women of the Old South* (University of North Carolina Press, 1988), coauthor with Eugene D. Genovese of *Fruits of Merchant Capital: Slavery and Bourgeois Property in the Rise and Expansion of Capitalism* (Oxford University Press, 1983), and numerous other works on comparative and women's history.

George Fredrickson is Edgar A. Robinson Professor of United States History at Sanford University. His many works include *The Black Image in the White Mind: The Debate on Afro-American Character and Destiny, 1817–1914* (Harper & Row, 1971), *White Supremacy: A Comparative Study in American and South African History* (Oxford University Press, 1981), and, most recently, *The Arrogance of Race: Historical Perspectives on Slavery, Racism, and Social Inequality* (Wesleyan University Press, 1988).

194   Contributors

Eugene Genovese is Distinguished Professor of Arts & Science at the University of Rochester. Among his books are *The World the Slaveholders Made* (Pantheon, 1969), *Roll, Jordan, Roll: The World the Slaves Made* (Pantheon, 1974), *From Rebellion to Revolution: Afro-American Slave Revolts in the Making of the Modern World* (Louisiana State University Press, 1979), and together with Elizabeth Fox-Genovese, *Fruits of Merchant Capital: Slavery and Bourgeois Property in the Rise and Expansion of Capitalism.*

Kees Gispen is associate professor of history at the University of Mississippi. He is the author of *New Profession, Old Order: Engineers and German Society, 1815–1914* (Cambridge University Press, 1989) and a number of articles and reviews in German history.

Richard Graham is Frances Higginbotham Nalle Centennial Professor of History at the University of Texas at Austin and has written extensively on Latin-American, especially Brazilian, history. He is the author of *Britain and the Onset of Modernization in Brazil, 1850–1914* (Cambridge University Press, 1968), *Independence in Latin America: a Comparative Approach* (A. A. Knopf, 1972), and most recently *Patronage and Politics in Nineteenth-Century Brazil* (Stanford University Press, 1989).

Steven Hahn is professor of history at the University of California at San Diego. He has written numerous reviews and articles on southern and comparative social history, as well as *The Roots of Southern Populism: Yeoman Farmers and the Transformation of the Georgia Upcountry, 1850–1890* (Oxford University Press, 1983). He is also coeditor of *The Countryside in the Age of Capitalist Transformation: Essays in the Social History of Rural America* (University of North Carolina Press, 1985).

Richard King is Reader in the American Studies Department at the University of Nottingham. In 1989–90 he was Visiting Professor in Southern Studies and History at the University of Mississippi. Among other works he has written *The Party of Eros* (University of North Carolina Press, 1972) and *A Southern Renaissance: the Cultural Awakening of the American South, 1930–1955* (Oxford University Press, 1980).

Peter Kolchin is professor of history at the University of Delaware. He is the author of *First Freedom: the Responses of Alabama's Blacks to Emancipation and Reconstruction* (Greenwood Press, 1972) and of a major comparative study, *Unfree Labor: American Slavery and Russian Serfdom* (Harvard University Press, 1987).

Index